THE LAND CALLED

A HISTORY OF LEWIS COUNTY, WASHINGTON

SANDRA A. CROWELL

Published in the United States by:
Panesko Publishing
222 S.E. Spring Street
Chehalis, Washington 98532

Copyright © 2007, Panesko Publishing

All rights reserved. No part of this publication may be reproduced, stored in any retrieval system or transmitted in any form - by any means, electronic, mechanical, photocopying or otherwise - without advance written permission from the publisher.

All photographs are reprinted with permission from the Lewis County Historical Museum unless otherwise attributed.

ISBN 978-0-9794515-0-8
Library of Congress Control Number: 2007924920

The paper used in this publication meets the minimum requirements of American National Standard for Information Services—Permanence of Paper for Printed Library Materials.
ANSI Z39.48-1984∞™

Printed in the United States by
Gorham Printing
Centralia, Washington 98531

Cover designed by: Kathryn E. Campbell

Cover photo: Mt. Rainier across a fenced pasture in Centralia, 1908.
Photo this page: The Michigan Hill Road in the Lincoln Creek area, circa 1913.

Table of Contents

Chapter	Page

1 First Inhabitants 1
2 Exploring the Northwest 10
3 Manifest Destiny 19
4 Times of Unrest 32
5 Lewis: The Mother of Counties ... 37
6 Canoes, Coaches, Steamboats 42
7 Trails to Rails 51
8 Railroad Boom Years 59
9 The Towns Came 70
10 The East End 84
11 Timber! 92
12 Mill Town: Onalaska 115
13 Tragedy in Centralia 119
14 Lodes of Ore 124
15 Crops and Hops 132
16 Quest for Power: Dams on the
    Cowlitz 146
17 The Great Melting Pot 150
18 The Great Depression, World War II,
    and Post-War Times 158
19 War Memorial 168
20 Living in the Land Called Lewis . 170
21 Rotogravure 180
Historical Time Line 192
Acknowledgments 194
Selected Bibliography 197
Index 200

Introduction

Lewis County is in southwestern Washington, stretching 96 miles from the rolling Willapa Hills to the crest of the Cascade Mountains. Mt. Rainier can be seen from some vantages, Mt. St. Helens from others and Mt. Adams from still others. Within its boundaries are a web of forests and rich farmland. Two major river systems, the Chehalis and the Cowlitz, flow through the area, carrying the names of the Native Americans who lived on their shores. Lewis County is the sixth largest in the state, but its boundaries once encompassed most of western Washington and British Columbia. The land attracted the earliest explorers and settlers north of the Columbia River, those who came up the Cowlitz River to shape the history of Washington State. They created government, churches and schools, farms, mines, industries, businesses--and homes. Their role and that of the following generations provide us a vivid slice of Pacific Northwest history.

Join us on a journey into the past in *The Land Called Lewis*.

Chapter 1

The First Inhabitants

As his oars strained against the current of the river, the young man observed the rich overhang of a forest canopy opening up to an occasional grassy prairie. Overhead a disturbed raven squawked a warning to his relatives, and rain from recent showers dripped softly from the branches.

While he pushed his way upstream in the winter weather, the strapping teenager absorbed the details of the land in the tradition of his fellow French adventurers. A stream such as this would be a fine territory for beaver—and the precious pelts for tall stovepipe hats so fashionable among prosperous men throughout the civilized world. Surely his employers back at the fort near the mouth of the Columbia River would be happy to hear of this stream and bountiful countryside. Ahead he spotted an opening and piece of land jutting into the river, a perfect landing place for his flat-bottomed bateau and maybe for other boats later. He unfolded his six-foot frame from his boat and examined his surroundings.

Yes, he would definitely return. Since he carried no arms on this trip, he would be sure to bring other trappers for protection next time. If they met Indians, perhaps they

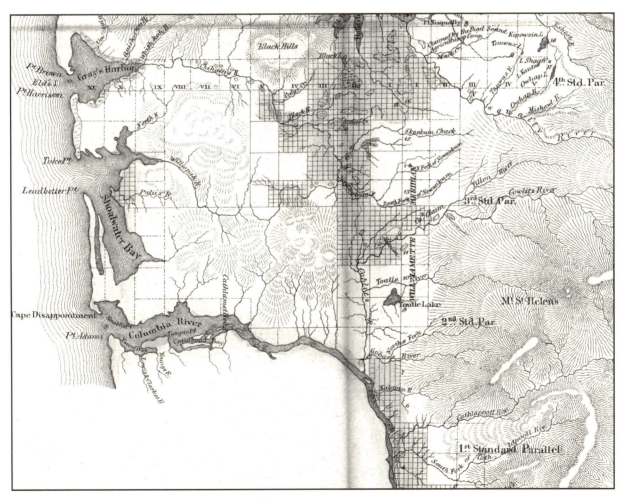

Southwest Washington, 1840, with future survey lines and river names.

could trade…or perhaps he might just stay in this appealing land… His imagination glowed with all the possibilities and his young man's dreams.

His name was Simon Plamondon, and the stream was the Cowlitz River. In this winter of 1818-1819, he was one of the first white men to set foot in present day Lewis County, Washington.

His lifetime would span a century of exploration and settlement, and this land would represent a slice of history in the settling of the Pacific Northwest.

The area of the Cowlitz River and what was later to be named Lewis County was indeed rich with possibility. What Plamondon didn't realize on his first trip up the river was that people had lived productive lives here for eons before.

The First Inhabitants

Prior to European explorers casting their sights on the Northwest, the land comprising today's Lewis County supported two groups of Native American people — the Upper Chehalis and three bands of the Cowlitz. Anthropologists believe the idea of a "tribe" was introduced by non-Indians who often took the river system name and applied it to Native Americans living in the area who shared similar cultures. The Upper Chehalis, which stands for the "Shining Sand" at the mouth of the Chehalis River on the coast, and the Cowlitz, which means "People who Seek Their Medicine Spirit," lived inland in cohesive communities. Traversing prairies and mountainous forests of cedar and Douglas fir, both the Chehalis and Cowlitz were expert canoeists and horsemen. They charred logs with fire, and then carved them into thin-sided, blunt-nosed canoes which easily crossed sand bars and rapids. They bred and trained horses for riding and hauling goods. In competitions they bet enthusiastically on their own riding skills.

The Upper Chehalis lived on the land running north from Lewis County and encompassing the headwaters of the west and east forks of the Chehalis River, an area called Satsop country. To the east their territory included the west flank of the Deschutes River watershed and touched Puget Sound at Eld Inlet. Westward, beyond the Chehalis Indian Reservation, their territory extended north of the Willapa Hills, heading along the ridges that separated the Upper Chehalis from the ocean-oriented Lower Chehalis. Two distinct language patterns were spoken by the Upper Chehalis, one spoken from Grand Mound east and the other west of there. Major villages were located at the mouths of Lincoln Creek, Scatter Creek, Skookumchuck River, Black River, Cedar Creek and at Grand Mound. The permanent village at the mouth of Lincoln Creek was a prime fishing place. Nearby was a prairie rich in camas (a blue-flowering plant with an edible root) and foothills where elk ranged—a combination that drew other villagers and

A Nisqually tribe blunt-nosed canoe is displayed in Chehalis at the Washington Territorial Centennial, 1953.

tribes to visit. Other sites were at Fords Prairie, Newaukum River, along the Chehalis River, and at Rainbow Falls.

In aboriginal times the Cowlitz had the largest land-base of all Western Washington tribes, according to Roy Wilson of the Cowlitz Tribe. Although boundaries were loosely defined, their area covered the western watershed of the Cascade Mountains. In the southwest the Upper Chehalis and Lower Cowlitz jointly occupied a triangular area encompassing Boistfort on the Chehalis River's south fork and the area known today as Pe Ell. South of Pe Ell the Lower Cowlitz territory continued on its west side to the Germany Creek drainage (west of today's Longview) and south again, just inland from the Columbia, near Vancouver Lake. Another band lived along the banks of Lewis River in Cowlitz County. In Lewis County, Cowlitz territory extended south of the present city of Chehalis to include the rest of the county eastward to the crest of the Cascades.

In their rounds the Lower Cowlitz wandered across the area's open prairies, from the Newaukum Prairie to the Cowlitz Prairie where camas fields and horse-grazing range intermixed with copses of evergreens. Beyond, the forested Cascades rose with sharp ridges and rugged terrain. Near the present town of Morton, the Upper Cowlitz Indians lived, fished and hunted deer, elk, bear and mountain goats valued for their hair and horns. These Upper Cowlitz families intermarried with the Sahaptain-speaking Yakima and Klickitat from east of the mountains. Sahaptain-speaking Cowlitz are called "Taidnapam" ("People of the Teiton River"). In historic times the Taidnapam traversed both the upper Cowlitz River and the Cathlapootle (Lewis River) watersheds to the Columbia.

Some Upper Cowlitz names are familiar in contemporary times, Roy Wilson

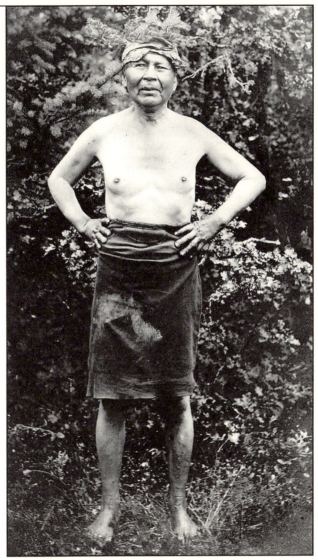

Jake, a Chehalis Indian, demonstrates a wrap-around skirt and a headdress of fir boughs, circa 1930.

notes in his book, *History of the Cowlitz Tribe*. Cispus is the name of a mythological Cowlitz warrior; Salkum is the Cowlitz name for Mill Creek; and Takh Takh Meadow in the Randle area means "small prairie." While most Cowlitz place names have been lost to common usage, they were based on physical characteristics of the land. Landers Creek, now flowing into Riffe Lake, once had a name meaning "steelhead place" and Craggy Tongue Mountain in the Cispus River Valley had a Cowlitz name which meant "tongue place."

Another group of native people, the Kwalhiokwa (which means "A Lonely Place in the Woods"), were considered to be a band of the Cowlitz. They lived in the secluded mountain valleys of the Chehalis and Willapa Rivers, the later location of Boistfort and Pe Ell. Other branches lived near the Willapa and Elochamon River headwaters.

The language of the Kwalhiokwa tells an interesting story. Anthropologists theorize that in ancient times the people migrated to the Willapa Hills area from northern Alaska, where they spoke an Athabascan dialect. Perhaps because of a lack of game, part of the group eventually migrated south to the Oregon coast. They carried their dialect with them, and they became known as the Umpqua. Some continued to migrate to the Southwest, to become known as the Apache, still using the same language patterns. A small number remained in the Willapa Hills where they became absorbed by the Cowlitz and were known as "Mountain Cowlitz." During the 1855-1856 war scare, the Indian Services removed the remaining Kwalhiokwa from the Boistfort area to the Cowlitz River internment camp.

Situated between the Columbia River and Puget Sound, and between the Cascades and the Coast Range, Cowlitz and Upper Chehalis villages were strategically located for trade. They accrued wealth by trading dried camas and the potato-like wapato, smoked smelt and salmon, dried berries and venison, supple buckskins and furs, and their especially fine baskets and horses.

Attuned to nature's cycles, the indigenous people followed seasonal rounds, according to Cowlitz historian Judith Irwin. They observed the orbit of sun and moon, the patterns of wind and rain and the ways of wildlife, such as the annual upstream run of the salmon.

Interior of an abandoned Chehalis Tribe longhouse.

In the spring villagers left their longhouses for prairies blooming with blue camas. The people dug the potato-like roots of the camas for a dietary staple. Women smoke-dried them and other foods over a low fire or baked them in an earthen oven under slow burning logs. At mealtime they boiled roots or berries with meat or fish, heating the water by placing smoldering stones in tightly woven baskets filled with liquid. In order to encourage the growth of berries and camas, tribes burned the prairie lands every two or three years to clear them of encroaching forests.

A Chehalis Indian basket.

Indians in more modern times picking huckleberries.

In the warmth of summer when blackberries and huckleberries ripened, the people moved to higher elevations to gather with other tribes and clans to pick berries. For temporary shelter in the summer season, they draped woven tulle-mats over a framework of sticks or other materials at hand.

Before winter arrived the families transported their stock of food to their permanent longhouses at lower elevations. These large cedar plank structures were built with the ends facing the rivers and housed several families who shared cooking fires. Winter was the season for carving, sewing and weaving. They turned wood, cedar roots, rushes and hides into bowls, baskets, mats and clothing. Winter was also the time for drumming and dancing, for ceremonies and for sharing legends and oral history. Their stories and myths carried a moral code of behavior for their children to follow.

Myth Times

Growing up along cold mountain streams, the children were sent out to swim before bedtime. This discipline toughened them up to withstand changes in the weather, historian Judith Irwin recounts. After their chilly baths the children snuggled into fur blankets near glowing coals and waited for the story teller to say, "A'unac tca'q(w)tlkta wat i't ac'." ("Now I will untie the myth.")

Cowlitz myths told how the world came into being, how all creation was interrelated, how Dangerous Beings were transformed into ordinary creatures and how codes and values were to be followed. They told how Coyote created sun, moon and stars for heat and light, and how he created and named the varieties of trees, the special places where camas and strawberries grew, and the churning waters which brought fish to the surface where they could be captured.

Legends said that Coyote taught the people to twirl a dry stick between their hands to spark a fire in cedar-bark shavings, and how to craft axes, bows, arrows, spears, basket fish traps and dip nets of soft maple and willows. They said that Mosquito and Flea, before being reduced in size and power, were Dangerous Beings — cannibals. Other Dangerous Beings took the

Mary Kiona of the Cowlitz Tribe and four of her great-great-grandchildren, Magpie, Anna Marie, Joanie, Raymond Eyle Jr., 1970.

form of grizzlies, clouds and earthquakes. Coyote also described the "new people" who, with a stronger sense of community, lived together in a lodge with many families. The new people shared food, cherished children of both sexes and tabooed cannibalism and incest.

Underlying their mythic view was the conviction that everything is alive, according to Irwin's research. They believed that spirit entities and energy animate all things, that Earth is a mother, the sun a father and all creation are brothers and sisters who may supply humans with personal spirit guides. Legends stressed the importance of spirit ("tomanawas") quests for young men and women.

The Village

When the white man arrived, the tribes' basic political unit was the self-sufficient village made up of allied families. Village groups varied, depending on their strengths and needs, but most people within the group were related to each other. Since intermarriage between groups was customary, families within one village were affiliated with other groups.

Each village had headmen or chiefs and commanded at least one winter fishing site where residents built their weirs and set their nets. The headmen were little more than first-among-equals, having no right to issue orders. Rather, they employed persuasion, wisdom and resolve to convince the villagers that their words should be heeded. In other words, they had good people skills.

Hunters and warriors led hunting excursions and sometimes raids on other villages. Men gained status and wealth through success in war, slave raids, contests and hunting or fishing expeditions. If they accrued enough wealth, they could have a second or third wife — sometimes at the instigation of an overworked first wife.

Smile from an Indian skan. Northwest tribes used cradle boards such as this to flatten babies' heads as a sign of social status.

Such marriages protected widows. "When a woman's husband died ... then the nearest, oldest male relative took his place," explained George Umtuch of the Yakima-Cowlitz. "This way no one would be left alone."

Intermarriage between groups could also increase a chief's authority. By having seven wives, Cowlitz Chief Scanewa became known as a "man of influence" among the tribes ranging from the Columbia to Vancouver Island. (It was no accident that he offered his daughter to the French Canadian trapper who would become Lewis County's first white resident.)

A man seeking a wife typically offered the young woman's parents a gift. If the gift was accepted, the man compensated the parents with more valuables at the wedding, where the bride's parents distributed their own presents to the guests. Later, these extended families gathered from great distances to socialize while hunting or gathering berries.

A woman's rank depended on her abilities and her husband's influence. Women had a strong voice in determining political and medical decisions, but not in war. Almost always, they dominated household matters,

Cowlitz Indians Kitty Tililikish and Mary Stockum by Arrington's store, Toledo,

such as food, children, festivals and packing the horses. If a marriage failed, the wife and husband could separate easily, and the younger children lived with their mother and her people.

The Lower Cowlitz were a hierarchical people, and their upper ranks included the wealthy, warriors and shamans. Medicine men and women studied the healing properties of plants and led various ceremonies. To ensure future salmon runs, for example, they conducted the first-salmon ritual when they thanked the season's first captured salmon for the gift of its life. The lowest ranks were reserved for slaves who were either captured or obtained in trades. At birth, head-flattening assured the Salish child of its free-born status and distinguished it from the slaves who were "round-heads."

Tribal leaders settled conflicts through compensation or mediation. In battle, however, warriors fought with bows and arrows, doubled-edged broadswords, spears and clubs. Some wore a kind of armor with a helmet — a thick, pliable elk hide which hung to the thigh or ankle. Over this they might sport a vest of twined hardwood or carry a shield. When someone was injured or killed during battle, an umpire stopped the fight and urged negotiations.

The Kwalhiokwa had a lifestyle of hunting, fishing and gathering that was

See-See-Nah was the oldest living Chehalis Indian in 1906. He was born in the 1790's.

similar to that of the Chehalis and Cowlitz. But they were distinctive in their use of "microblades" — small, sharpened "teeth" inserted into a fire-hardened wood shaft — which were employed as tools for sawing and cutting or as lances. The teeth were made by end-snapping them from a prepared core of chert, jasper or agate.

Mary Kiona

The remarkable Mary Kiona (1855-1970) represents both the native heritage and the course of history in Lewis County. Claiming descendency from the Yakima and Cowlitz tribes, this tribal matriarch's lifetime spanned the coming of the white settlers to modern times. Her birth on the banks of the Cowlitz River at Silverbrook near Randle was documented by Indian agencies as being in 1855 during the Indian War and the administration of President Franklin Pierce although her actual age has never been verified. She died at what may have been the age of 115; some sources say 118, others 122. She may have lived in the land called Lewis longer than any other human being.

Mary Kiona spoke in the unwritten language of the Upper Cowlitz dialect, the basic language of which is Sahaptin. In interviews conducted through an interpreter, she recalled her first experience of seeing white people and covered wagons arriving in Washington Territory. She remembered Hudson's Bay trappers at Cowlitz Landing and specifically a one-eyed French-Canadian trapper, Pierre Charles, for whom Pe Ell was allegedly named. A niece of the prominent Cowlitz Chief Scanewa, she lived to see the coming of steamboats, trains, automobiles, jetplanes--and many more white people.

When Mary Kiona was a child her people moved freely over the land to gather food in a cyclical life based on the seasons. In the spring they fished and dug camas and other roots. In the late summer and fall they moved by horseback to the high country to hunt and gather blackberries and huckleberries in large woven baskets which they hung on their horses. For many years her family continued their trek to Packwood where they set up rough shelters (and later tents) for a month or so of food-gathering. (Another uncle, Jim Yoke, discovered the hot springs at Ohanapecosh, east of Packwood.) She recalled times when the Cowlitz and Yakima tribes met to trade goods at Packwood. In the winters her family used fire to chip arrow heads, dry venison and smoke salmon, boil Hemlock bark for tanning deer hides, and hollow out cedar-log canoes. Winter was also a time for making baskets.

At about the age of six Mary began making baskets, and for over a hundred years she crafted some of the finest and most famed baskets of the Northwest. Besides being utilitarian, the Cowlitz basket was deeply imbedded in tribal myth and culture as an object of beauty. Anthropologist Otis T. Mason wrote in 1902, "The most absolutely beautiful and perfect baskets...were made on the Cowlitz and Lewis Rivers in Washington." Mary Kiona's cedar root baskets, in a vast array of shapes and

A Mary Kiona basket at the Lewis County Historical Museum. The basket is about five inches across and is intricately woven.

The First Inhabitants

Mary Kiona in 1970, the year of her death. She may have been the longest lived person in Lewis County.

sizes, could take up to two years to make. In the wooded areas near Chehalis and Cowlitz Landing, she collected sturdy horsetail roots, Oregon grape for tawny color, alder bark for red dye, and at higher elevations, creamy-colored bear grass. Coiled in the sand-colored cedar root were intricate designs, partially overlapped, in different colors of the natural fibers. Her baskets are in museums and private collections today.

Mary Kiona's beauty treatment was a facial masque of spruce pitch which she removed with bear and deer grease. If the unusual beauty trick didn't contribute to her longevity, it certainly didn't harm her. She continued berry-picking, basket-making, and canoeing well past her 100th year, and in the 1960s at age 107 she was called upon to testify in government hearings about the dams on the Cowlitz River.

She stated in court that, "It is not right to move people off their lands. The Indian had many rights--fishing, hunting and berry picking--before the white man came. Now, some of these rights have been taken away from the Indian."

On June 16, 1970, she told her granddaughter of a gate opening up through which she would go. But first she wanted a good, old-fashioned Indian meal of boiled venison, mashed Yakima peaches, bitterroot greens, and strong black coffee. Afterward, she saw the gate open wide, and Mary Kiona left her birthplace, the land called Lewis. Kiona Creek, Kiona Road, and Kiona Mountain in the Randle area carry her family name.

With the arrival of European explorers and the subsequent waves of white settlers, the way of life of the early people disappeared into the mists of prehistory. Diseases ravaged the tribes and obliterated entire villages. The Cowlitz Tribe population, once estimated at 50,000, was reduced to 2,400. The people became assimilated into the culture of the white man, leaving their own culture and many traditions behind. However, the memory of their lifestyle contributes to the richly textured tapestry of Lewis County. It serves as a reminder that the land has long supported cultures other than the contemporary one and if treated respectfully, the land will provide and endure.

—

Simon Plamondon, the French Canadian trapper, entered into this world on his exploratory trip up the Cowlitz River. Curious, he disembarked from his canoe on the open finger of land —to be instantly taken hostage by braves guarding the domain of Chief Scanewa of the Cowlitz.

The chief, with an ever-canny eye for opportunity, soon realized the advantage of having the handsome young white man become a part of his family.

Chapter 2

Exploring the Northwest

The Columbia River pushes through the Northwest to the Pacific near the 47th parallel. It divides Washington and Oregon, and its numerous tributaries stretch into Canada, Montana and Idaho. These waterways were thoroughfares for early travelers and avenues of exploration into an unknown land. The Cowlitz River was the tributary that led settlers to the land north of the Columbia. But the exploration leading up to the early recorded history of what became Lewis County is a tale of adventure and sharp competition among the world's 18th and 19th-century powers — Russia, Spain, Britain and America. All were in search of the elusive Northwest Passage and determined to establish the newly discovered land under their own flag.

America joined the quest for the Northwest Passage in the 1780s when Boston merchants heard dazzling tales of riches gained from the China trade. Under the leadership of Captain Robert Gray a two-ship expedition, consisting of the *Columbia Redeviva* and the *Lady Washington*, set sail to the northwest coast of North America. On his first voyage Captain Gray failed to locate the cross-continental waterway but succeeded as the first American to circumnavigate the world. During his second voyage in May of 1792, at the 47th parallel he discovered "a large river of white water," an estuary he named the Columbia River and claimed for the United States. The mystical river, so long sought, had been found and America's colonization rights established. Nevertheless, Britain maintained a tight grip for another half a century.

In the early 19th century President Thomas Jefferson declared the charting of the western territory a national priority. After the Louisiana Purchase in 1803, it was in the nation's interest to know what lay beyond the Mississippi and prevent the British from claiming the territory. With Congressional backing Jefferson ordered an overland expedition that would map the landscape, record the botanical specimens and set up trade ties with Native Americans. He assigned two Virginians, Meriwether Lewis and William Clark, to head the famous trek into the wilderness. In 1804 their expedition headed up the Mississippi

Meriwether Lewis and William Clark, circa 1800. Two Washington counties carry their names.

and Missouri Rivers, across the Rockies and to the Pacific. The result was an extensive report to Jefferson that stressed the vast potential of the Northwest for American settlement.

Although Lewis and Clark did not enter the land of today's Lewis County, they did camp on the Cowlitz River on March 27, 1806, calling it by its Indian name, "Cowlitskee." They described the Cowlitz and Willamette valleys as a "desirable situation for a settlement" and noted the region's fertile soil, mild climate and abundant timber. Two counties in Southwest Washington were later to carry the names of the explorers. While settlement didn't occur for decades, it wasn't long before fur traders penetrated the land of the Cowlitz.

Simon Plamondon was not the first white trapper to visit the Cowlitz River. French trapper Gabriel Franchere left a clear account of the first recorded visit of white men to the Cowlitz in 1811. His party traveled thirty miles up the Columbia to a large Indian village where "...we landed to obtain information about a little river that empties into the Columbia here. It comes from the north and is called Cowlitz by the natives. Mr. McKay embarked with Mr. Montigy and two Indians to examine the course of the river a certain distance upstream… after ascending the Cowlitz about a mile and half, on rounding a bend of the stream they suddenly came into sight of about twenty canoes full of Indians, who made a rush upon them with the most frightful cries and screams." It seems the traders were caught between two warring tribes, the Cowlitz and the Chinook.

The native people "who had never seen white men regarded us with astonishment and curiosity, lifting our trousers and opening our shirts to see if the skin of our bodies resembled that of our faces and hands." The party returned gratefully to the Columbia. Several years would pass before another white man ventured into the Cowlitz country.

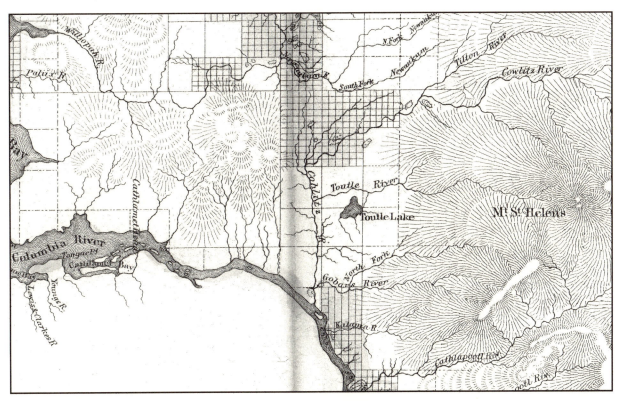

The lower Columbia River and the Cowlitz River Valley, before roads or rail lines, 1840.

The First Settler

As massive and colorful as the land he inhabited, Simon Plamondon, the young man with the dreams, became the first settler of Lewis County. His life spanned the entire 19th century from 1800 to 1900, and his "long walks" covered major parts of the North American continent.

Historians have found some 18 variations of the spelling of his name, and undocumented sources claim that he fathered 60 children from 19 marriages! That and other legends about him are highly unlikely, including the story that he was seven feet tall. But he was a giant of a man for his times, straight and ruggedly handsome, even in his later years. Local families considered him "a rogue," which added to his allure.

Born a French-Canadian and later naturalized as an American citizen, Plamondon stumbled into the midst of Britain's and the United States' battle for the Northwest. His part in the development of a huge and prosperous farm on the Cowlitz Prairie for Hudson's Bay Company showed the world that the land north of the Columbia offered untold prosperity. His discovery of a landing near the present site of Toledo on the Cowlitz River, which for many years bore his name, became a major mooring for both American and British travelers. It was Plamondon who guided the American naval expedition of Lt. Charles Wilkes through the area in 1841. He had a role in bringing the "Black Robes" and Catholicism to the Northwest. His "X" appeared on the earliest legal documents of Oregon Territory, Washington Territory and Lewis County. And it was he who fed and placated Native Americans and settlers during the Indian uprising of 1855-1856.

Born Simon Bonaparte Plamondon in Quebec in 1800, he was the youngest of seven children and grew up speaking sev-

Simon Plamondon, the first settler of Lewis County.

eral Indian dialects as well as French. After his parents and an older brother died in 1810, he chose to follow the tradition of the *coeur-de-bois*, or "one who runs or goes into the forest." These were the French adventurers who became voyageurs, fur traders and liaisons with Indian tribes. Infatuated by their tales, 14-year-old Simon took the first of his long walks; he journeyed from Quebec to New Orleans, and then up the Mississippi and Missouri Rivers to the Columbia and on to the Pacific coast.

Two years after he had embarked on this trek, Plamondon, now a lanky 16-year old, landed work as a trapper for the North West Fur Company, a Canadian firm located at the present site of Astoria. In the winter of 1818-1819 he canoed unarmed up a Columbia River tributary into a land seen by few white men and scouted the Cowlitz

River, paddling against its currents into the present day Lewis County, where he was captured by the Cowlitz Indians. Simon's ability to speak several Indian dialects and the fact that he was unarmed soothed hostilities. Some accounts say that Chief Scanewa escorted him on a tour of the Upper Cowlitz territory, into the lush Big Bottom Country as far as the present site of Randle.

After several weeks, Chief Scanewa released Plamondon only if he promised to return with trade goods, a promise enforced by two warriors who accompanied him back to Fort George. He reported back to his superiors at the fort that trade prospects looked good and the country bountiful. True to his word, he returned to Cowlitz Prairie bearing gifts of blankets, clothing, tobacco and beads. Plamondon had succeeded in being one of the first white men to explore the Cowlitz River.

Chief Scanewa called Plamondon "a man of his word." He offered Plamondon one of his three daughters in marriage. The explorer chose for his wife the woman Thase-muth who was later to be known as Veronica. In keeping with Cowlitz custom the couple was presented with 20 to 30 young braves as a gift from the father of the bride. The union formed a strong basis for trade in the Cowlitz corridor, and Plamondon's new father-in-law became one of the three most important chiefs in the Northwest and a major player in the fur trade. In about 1821 Simon and Veronica had a daughter, the first child of white ancestry in Lewis County.

In the late 1820s the native population of the Northwest was stricken by a terrible epidemic, perhaps malaria, called ague fever by the whites and "Cole Sick" by the Indians. In a sweeping death march, at least three-fourths of the coastal tribes were wiped out, almost depopulating the Columbia River region. Historian Judith Irwin points out that the usual therapy for curing fevers — purification in the sweat bath and cleansing in cold water — made the Cole Sick deadly. Although the percentages of the dead varied from village to village, the tattered remnants of the tribes lived in terror of a recurrence, and the Cowlitz people mostly fled to the coast.

The Plamondon family survived, perhaps because of a gift of quinine from the Hudson's Bay Company or because their Caucasian blood was a natural immunity, according to Roy Wilson's book *History of the Cowlitz Indians*.

Plamondon continued to work for Hudson's Bay Company, which by then had absorbed the North West Fur Company. He assisted the company in its move from Fort George (Astoria) to Fort Vancouver on the Columbia River, and influenced its shift to include farming as well as fur trading. Hudson's Bay records indicate that Plamondon was hired as a "middleman," one who mans the oars in the middle of a canoe, at three different Company locations in the years of 1821 to roughly 1835. He also assisted in carpentry, planting orchards and clearing farm land.

Around 1827 Veronica died while giving birth to the couple's fourth child. Driven by grief or perhaps wanderlust, Simon left his children with an Indian family and set out for the Yukon on another of his "long walks" with his favorite dog and a gun. The next year his father-in-law Chief Scanewa was murdered, an act that heightened tension on Puget Sound.

It is believed Plamondon unofficially remarried and fathered another child while returning home through British Columbia. In Spokane, however, he met Emilie Fenlay Bercier, whose husband had just died and left her with several children. By 1837 the charming French-Indian woman would become the next Mrs. Simon Plamondon. Five children were born to this union.

In 1838 the Hudson's Bay Company established the Puget Sound Agricultural Company. Simon Plamondon put down roots to supervise a 4,000-acre farm in the Cowlitz Prairie, just north of present-day Toledo. His prosperous settlement included six ploughmen, three sheep herders, two carpenters, a blacksmith and ten servants. Soon other French Canadians, many with Indian wives, developed their own farms nearby. Thus, the names of Bernier, Cottonaire, Gobar and Sareault appear on early maps, while Pierre Charles took out a claim in the area he named Boistfort before moving over the hills to Pe Ell.

The Revs. Francis Norbert Blanchet and Medeste Demers.

By the late 1830s the area of the future Lewis County became a main corridor of travel — the first direct inland route from the Columbia to Puget Sound, nearly two decades before the settlement of Seattle, Tacoma, or Olympia.

Black Robes Arrive

In 1838 Lewis County became the home of the first permanent church north of the Columbia River. Between 1834 and 1836 the French Canadians in the new land had petitioned the Catholic Church to send them missionaries so that their children could be raised in the faith of their upbringing. Most accounts say that Simon Plamondon, always ready for adventure, trekked 3,000 miles to Red River in Manitoba, Canada, to lead priests back to the Cowlitz settlement. Revs. Francis Norbert Blanchet and Medeste Demers arrived at Fort Vancouver in the fall of 1838 with instructions to found a mission on the Cowlitz River "where it would not be ground whose ownership was disputed by Great Britain and the United States."

They immediately chose a section of land for a mission and made arrangements for the construction of a house and barn. On December 16, 1838, Father Blanchet celebrated mass in the Plamondon home, an event that officially marked the "Black Robes" arrival in the new land, and within two months they built the St. Francis Xavier Mission, the first permanent church in Washington. Built without doors or windows, Father Demers wrote that it had a "roof like a wolf's head, no ceiling and a floor leveled with an axe." The brick chapel of the same name became the fifth building to occupy the site.

Besides the French Canadians, the mission's first parish included a number of Hudson's Bay employees, perhaps indentured servants, and their families. In time the two priests founded missions at Astoria, Okanogan, Colville, Vancouver, Whidbey Island and Walla Walla, and be-

Sketch of Father Blanchet's St. Francis Xavier Mission a 30 ft. by 20 ft. log building to replace the original log mission which became the priest's residence, 1857.

The third mission was built in 1902, and both the rectory and church were destroyed by fire in 1916.

The fourth mission was built in 1917 and burned in 1932.

The fifth mission was built in 1933.

came leaders within the Catholic hierarchy in the Northwest.

Simon Plamondon, who became a naturalized citizen, participated in incredible changes as the new Lewis County developed during the rest of the century. At his death in 1900 Plamondon was three months shy of his 100th birthday. Despite his pivotal role, Plamondon's life has been largely forgotten. Unable to read or write, he kept no diaries or records, and as a French Canadian Catholic employed by the British, his role was ignored by Americans. A marker in his name can be seen at the pioneer cemetery by the St. Frances Mission and St. Mary's Center in Toledo, not far from his beloved Cowlitz River. Today only Plomondon Road (note the different spelling) near Toledo and hundreds of descendants are reminders of his role.

The First Farm: A Corporate Operation

The handful of travelers who came upon the Cowlitz Prairie in the 1840s looked with amazement at a bustling settlement. With Mt. Rainier and Mt. St. Helens as a backdrop, a small village of French Canadian buildings was nestled on the prairie amid prosperous grain fields and livestock. On a summer day one could see some forty men cutting wheat in the fields, while others herded pigs, prepared wool or tended the large dairy. The sound of construction reverberated through the bright sunshine as new granaries and piggeries were built, some eleven outbuildings in all. Children from as many as 90 families shouted to each other in French, English and Indian dialects. At the Cowlitz Landing large canoes and flat-bottomed boats, known as "bateaux," rocked on the water, ready to haul fresh edibles downriver to Russian and English ships anchored at the mouth of the Cowlitz.

This early settlement was not only the first in Lewis County but the first in Washington after Fort Vancouver. The settlers weren't American but rather from a giant British corporation that spanned the entire North American continent. The Cowlitz Farm, as it was called, was a subsidiary of the massive Hudson's Bay Company. Its formation and that of its sister farm at Fort Nisqually were proof to the world that agriculture could thrive in the unsettled lands of the Northwest.

Hudson's Bay Company operated a world-wide fur monopoly. Fort Vancouver became a prosperous trading hub with some 63,000 beaver pelts passing through its portals in 1843 alone. Three different units of 150 traders, families and all, set out every six months in fur-trading expeditions to the south, the west, and to the country north of the Columbia. A system of trading posts formed the backbone of the fur trade; some 20 trading locations existed north of the Columbia in 1840.

At the edge of the continent, surrounded by wilderness, Fort Vancouver became a bastion of civilization. Clerks, drafted into service from London, kept impeccable records, three copies of every transaction. One clerk was a young man named George Roberts, who later played a key role in Lewis County history and whose writings survive to document the county's development.

Hudson's Bay Company traders and trappers became the first Europeans to use the Cowlitz Corridor extensively. Transporting their trade goods, they turned the milky waters into a regular highway of commerce. The remains of their camps have been discovered as far upriver as Eastern Lewis County.

In the 1830s Chief Factor (director) John McLoughlin realized the fur trade was abating, while trade in grain, fruit, and livestock at Fort Vancouver was prospering far beyond expectations. The new land he wanted for farming and grazing: Cowlitz Prairie. George Simpson, the company's governor, wanted farms north of the Columbia to strengthen England's claim to the Northwest.

In 1838 a separate British entity, Puget Sound Agricultural Company, was set up specifically for farming. Soon cultivation began in the Nisqually area on Puget Sound, between the Nisqually and Puyallup Rivers, and on Cowlitz Prairie. The new subsidiary satisfied an agreement with the Russian settlement in Alaska to supply farm products and 15,000 bushels of wheat annually. By 1841 the Cowlitz Farm and the Puget Sound farm produced a phenomenal amount of goods, no less than 4,000 pounds of wool in 1842, as well as acres of hay, wheat, oats, peas and potatoes. In 1852 the Cowlitz Farm had herds of 7,000 cattle and sheep and 300 horses.

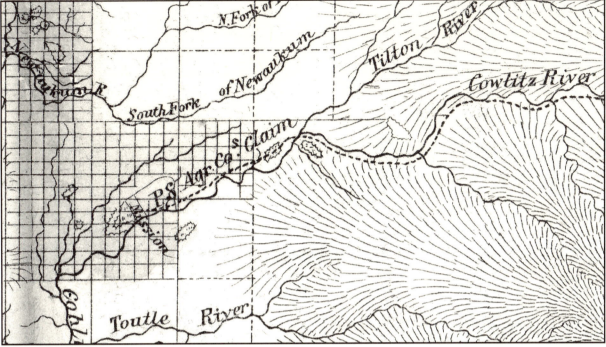
The Puget Sound Agricultural Company farm is shown on this map adjacent to the St. Francis Mission, north of Toledo, 1857. The British-owned farm dated back to 1838.

Simon Plamondon, in court hearings in 1865, dictated this description of the Cowlitz farm: "(The farm was)...bounded on the South by the Claim of the Roman Catholic Mission, on the West by a Swale (a low-lying, wet area), on the North by a small stream used by the Company as a sheep wash and on the East by the Cowlitz River. ... the farm was established in 1838 and that about 2,000 acres of land was enclosed and under tillage prior to and after the year 1846. The remainder of the unenclosed prairie land was used for grazing purposes...the whole occupancy covering about three miles square of land." (An "X" for Plamondon's signature appeared after his testimony.) The farm's entirety was estimated as being almost 3,600 acres, located in the approximate vicinity of the Toledo airport. The buildings were mostly at what is now the area of Spencer and Howe Roads north of Toledo.

To induce British settlement, the company persuaded 13 families (116 persons) of Scottish and Irish descent to relocate on the Cowlitz and Nisqually farms from the Red River Valley in Manitoba, Canada. They stayed only a year before moving to the Willamette Valley, south of the Columbia River.

Farming for the Puget Sound Agricultural Company continued after the area was declared American soil, but violence and vandalism took a toll on those employed to maintain the Cowlitz Farm. Americans, known as squatters, illegally staked out land hoping to acquire ownership later. George Roberts, the one-time clerk, had become Cowlitz Farm's intermittent manager and had to battle squatters for 12 years before violence forced him off the land.

Roberts was later to write that, "These squatters were determined at all hazards to get rid of me. They burned my buildings, shot through the windows, shot at my son, killed my lawyer, poor Kendall, stole my crops, and I stood all of this for upwards of ten years."

Roberts and his English wife endured

great heartache on the Cowlitz. First an epidemic of measles in 1846 struck the servants and laborers, and a typhoid onslaught in 1848 took Mrs. Roberts' life. She became the first European woman buried in Washington; her grave and those of her two daughters are still visible on a Toledo farm. Roberts was also plagued with sickened sheep and cattle, decaying buildings, and a vicious winter in 1860 which nearly decimated his livestock.

Attempts at justice in American courts proved futile. Finally in 1869 the holdings of Hudson's Bay Company and its monopoly on the fur trade officially ended in the United States with a settlement of $650,000 for its holdings, $200,000 of which represented the value of the Puget Sound Agricultural Company, including the Cowlitz Farm. A sadly disillusioned George Roberts moved to Cathlamet where, despite his misfortunes in Lewis County, he operated a store and became an active American citizen in county government.

The memory of the British settlement in Lewis County has vanished. Pioneer recollections have deleted the story, ignoring the French Canadians, George Roberts, and even the fact that the settlers were drawn here by the successful British farming operations. Nary an artifact remains of Hudson's Bay Company nor a marker for the prosperous Cowlitz Farm, obliterated by patriotic Americans declaring the land as their own.

Chapter 3

Manifest Destiny

Manifest Destiny carried with it many meanings. Why were those first settlers so eager to come? They were driven west by the dream of adventure, by ambition and greed. Their burning patriotism urged them to claim the land for America and push the British out. The land and its untold potential for agriculture grasped their souls. So it was that the prairies of the land of Lewis attracted the first settlers, most of whom were farmers by necessity.

They chose prairie land, much of which had been burned clear by the Indians for harvesting camas and grazing ponies. They located claims near creeks and rivers so they could transport their goods upriver and their farm products to market. Most of them gratefully returned the friendship and assistance they received from the Upper Chehalis and Cowlitz Indians. The settlers made lasting contributions as they carved out their places in the wilderness.

Taming the Land: The Jacksons

John R. Jackson, a rugged, intelligent man, stood over six feet tall with a build reminiscent of President Abraham Lincoln. Although he had lost an eye at 21 by being thrown by a horse into a hawthorn bush, Jackson did not suffer from a lack of foresight. He was Washington Territory's first American landowner and served as sheriff, judge, clerk of both Lewis County and U.S. District Court, legislator, and justice of the peace. He owned 2,200 acres of land and an impressive list of livestock. "The Highlands," his log cabin which was built in 1848 and now a historical site on Jackson Highway, held the first U.S. District Court

John R. Jackson, Washington Territory's first land owner and owner of Lewis County's first courthouse.

north of the Columbia River on November 12, 1850, and became one of the main stopping places north of the Columbia River.

Born in England in 1800, Jackson arrived in New York in 1833 by ship, then crossed the plains from Illinois as a driver of an ox team, to arrive at Clackamas Bottom on November 5, 1844. At Fort Vancouver, he let it be known he was looking for a good homestead site and neglected to mention to Chief Factor Dr. John McLoughlin that he was a naturalized American.

Thinking Jackson was British, McLoughlin allowed him to settle north of the Columbia. Jackson's arrival coincided with the arrival of the Michael T. Simmons/George Bush party in 1844 to the Tumwater/Olympia area defying McLoughlin's ban on Americans to the north. (Accounts of northwest history

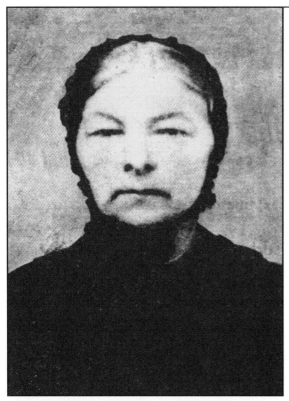

Matilda (Koontz) Jackson was highly respected.

credit Simmons for his formation of Olympia, but Simmons was also a property owner in Lewis County and died on his claim near Toledo.)

In July of 1845 Jackson made his claim in Lewis County a year before it was conceded to be in the U.S. On a trip to Oregon City for supplies two years later, he met and married Matilda Glover Koontz.

A heroic pioneer in her own right, Matilda Koontz had witnessed the drowning of her husband in the Snake River along the Oregon Trail. Matilda found herself a widow with four little boys, two thousand miles from her home in Missouri. To add to her grief, the next day she gave birth to a baby girl who died a few days later. One source says she recuperated from her illness at the Whitman Mission before journeying on by canoe, escaping by less than a month the fate of the angry Cayuse Indians who massacred the Whitmans. A family source says she rested two weeks at the Dalles where she was greeted with more bad news: her livestock had been stolen.

After her marriage to John Jackson, Matilda Jackson established a warm, inviting home which was open to many travelers, including Ulysses Grant, George McClellan, Phillip Sheridan, all of whom later became generals, and Gov. and Mrs. Isaac Stevens. While her husband is credited with having a store, an inn, and being postmaster, Mrs. Jackson was in the background assuring that all the pieces came together. "His-story" tends to overshadow "her-story," the story of the many women like Matilda Jackson who tamed the frontier by making it "home."

John R. Jackson died May 23, 1873 at his home on Jackson Prairie; his remains were moved from a fir grove on his property to Fern Hill Cemetery (once named Urquhart Cemetery) in Chehalis. Matilda Koontz Jackson lived to be nearly 90. She died February 14, 1901, one of the most highly respected of pioneer women. Her sons settled in the area, leaving their name on Koontz Road.

The Jackson home (shown before its first restoration in 1915) also served as the Jackson Courthouse.

The Claquato Church, here in 1891, is the oldest Protestant church in Washington. It was built in 1858 on land donated by Lewis Hawkins Davis, one of Lewis County's first settlers. Note the "crown of thorns" steeple.

Claquato

Lewis Hawkins Davis, his family, and five stalwart, grown sons came in 1851 to claim the land on Claquato Hill, a Native name for "high place." The Davis family wasted no time in creating a settlement; Davis cleared the land and erected a home, platted a town site, and built a grist mill on the Chehalis River. He donated land for the community church and provided lumber for its construction. He set aside a block for the county courthouse and later constructed a two-story building to attract the county seat; and in fact, Claquato was named the county seat in 1862, replacing the Jackson Courthouse. In another act of foresight, he set aside land for Claquato cemetery, one of the county's most historic and well-maintained "resting places" for the pioneers.

The Claquato courthouse is shown in 1869 with members of the Masons and their wives. The courthouse was designated the county seat in 1862, succeeding the Jackson Courthouse south of Chehalis.

The Land Called Lewis

Borst Family: *Mary A. Borst, Allen Borst, Joseph Borst, Eva Borst McElfresh and Ada Borst Blackwell, circa 1875.*

Adventure and opportunity brought many young men with large dreams. Joseph Borst was one of them. Borst, age 24, arrived with the Sidney Ford party. To earn money, he split rails for Hudson's Bay Company at Cowlitz Farms. Legend has it that he split 800 rails to earn $4 for a bushel of wheat, which he carried on his back for

The Borst barn, the promised Borst home and the storage blockhouse on the Chehalis River, 1909.

Manifest Destiny

Mary A. Borst on her 74th birthday, 1912.

25 miles back to his claim. To get lumber he traveled to Tumwater to the Roundtree mill on Black River. There he met his future bride, another pioneer, Mary Adeline Roundtree whose parents had originally settled in the Grays Harbor area. She agreed to marry him if he would build her a house. The "fine wooden house" he built for her of wood dipped in white lead has lasted so long that it can be seen today at Borst Park. After losing seventy head of cattle during the winter of 1860-61, Borst also constructed a huge barn so big that a four-horse team and wagon could be turned around inside it.

Borst was very prosperous during his lifetime. Beginning with his donation land claim, he added an extra 100 acres, bought a farm on Scammon Creek, added two farms at Adna and a large ranch near BawFaw Peak in the BawFaw (Boistfort) Valley. He also had a large ranch east of the Cascades near Ellensburg, where he died.

Tansunshun: The Resting Place

The Chehalis Indians who lived on the prairie near the Skookumchuck and Chehalis Rivers called the place "Tansunshun," meaning "resting place," where they came to bask in the sun. The Sidney Ford family settled at this resting place in 1846, after a treacherous trip in a wagon train from New York. They chose 640 acres on the strawberry-covered prairie northwest of the confluence of the Skookumchuck and Chehalis Rivers. It is still known as Fords Prairie.

The Ford home became the "Tansunshun" of hundreds of settlers en route to the Puget Sound. When Gov. and Mrs. Isaac Stevens made their way to Olympia for the first time, their son Hazard Stevens wrote, "It was another rainy, drizzling day. The road was almost impassable. At Saunders' bottom, where the town of Chehalis now sits, the mud was knee-deep

Sidney S. Ford and his wife Helen Ford, circa 1880.

for two miles, terribly wearing on the animals. At length after fording the Skookumchuck at its mouth, and traversing an extensive prairie, the wet, tired, and bedraggled party reached the log house of Judge Sidney S. Ford, and found hospitable shelter for the night, having traveled about twenty-five miles that day."

Besides being a judge in the new land, Sidney S. Ford was also an Indian agent for several tribes and signed the Indian Treaties negotiated by Gov. Stevens. Both father and son, Sidney Ford, Sr. and Jr., learned the Chehalis language and laid the groundwork for federal assistance and the Chehalis reservation at Oakville. Sidney Ford, Sr. attended the Cowlitz and Monticello Conventions to form the Washington Territory.

In 1851 Sidney S. Ford, Jr., his brother Tom, and future brother-in-law Sam Williams were held captive by the Haida Indians for fourteen months in the Queen Charlotte Islands where they were prospecting for gold. Stripped of their clothing and made to serve as slaves, the men were forced to dance for half the night for a piece of bread to fend off starvation. The prospectors came out with their skins intact, albeit flea-bitten and half-starved. Judge Ford, who was a member of the rescuing party, bought a grateful Haida slave who had been tortured. He served as the slave of Judge Sidney S. Ford for several years until the Judge freed him from bondage.

The Ford family members contributed immensely to the development of communities in southwest Washington. One daughter married John S. Shelton, for whose father the town of Shelton is named. Sam and Harriet Williams were instrumental in forming the first school at Peterson's Point, now called Westport. Other Fords settled in Rochester, Aberdeen, Cedarville (across the river from Oakville), Tenino, and Centralia. The numbers of Ford descendants are in the hundreds. Each year they hold a picnic at Borst Park, commanding a major section of it.

Napavine

Several were attracted to the Napavine area in the early years. The John Cutting family came from England in 1852 to join a relative at Cowlitz Prairie, Hudson's Bay Company clerk George B. Roberts. En route to San Francisco, their ship was attacked by pirates. When they docked in San Francisco, the Cutting's daughter fell into the bay and was rescued by a customs house officer named MacDonald. He later married the young woman and settled on MacDonald's Prairie. The Cuttings took up a Donation Land Claim just south of Napavine where they built a log house in 1853.

Napavine originally was named Napawana, according to some sources, for the daughter of an Indian chief; other sources claim it meant "small prairie." There are several native legends attached to Napavine's past, however. Eugene Evans in an unpublished memoir cites a story told by J. W. Cutting, of the last great battle between the "East-of-the-Mountains Indians" and the Cowlitz tribes, fought on the Newaukum Prairie. The local Indians won the battle but lost their chief to wounds incurred in the fray. After his death, the tribe held a big council to arrange for a new chief. In preparation for a feast, some of the Indians went to Puget Sound for shellfish while others hunted elk and deer in the Boistfort hills. They dug holes in the ground three feet deep by twenty feet wide and built huge fires for beds of coals on which to roast the meat. Over this they placed green ferns. Cutting claimed that the council and barbeque was held on the land his father homesteaded and that in his later years, evidence of some of the pits still remained.

The leader selected, Cutting said, was Chief Scanewa, the father-in-law of Simon Plamondon.

Manifest Destiny

Urquhart Store and Post Office at Napavine, 1905.

In the late 1860s when news of the passage of the railroad came, Horace H. Pinto was teaching school at Cowlitz. He decided immediately to open a store near the present site of Napavine. Hearing of Pinto's plans, John Cutting rode all night to Olympia to arrive at the land claims office at dawn and file his claim on the land instead. Later he gave two acres to Pinto for his store. Cutting and his wife Lydia adopted a child born in Mossyrock, and a pioneer story relates that Cutting carried the baby in his arms by horseback from Mossyrock to Napavine. The child, Otis Plant Cutting, grew up to become a well-known Northwest shipbuilder.

A dislike for Indian names supposedly prompted the name of the settlement to be changed to Napavine when the James Urquhart family bought out both the Cutting claim and Pinto's store. Later several members of the Urquhart family served as postmasters of the Napavine post office, county officials, and as pioneer citizens of Chehalis.

Boistfort/Pe Ell

One settler harkening back to the days of the Hudson's Bay Company was former HBC employee, the French Canadian trapper Pierre (Peter) Charles and his Indian wife. Not only one but two mispronunciations are associated with Pierre Charles. He claimed and named the Boistfort valley; Boistfort is a French word supposedly for "small valley" and is actually pronounced "Baw Faw." The highest point in the area still carries the name of Baw Faw Peak. Nearby land was claimed by Charles F. White near a big mound which had been an Indian burial place; he was joined by Turner R. Roundtree and Henry Stillman. Pierre Charles didn't stay long, perhaps because the new residents did not approve of his affiliation with the British. He moved on to another settlement which bears his name as another mispronunciation, Pe Ell. Oral tradition claims that the Indians could not pronounce Pierre and called him and his home Pe Ell. The odd name has stuck, despite the attempt to name it Mauermann after a family of Austian settlers who declined the honor.

Will Mauermann left, Albert Mauermann right, on a fishing trip at the Chehalis River, August 1909. The Mauermanns settled in the Pe Ell area.

Had they chosen to accept the name, the Mauermann family certainly would have earned it. After leaving their homeland in 1848, the ship on which they set sail sank in the English Channel. Surviving that ordeal, they journeyed on via another ship to New Orleans and on to St. Louis where they worked to save money. They decided to move to California but took the northern route instead. En route cholera struck their wagon train. An infant son died and Mrs. Karolina Mauermann was the only afflicted woman to survive. Shortly after their arrival at Boistfort, they fled to the Boistfort blockhouse for protection during the Indian uprising. Settling at the site of Pe Ell with their eight children, the Mauermanns faced the ravages of gray timber wolves and the challenge of using cougar and deer tallow for their only source of light. Karolina lived a lonely life without a single guest for nine years!

Nevertheless, the Mauermanns accumulated enough money for Joseph to return home to Austria in 1872 in search of brides for his sons. He came back with two young women who soon became members of the family.

Education has been important to Boistfort since its inception. Not only did the early settlement of Boistfort open the first school in Lewis County, but when Washington became a territory in 1853, Boistfort was considered as a site of the University of Washington. Knowing "U-Dub" as a significant establishment in Seattle, the idea of the University of Washington being at Boistfort conjures thoughts about the course of history for Lewis County had that happened.

Boistfort School with new school buses, circa 1925.

Mossy Rock

Another early settler chose his claim near a large moss-covered ledge in central Lewis County in 1852, a year before Washington became a territory. Henry Busie (also spelled Bucey and Bucie) established a claim at the area which his neighbor, Mr. Halland, named Mossy Rock. Mossy Rock was typical of many areas of the West in that a few settlers established claims in the 1850s but not many followed until after the Civil War. The Berry brothers, Hendricks, Dosses and Millers came to Mossy Rock in the late 1860s. Their first post office box was just that — a soap box kept under the bed. The official Mossy Rock post office was established in 1875 and renamed as Mossyrock (one word) in 1895.

George Washington Had A Dream

One settler in Lewis County has brought more positive attention to Centralia than perhaps any other single individual. He is the main character in several children's books and the feature of numerous books and articles. The founding father of Centralia was a benevolent black man, George Washington, who had a reason of his own for moving west: persecution because of his color. Washington braved all odds by having his own claim in a territory forbidden for black settlement — and founded a prosperous town on the railroad line. An ambitious entrepreneur who amassed a substantial estate, he was willing to give major portions of his land and good fortune to his community. Washington's dream was a town called "Centerville" for its location midway between Tacoma and Kalama on the Northern Pacific Railroad.

Named for the nation's first President, George Washington was born in Virginia to a white woman and a black slave on Aug. 15, 1817. Shortly after his birth and the sale of his father to another master far away, Mr. and Mrs. James Cochran agreed to raise him until he was 21. The couple and their adopted son lived in Virginia and Ohio before moving west to Missouri where the young boy learned how to tan hides, sew, knit, and cook and later how to make his own shirts in a hour and half. Although by law he was not allowed to go to school, he taught himself to read.

At the age of twenty he built himself a handsome brick home in Bloomington, Missouri and then rented a sawmill with a partner only to be arrested for owning a business. When his sawmill flooded, he moved to Illinois and purchased a patent for making whiskey. An empty whiskey barrel may have been the germination for the founding of Centralia, for legalized prejudice forced Washington to abandon

George Washington, the founder of Centralia.

his distillery because Blacks were forbidden from manufacturing or selling alcohol. Disgusted by laws that would not grant a person a chance to succeed, Washington looked to a place for the freedom to develop his dreams. The West.

His adoptive parents, the Cochrans and their ten-year-old granddaughter, agreed to join him in a wagon train to Oregon. After his recovery from an illness at Fort Vancouver, he and the Cochrans traveled to the mouth of the Cowlitz where they built a boat to travel upstream to the Cowlitz Landing. George built a cabin for the Cochrans and then established his own claim at the mouth of the Skookumchuck and Chehalis Rivers. He hoped to be a legal owner of the land.

His neighbors, the Chehalis Indians who camped each summer along the banks of the Skookumchuck called him "Noclas" meaning "black face" and "Myeach" for charred, blackened wood. The settlers referred to his claim as "Black George Prairie." On the northwest portion of his land were more than two hundred graves of those who had died in the smallpox epidemic of the 1830s. The tribe continued to use the area as a funeral site where they placed their dead in canoes in the trees.

Soon other squatters coveted his land, which was fenced, cleared and planted in crops. However, Washington was not free from the laws of the Oregon Territory prohibiting blacks to settle. One night two visitors hinted at their plans to go to Olympia and file claim on his land. Without a minute to waste, he walked to Cowlitz Landing and sold his claim to the Cochrans for $200. They moved in with him to "prove up" on the claim of 640 acres, which soon included a dock and a toll ferry to be known as Cochran's Landing. After four years' of proving up, Washington bought the claim from the Cochrans for $3,200. One early newspaper article refers to "Cochran's claim" and "his black slave." The same year that George Washington almost lost his homestead, a bill, filed in the Oregon Territorial legislature read:

"...Be it enacted by the legislative assembly of the territory of Oregon that George Washington, a man of color, of Thurston County (the county border was then south of the Centralia/Chehalis area), be hereby exempt from the provisions of the act ...to prevent Negroes and mulattoes from coming into or residing in the Oregon Territory...Passed Dec. 17, 1852."

The Chehalis River ferry at Lincoln Creek, 1896, similar to the ferry at Cochran's Landing.

Washington nursed his aging adoptive parents with compassion until their deaths in 1859 and 1861, and for nearly a decade, he lived alone, expanding his property in relative peace while the Civil War raged on far away. He built a new two-story home in 1868 (near the present Washington Park) to which he brought his first wife a year later. A widow from Tumwater with one child, Mary Jane Cooness was black and Jewish. The new Mrs. Washington had the first sewing machine in the area, such a curiosity that visitors traveled from miles to admire it. George himself made all his own clothes on it.

Mary Jane (Cooness) Washington, named Centralia's first streets.

In 1872 George Washington watched the railroad cross his land. He and his wife filed a plat for the new town of Centerville on January 8, 1875. The four-block square ran north from Locust Street on Pearl Street to Pine, east to Diamond Street and south to East Locust. In one year his town grew to a population of 50. Centralia owes the naming of its core streets to Mary Jane, who may have had images of heaven in mind when she chose the names of Pearl, Gold, Silver, and Diamond. Washington donated the land for a park which bears his name. Later it became the home of the Carnegie (later Timberland) Library. In 1883 the name of his town was changed to Centralia, suggested by a newcomer from Centralia, Illinois, because of confusion with another Centerville in eastern Washington.

George Washington, a man who lived by his word and a generous spirit, sold lots for $10 each at first, and never more than $150. He interviewed prospective buyers and sold only to those who intended to build in his town. He helped to found and build the first church. By 1883 he had watched the town boom to a thriving population of 5,000 with ten lumber and manufacturing mills. Then he observed it deflate during the severe depression of 1893. When families were close to starvation, he personally bought food and carried it in wheelbarrows to his neighbors. He forgave debts, allowed people to work for food and clothing, and literally kept the town going until the economy recovered, although the town had declined to 1,200 people.

When Washington died on August 26, 1905, his estate was worth some $150,000. His town of Centralia was well-established, as was his reputation as a man of sterling character. In 1976 his memory was honored by two national organizations, the Association for the Study of Afro-American Life and History and the Amoco Foundation, Inc., the charitable arm of the Standard Oil Company. Governor Dan Evans proclaimed, "George Washington Day: Friday, Oct. 22, 1976."

Today George Washington's dream is alive and well in the "Hub City" of Lewis County.

Schools and Churches

As soon as they could, settlers established roots through two institutions: their schools and churches. The first schools were almost always rough-hewn, one-room affairs. The school sessions often lasted only three months out of the year, and teachers boarded with local families, receiving wages of $45 to $50 a month.

Alder School, near Alder Lake, north of Morton, 1890.

Sometimes teachers faced more adventure than they bargained for; a teacher at Saundersville (Chehalis) once shot a cougar on the front porch and was so shaken by the event, he dismissed school for the day.

The churches were built with donated labor and true devotion. Pioneer churches in the area included the lovely Claquato Church, the St. Francis Xavier Mission at Toledo, and later the Harmony Church near Mossyrock and the St. Urban Church near Winlock.

Land Claims

The settlers came under the auspices of the Donation Land Claim Act, but like many legislative acts it had its unusual consequences. One had a direct effect on the female population, for in order to have 640 acres, men had to be married. With the scarcity of females in the new land, everyone with a skirt was in great demand. Girls as young as twelve were married to men much older. The 1860 census lists some married women who were a mere fourteen years of age.

One young man, determined to have female companionship for a New Years Eve party, traveled by horseback all one day to the home of his sweetheart. The two rode all the next day to attend the party, returned to her home the following day, and he rode back the fourth day. A four-day journey for a date!

Our Lady of Assumption Catholic Church, St. Urban, circa 1985.

One unfortunate aspect of settlement reared its ugly head in the form of greed. Judith Irwin, Longview historian, provides this account of a settler at Cowlitz Landing: "Later settlers were not always neighborly or so careful of the Native Americans' indigenous rights. In fact, some boasted of taking advantage of their American Indian neighbors, at times getting them drunk in order to cheat them. By a 'sharp Yankee practice,' E. D. Warbass usurped Simon Plamondon, Jr.'s, right to his donation land claim next to Cowlitz Landing. While Simon, Jr., was on a trip north, E.D. Warbass got Simon, Sr., drunk. Whether Plamondon, who could not read or write, or Warbass himself put the 'X' to a quit-claim deed for the younger Plamondon's property cannot be known. According to Simon, Jr.'s, later affidavit, when he returned, E.D. Warbass met him with a gun in his face, ready to shoot if he set foot on his own property. Unfortunately, as pioneer law was practiced, if an Indian (or a half-blood) killed a white man, he was hanged. If a white man killed an Indian, no court of law, even if the case should go to trial, would hang the white man."

An ironic twist of the Land Claim Act was the isolation it caused. The large plots of land separated people from their neighbors and created isolation rather than communities. Once prime prairie land was chosen, few newcomers were attracted to the area, and the population remained low during the decades of the 1850s, 1860s, and the 1870s. Washington Territory was to remain an inaccessible frontier until the rails of the Iron Horse replaced the muddy trails of the packhorse and work oxen of the first pioneers.

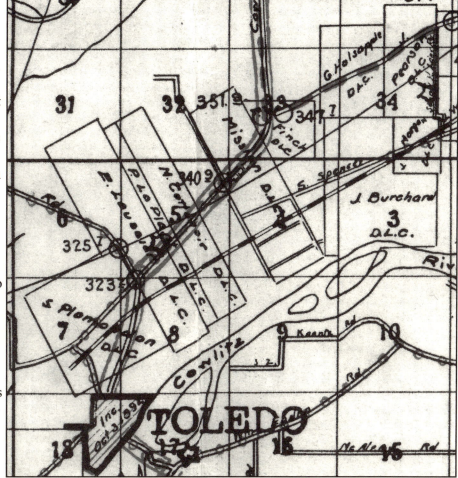
Map of early donation land claims, including the Plamondon DLC near Toledo.

Chapter 4

Times of Unrest

For the Native peoples the arrival of the settlers marked the end of their traditional way of life. The new arrivals built fences around grazing prairies for the Natives' ponies, and metal plows and rooting hogs ruined their best camas patches. They also brought new diseases, along with guns and liquor. Adding to the list, the territory's aggressive new governor, Isaac Stevens, wanted to place the Northwest tribes on reservations in order to secure safe passage of the northern route of the railroad and open the land to settlement.

The white settlers had a neighborly interdependence with the tribal people and occasionally intermarried, but most settlers felt threatened by the Indians whose ways and traditions they found alien. The 1847 Whitman massacre in eastern Washington, in which Indians killed a group of unsuspecting missionaries, was fresh in their memories. Stevens moved quickly to get the tribes to sign treaties that relinquished their right to the land so the settlers could feel safe and the Indians could be "domesticated" on the reservations. With the Medicine Creek Treaty of 1854, he collected signatures with an amazing speed, choosing tribal representatives arbitrarily and providing sketchy treaty translations in several tongues, including one in the 300-word Chinook trade jargon. Historians theorize that few Indians realized what they were signing.

Stylized painting of Gov. Stevens, foreground, Sidney Ford, Sr. of Centralia in the back and the Chehalis Indian Tribe at Cosmopolis negotiating their treaty. Northwest tribes had neither feather headdresses nor teepees.

Duplicitously, Stevens told the Indians they wouldn't have to leave their lands until the treaties were ratified, while, at the same time, on the eastern side of the mountains, he advertised that the land was available to settlers. However, the treaties failed. For one thing, each tribe wanted its own reservation near its ancestral burial grounds, and each refused to share a reservation with its rivals. For another, the governor's obstinacy prevented him from compromising. The result was the Indian War, called by some, the "Indian-Stevens War."

In 1855 the ink on the treaties was barely dry when the discovery of gold along the Colville River brought a frenzy of prospectors across the Yakima Valley. The Yakima Indians reacted angrily by killing many miners. A militia from the new Territorial capitol in Olympia marched in to defend the prospectors, but while the soldiers were east of the mountains, the western tribes attacked settlers near Puget Sound and threatened the village of Seattle. When settlers and soldiers were accosted at White River, north of Fort Steilacoom, the assault shook the nerves of settlers in nearby Lewis County.

Local settlers were startled in the middle of the night with the warning: the Indians were planning an attack in Lewis County! Supposedly, the rumor went, the Yakima Indians would join forces with the White River Indians and strike from the east, while the Puget Sound Indians would hit from the north. The Chehalis tribe, the wide-eyed settlers believed, was already lurking nearby, ready to attack. The settlers momentarily forgot that most of the Natives were their friends and neighbors.

According to an account written by Evelyn Walking in *Centralia: The First Fifty Years*, a friendly Indian in the Grand Mound area, John Highton or Heyton, "mounted his horse and rode through the night, Paul Revere fashion, warning the settlers. The men, women, and children of five prairies hurriedly packed their utensils and bedding in wagons and urged their oxen to the half-finished stockade on Mound Prairie (Grand Mound)." So 30 families, some 224 people in all, arrived at the partly completed fort where they were to live for 16 months during the Indian War of 1855-1856.

On October 17, 1855, settlers from the nearby prairies of Grand Mound, Fords, Frost, Baker, Mima and Waunch gathered to build a defensive stockade. They named it Fort Henness after Benjamin Henness,

A model of Fort Henness on the ground at its original site near Grand Mound, 1982.

Lewis County Museum volunteers, Harlan Shepardson, Hamlet Hilpert, Don Bunker and Minnie Lingreen hold up a scale model of Fort Henness in Grand Mound, 1982.

captain of the hastily formed local militia. The fortress walls consisted of 16-foot pointed logs planted in a 100 by 130 foot trench, while at the southeast and northwest corners stood two-story bastions and in the middle loomed a guardhouse. Inside stood a schoolhouse, barracks for single men and split cedar cabins for families. A well dug within the walls supplied water for the inhabitants. Children played "Settlers and Indians" when they weren't in school, which for many was their first formal education. Women, often isolated and lonely on their land claims, socialized with their neighbors. Yet despite the rumors of an impending attack, the Indians never came.

Not all the settlers headed to Fort Henness. George Washington, the founder of Centralia, built a small fortress on his own land. The Ford family fortified their log cabin while Indian agent Sidney Ford confiscated weapons and promised protection for those natives who complied with the government's directives.

At Mossyrock, settlers constructed a three-story, split-cedar blockhouse. Another one was erected at the Joseph Borst claim, not to protect settlers but to store grain for the soldiers and settlers hunkered down in other places. Wagons regularly delivered supplies of grain to and from the Borst farm. The driver of one supply wagon from the fort was found near Rainier, thrown from his wagon and scalped. The Borst blockhouse, solidly built in the 1850s with skillfully hewn logs, has lasted to this day. After the river bank where it stood eroded, it was moved to Riverside Park, and then in 1922 back to Borst Park as a historic structure visible from Interstate 5.

The eroding Chehalis River bank threatens the Borst blockhouse in its original location, circa 1915.

Ironically, some of the Indian War's most colorful anecdotes stemmed not from heroic struggles, but from the settlers' own paranoia and irrational fears. A Mossyrock settler had a cabin on the Cowlitz River near a frequently traveled Indian trail. When a band of war-painted Indians approached his cabin, he was convinced of his impending doom and, with gun in hand, dashed from the cabin and shot himself on the spot. The Indians passed by without touching his body or gun. He was buried later by his neighbors exactly where he fell. If the story is true, he may have been the only Caucasian casualty within the boundaries of Lewis County.

At Claquato, Lewis Hawkins Davis built a blockhouse in which cramped conditions and fear of Indian attacks drove the inhabitants to the brink of insanity. In his memoirs about Claquato, Roscoe Britten Doane wrote that "the confinement of a number of families in such close proximity soon brought about discontent and some ill feeling so most finally decided to take their chances in case of attack." Other accounts tell of a man who went insane, raving and singing wildly for nights on end.

Accounts of those times don't mention what happened to the settlers' homes while they were in the blockhouses. But Schulyer and Elizabeth Saunders, whose claim would become the town site of Chehalis, had their cabin burned and their stock killed during their time living in the protection of the Claquato blockhouse.

Other blockhouses were erected, one by the Layton family near Toledo, and one by Javan Hall across the Cowlitz River. The White family had one at Boistfort, and one was at the Camas Land Claim near Winlock.

During the Indian War the indefatigable Simon Plamondon played a key role in Indian affairs. In a gesture of peace some 450 members of the Lower Cowlitz tribe surrendered their arms and went to a temporary reservation on Cowlitz Prairie. Plamondon, also an Indian agent, supervised the proceedings, and since the Indians were not allowed to hunt, he personally fed them from his own cattle and hogs for the duration of the conflict.

He later submitted vouchers for $4,000 to the government. Correspondence from Gov. Stevens to Plamondon dated April 4, 1856, reveals the mistrust of those times:

"Sir: Great Complaints are made by the citizens of Lewis County in regard to the Indians under your charge, and I have requested Col. Croski to make an examination into the matter, and see where the fault lay. It is the intention of the (gov't?) to supply them with the food they really need. It is absolutely necessary they not roam at large, for we know not when the county may become the war ground of the hostiles. Any direction which Col. Croski may give you in reference to the Indians you will conform to."

Stevens' curt letter may have been prompted by his distrust of people like Plamondon -- French Canadians and former Hudson's Bay employees with Indian wives. During the Indian War he had ordered a group of them from the Steilacoom area to leave their farms and report to blockhouses where they could be supervised. In an uproar that later earned Stevens a reprimand from the White House, Stevens declared martial law to enforce their imprisonment. The chief justice of the territory ordered Stevens arrested; Stevens in turn ordered his militia to arrest the judge and close the courts. The commission appointed to resolve the altercation ruled that Stevens had no grounds to declare martial law, but the case was referred to civil court and dismissed. The French Canadians went free.

By 1858 the winds of war had calmed and settlers returned to their regular routines. On March 8, 1859 Congress ratified

Stevens' treaties, which to this day are the cause of much debate, especially over the Indians' rights to traditional hunting and fishing grounds. Although many historians agree that Stevens' treaties were more equitable than most, they are viewed less charitably by those whose lives were affected.

Five years later in 1864 the Chehalis Reservation was created at the juncture of the Black and Chehalis Rivers. In 1939 The Confederated Tribes of the Chehalis Reservation became a self-governing, independent political unit, Over time both Upper and Lower Cowlitz tribes were dispossessed of their homeland without a reservation. After nearly a century and a half the Cowlitz Tribe was federally acknowledged as an American Indian tribe on January 4, 2002.

The Chehalis Reservation, near Oakville, circa 1900.

Chapter 5

Lewis: The Mother of Counties

In the history of settlement of the land north of the Columbia River and the formation of Washington State, the early role of Lewis County was pivotal, though sometimes overlooked.

Its creation and its amazing boundaries date back to a time when the land was in British territory, and its first government operated outside of United States jurisdiction. Incredibly, Lewis County stretched all the way to the Russian settlement of Sitka, Alaska, encompassing not only most of Western Washington but also most of British Columbia! It became known as the "Mother of Counties" for the thirteen Washington counties carved from its borders. Furthermore, the first civic actions of government, indeed the very decision to petition Congress to break away from Oregon Territory to form a separate territory, occurred within the land called Lewis. Consequently, the first courts and the first formative government began operation in Lewis County as well. Washington's first legal documents bore the signatures of the county's first settlers, including the "X" of the indefatigable Simon Plamondon.

Like salmon hurling themselves upriver, the first settlers forced their way up the Cowlitz River to form a new life. Their determination gave birth to the county that spawned most other counties in Western Washington — Lewis County — and their drive upstream resulted in formation of the Washington Territory.

The future of the land called Lewis was yet to be determined in the early 1840s, for Britain and the United States were still in a fierce competition for much of the Oregon Territory — that expanse of land encompassing most of the current states of Oregon, Washington, parts of Idaho and Montana, and going all the way north to Alaska. While the British were willing to concede the land south of the Columbia, they still wanted to keep the land to the north. But Americans were filling up the Territory,

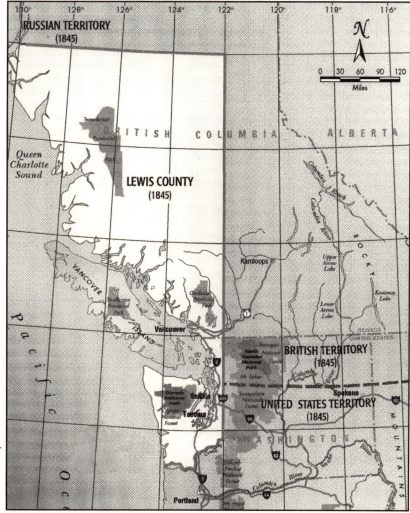

Lewis County, the mother of counties in 1845.

The Land Called Lewis

A prairie schooner at the Territorial Centennial display in the lawn in front of the Chehalis City Hall and Library in Chehalis, 1953.

and people from distant England had little interest in an area they equated with the bitter climates of northern Canada.

As early as 1836 American immigrants petitioned Congress to declare the Oregon country part of the United States. Several bills in Congress sought protection for U.S. citizens in the territory, and after several attempts at passage, the Oregon Donation Land Act of 1850 offered free land to American settlers, 320 acres to each white man and 640 to married couples who lived on the soil for five years. Slavery was also a keen issue to Americans, and in the Oregon Territory both slavery and Black ownership of land were prohibited.

Americans were coming in hordes to the Northwest, around the Horn by ship or by wagon train along the Oregon Trail, some 65,000 of them between 1830 and 1869, all driven by the hunger for free land. Terms like "Manifest Destiny" and tales of green, unfenced pastures fired the American imagination. With patriotic fervor, Americans took up the rallying cry for a northern parallel line, "Fifty-four forty or fight!" Not only did they want the land north of the Columbia, they wanted it all the way through British Columbia to the Russian holdings in southeast Alaska.

As this torrent of settlers deluged the territory, it was clear that a legal system was needed. Finally, on May 2, 1843, a group of Americans and French Canadians met, ironically in a British-owned Hudson's Bay warehouse, to discuss wolves but instead laid the groundwork for a provisional government. A settler who had packed along a book of Iowa law on his trek over the Oregon Trail contributed it as the basis for the law.

The Evolution of Washington Counties, compiled by the Yakima Genealogical Society in 1978, described the informal process: "With fine disregard of troublesome questions of local and international geography, ...[the settlers] drew lines toward the four points of the compass from their little center of settlement on the Willamette River, thus laying off the four pioneer districts, parents of all counties within this imperial domain." The Oregon Territory was defined as from the 42nd parallel, bordering Mexican-ruled California, east to the summit of the Rocky Mountains,

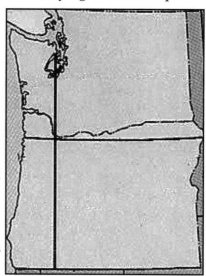

The north-south Willamette Meridian and the east-west Willamette Base Line meet in the Willamette Stone State Heritage Site two miles west of downtown Portland.

This stone was the point from which all land in Washington and Oregon was measured as either east or west of the Willamette Meridian and either north or south of the Willamette Base Line. The stone was destroyed by vandals in the 1980s and replaced by a brass marker.

and north to Russian Territory at the 54th parallel.

When Lewis County was created in 1845, it wasn't even a part of the United States. On August 18, 1845, the territory north of the Columbia was designated as the Vancouver District. Then on December 21, 1845, all the land west of the Cowlitz River — a rather vague designation — and north to 54 degrees 40 minutes near present day Sitka was given the name of Lewis County, after the explorer Meriwether Lewis. Thus, Lewis County, "the Mother of all Counties," extended to Alaska, encompassed Puget Sound, coastal British Columbia and the Washington coast.

The next day, on December 22, 1845, the word "district" was changed to "county" and so the remainder of the Vancouver District became Vancouver County.

In keeping with the name of Lewis County, Vancouver County was renamed Clarke (sic) County on July 16, 1848. The misspelling was not officially corrected until 1925.

To this day, the debate goes on about which county was actually formed first, Lewis or Clark. It would appear to be a matter of semantics and perspective, for Clark County was actually the Vancouver "District," while Lewis was actually named a county from the onset. Clark County's name was chosen after Lewis County's. Many have observed it certainly was not the Clark and Lewis Expedition.

The original Lewis County was eventually carved down to its current boundary with the addition of thirteen other Washington counties: Pacific (1851); Thurston, King, Jefferson, Pierce, Island (1852); Clallam, Chehalis (later renamed Grays Harbor), Cowlitz, Wahkiakum, Swamish (later renamed as Mason), Whatcom and Skamania (1854-57). Slaughter County (Kitsap) was carved from King County in 1857. The boundaries of Lewis County itself were changed several times. At one point what is now Centralia fell within Thurston County, and in the late 1880s Eastern Lewis County residents were certain they would have a county of their own. The rectangular boundaries were set by 1879.

For a period of six months and four days, Lewis County was not officially a United States territory, yet it operated with an American code of laws and form of government. Its affairs were administered by citizens, some of whom, such as Simon Plamondon, were not yet Americans. The settlers clamored for a resolution to the issue, but in 1846, the United States government was occupied with the Mexican War and the slavery controversy, and the Hudson's Bay Company was shifting its holdings to Fort Victoria in British Columbia, away from the Willamette and the Cowlitz Corridor. While the two long-time rival nations were preoccupied with other matters, the British and the Americans reached an agreement on the Northwest: the U.S.-Canadian border would lie at the 49th parallel. That, at least, was clear. But the question of British holdings within the new U.S. territory was subject to intense, even violent, controversy.

In 1848 Lewis County citizens, still including those of the Puget Sound, were so riled by the British-owned Puget Sound Agricultural Company's claims to the land that they met to make "serious charges" against the company. The commemorative booklet published by the Washington Centennial Association in 1945, reprinted the document from their meeting charging that the long-haired Spanish cattle owned by the British were running wild, consuming all the vegetation and endangering the domestic herds belonging to the Americans. They were enraged that the British refused to sell them sheep, and they were furious with Hudson's Bay Chief Factor William F. Tolmie. The rights (and perceived wrongs) of the British on what was now American soil raged for twenty more years until the British were awarded payment for their holdings.

Setting Up the Government

The work of setting up a government was not a simple matter for the new county. Its founders, including Plamondon, John R. Jackson, and Sidney S. Ford, were to play a vital role in not just one but three different governing bodies: the provisional (temporary) government before Oregon became a territory (1845-46), the Oregon Territorial government (1848), and the fledgling Washington Territory (1853). Some of the most significant decisions affecting the future state of Washington during those years occurred in the Lewis County homes of John R. and Matilda Jackson, Sidney and Nancy Ford, and at Cowlitz (Plamondon) Landing, prior to the settlement of the Puget Sound area.

For settlers north of the Columbia, the Oregon-based government proved unnecessarily cumbersome because of simple geography. Getting to the legislative sessions meetings or court hearings in Salem, Oregon, took days, and there were few places to stay en route. The only means of travel was by horseback or by passage in 30-foot boats, interrupted by grueling portages. There was no wagon road between Cowlitz Landing and Tumwater, then known as New Market. In order to discuss the issues of the day with one another, settlers had to either walk or go by horseback to meet.

After only three years, settlers north of the Columbia were clamoring for change; they wanted their own local government. A committee met at John R. Jackson's cabin in 1851 to plan an official plea to Congress for a new territory separate from Oregon Territory, and within six weeks, they met at the Cowlitz Landing to demand just that.

The first meeting-place to form the Territory of Washington was John R. Jackson's home south of Chehalis, shown after its restoration in 1915.

An artist's rendering of Cowlitz Landing and the Clarke Hotel, the site of the Cowlitz Convention in 1851.

The Cowlitz Convention met at the Clarke Hotel on August 29, 1851, a day which is considered the inception of the Washington Territory. A memorial was drafted to the United States Congress asking for a division of the Oregon Territory, and nearly every paragraph stressed either geographic isolation or inconvenience in travel. With the seat of government 300 miles from the principal settlements, "the rights of citizens must go unredressed, crimes and injuries unpunished."

The next year, Tumwater settler Michael Simmons headed a delegation at Monticello (south Longview) to draft a formal petition to Congress requesting a new territory named "Columbia" and the construction of military roads. Supposedly to avoid confusion with the District of Columbia, a short-sighted Congress chose "Washington" as the name for the new territory, and ever since that time, Washingtonians have had to explain their residence as "the other Washington." Isaac I. Stevens, a West Point graduate and military engineer, officially accepted the offer of the governorship.

The new Washington Territory came into being with the signature of President Millard Fillmore on March 2, 1853. Its eastern boundary stretched to the crest of the Rocky Mountains. It had eight counties at the time, seven of them created by Lewis, the Mother of Counties.

Signers of the Cowlitz Landing Convention and the Monticello Convention are listed on a memorial maintained by Washington State Parks in Longview near the original Monticello site.

Chapter 6

Canoes, Coaches, Steamboats

Long before Europeans came to the Northwest, a network of rivers and trails laced the land with passageways for travel. The Indians of the Lower Chehalis tribe living downriver relied heavily on waterways and came far up the Chehalis River in canoes. The Cowlitz and Upper Chehalis Indians who lived inland journeyed in canoes and on land with horses via a system of trails. When white people came, they relied on the same methods of transportation. First the trappers and then the settlers navigated by canoe and flat-bottomed bateaux, and like the Indians, developed overland trails. They built the rugged Military Road, and for half a century they steamed up the Cowlitz River aboard colorful steamboats. The mode of transportation dictated where early settlements were located and later where towns and cities grew.

From the time Michael T. Simmons and John R. Jackson journeyed inland in 1844, to 1872 when the Northern Pacific Railway was built, transportation was an ongoing challenge. Prior to 1850, passage up the Cowlitz River corridor was the only inland option for the handful of white settlers north of the Columbia. The road from Cowlitz Landing to Olympia was barely passable for wagons; few ferry crossings were available over the rivers, and mud holes during inclement weather were horror stories for road travelers in lowland areas. In 1854 a mail carrier's trip from Cowlitz to Olympia, 53 miles, took two days. Stories of pioneers carrying goods on their backs from Claquato to Olympia and from Chehalis to Randle and Packwood were legendary. To transport goods across rivers, wagons had to be unloaded, materials placed in canoes, the wagon and horses taken across, and the wagons reloaded. Imagine the temperament of the settlers after numerous river crossings!

Hacking their way through dense old-growth forests and underbrush, the settlers came nevertheless, determined to make the way passable for those who followed. They

Approaching the site of the Cowlitz Landing, also called Warbassport, 1889. This was the major debarking point for thousands of Washington settlers. Cowlitz River floods have washed away much of the natural landing.

demanded better routes of travel from the government, their demands dating back to the Cowlitz and Monticello Conventions. The answer was the Military Road.

Coaches

If Lewis County is the mother of counties in Washington, then the Military Road can be designated as the "Mother of Roads" in the region, for it was one of the first identifiable roads. It was used for years as the main stage road from the Columbia River to Olympia. Although it was planned to ensure military protection for settlers, the Military Road was also used to transport mail, freight, and passengers by stage coach. The first territorial legislature had approved a grant of $18,000 for the road, enhanced with a Congressional appropriation of $30,000. *The Columbian* newspaper reported that on October 1, 1852, "This road will be placed so as to make navigation of the Cowlitz River unnecessary and both time and distance will be saved to those traveling the route. The road will be finished early next season and will render communication between Puget Sound and the Columbia River both speedy and easy."

The road was not completed for five years, and nothing about it was speedy or easy.

One section of the Military Road was intended to connect Fort Vancouver on the Columbia (by then American-owned) to the newly constructed Fort Steilacoom on Puget Sound. The other part was planned from Fort Vancouver to Fort Walla Walla. But then the Indians went up in arms. Construction was delayed until the close of Indian trouble in 1856, although portions were used to transport military supplies from Fort Borst during the "blockhouse years." Fears sparked by the conflict fired the need for the road. In 1856 government contracts were issued for construction from Cowlitz Landing to Fords Prairie, a distance of 25 miles, with additional sections opened in 1857 to Fort Nisqually and Fort Steilacoom. In 1858 a seventeen mile stretch of road was built on the west bank of the Cowlitz from Monticello (Longview) to Cowlitz Landing. It was little more than a cow trail, barely negotiable by wagons or stagecoaches maneuvering around stumps and through mud.

Surveyors of the military road chose to build as many portions as possible on high plateau areas or foothills on the west side of the Chehalis River. They planned only two river crossings, one at the mouth of the Skookumchuck and another below Claquato, obviously the huge "sink hole" that travelers wanted to avoid. John R. Jackson, realizing the road's value, tried to wield political clout to establish the route

A team in 2005 recreates the experience of traveling early trails.

The Land Called Lewis

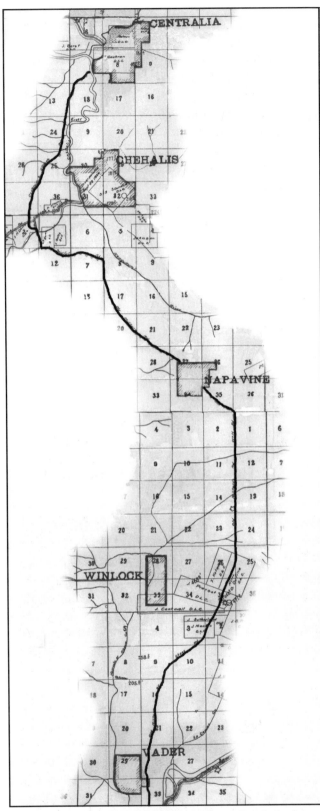

One estimate of the location of the Military Road, the first overland route that was more than a foot path, circa 1860. Town boundaries are shown after later development.

by his "Highlands" property, but instead it wound farther west on the higher plateaus near the future sites of Winlock, Koontz Road to Napavine, Claquato and Scheuber Road.

Jackson need not have worried. The road past his property would emerge as the major north-south route for travelers from Portland to Seattle. First known as the Cowlitz Trail, then Cowlitz-Puget Sound Road, it was also named the Pacific Highway, Highway 99, and the Jackson Highway. Historian Margaret Shields from the Lewis County Historical Museum notes that paving didn't occur until 1923.

In the 1960s Charles Miles, a teacher and historian whose birthplace was Claquato, discovered an old map which showed the route of the Military Road prior to its construction. Labeled as the "Advertised Section of U.S. Military Road — from Columbia Barracks to Fort Steilacoom," the place names of the time are used, which are a challenge to interpret in later times. The map showed the road skirting the west bank of the Cowlitz River at Cowlitz Landing, where it turned west. It took to higher ground in "Lacamas Creek" Basin, east to the edge of Drew's Prairie and to the center of Grand Prairie near present-day Winlock. It then connected with a road labeled "Road from Boistfort Prairie." After Cutting's Prairie (Napavine) the route bent to the west directly for Davis's Settlement (Claquato). Its route continued past Scheuber farm (southwest of Centralia), and although it was closed prior to 1900, the present Scheuber Road is nearby.

One section over the steepest part of Claquato Hill was so steep that it earned the name "Chain Hill" because the only way to get wagons down it safely was to chain up the wheels to act as brakes. This route over the hill has been long abandoned. The road connected to Fort Borst, and then some references indicate that it went up the Skookumchuck by "Cochran's Landing," which was George Washington's claim (Centralia). At some point it joined "the Territorial Road from Olympia to Monticello"—the Cowlitz Trail, which was the route used by Indians and the Hudson Bay Company to get to the British-owned Fort Nisqually.

A report of the survey contains this notation: "Higher ground, no serious hills to be surmounted; crosses the Chehalis River twice, bridge at farther crossing."

Inevitably the Military Road had to cross rivers such as the Chehalis by a primitive ferry or barge. The ferries operated by a cable attached to anchors on both sides of the river. An eyehook was latched to the cable on which the vessel slid. By steering the ferry into the river's current with a rudder, the ferry used the force of the river for propulsion. These early ferries transported wagons, passengers, livestock, and freight.

The original settler of Claquato, Lewis Hawkins Davis, was instrumental in determining the course of the Military Road. Davis realized the importance of all-season,

Ferry crosses the Cowlitz River at present site of Cora Bridge, above Randle, 1914.

passable roads. All roads would emanate from his town, he figured, and ensure its prosperity. Charles Miles noted that the section of the military road by Claquato "was built by Davis and his boys to promote the welfare of his settlement in competition with Saunders' Prairie." With his sons and teams of oxen, he cleared a six-mile road down the Chehalis Valley to the point where the Skookumchuck empties into the Chehalis (at Centralia). The next year he oversaw the construction of a nine-mile road over the densely timbered Newaukum Hill to the settlement at MacDonald's Prairie in the Newaukum Valley.

Earlier roads built by Davis and his neighbors were completed without government grants. Davis' excellent plans preceded even the surveys for the government roads, and they

A temporary footbridge at the Chehalis River crossing near Claquato, circa 1880.

The Land Called Lewis

were adopted as part of the military road system. "Thus, the historic military road of Western Washington had its true beginning at the Davis place on Claquato hill," explained historian Roscoe Brittan Doane in 1965.

Today much of the original Military Road through Lewis County is the subject of guesswork, with the exception of South and North Military Road near Winlock. As with many of the very early landmarks, it remains unmarked and lost with the passage of time.

Steamboats

In the early days so many pioneers came up the Cowlitz River that Cowlitz Landing and Monticello were actually considered to be on the old Oregon Trail. Cowlitz Landing in early territorial days was a bustling little place from the time of the Hudson's Bay Company farms and the fur trade. In 1850 Captain Edward D. Warbass had usurped the claim originally held by Simon Plamondon, Jr., with the idea of establishing the area as the head of navigation. A crude wharf accommodated the canoes and bateaux of the traders. The spot was generally known as Cowlitz Landing, although it was called Warbassport for a time. It consisted of a blockhouse, a hotel, a general merchandise store, a sawmill, grist mill, and tavern. People from all parts of Lewis County and the new territory congregated at the Landing for a common meeting place. It was here too that travelers could get horses for their trip to Puget Sound, or a stage if they were fortunate enough to find one in operation. In 1853 Rabbeson and Yantis formed the earliest known stagecoach operation, but it ran for only 13 months.

Once their donation land claims were producing crops, the settlers realized that the Military Road was only a partial solution to their transportation needs because it was still passable only in the dry season. Steamboat service on the Columbia and Willamette Rivers had started in the 1850s; within a decade steamers pushed up the Cowlitz River to begin the nostalgic era of steamboats in Lewis County. The destination: Cowlitz Landing.

Albert Kletsch, a long-time Toledo educator, compiled extensive research in the 1930s into the history of the steamboat era. His research indicates that as early as 1836, the side-wheeler *Beaver* plied the waters of the Cowlitz briefly under the British flag of the Hudson's Bay Company. By 1850, steamboats traveled on the Columbia from Fort Vancouver as far as Monticello.

Kletsch observed that although the Washington Territorial government in the late 1850s granted two different charters for

Log boom below the P. Brouse and Son mill, Toledo, circa 1900. The Cowlitz River was the major travel route as well as a way to transport logs to mills.

steamboat service on the Cowlitz, these efforts were unsuccessful. Apparently legislative restrictions and deadlines made it impossible for the companies to comply. In the interim, in the early 1860s, the first steamer, the *Bell*, clanged up the Cowlitz a few times. At last, the third attempt at forming an actual steamship company succeeded with the Monticello and Cowlitz Landing Steamboat Company which built the 95-foot *Rescue* at Monticello in 1864.

Along with the *Rescue*, a steamboat war was launched. Bitter competition flared up to determine who would serve the Cowlitz. The Monticello and Cowlitz Landing Steamboat Company, the Oregon Steam Navigation Company, and the Cowlitz River Steam Navigation Company were stem to stern in competition. The Oregon Steam Navigation Co. haughtily put the steamer *Express* in the water to compete with the *Rescue*. The *Rescue's* owners promptly filed suit, claiming "an infringement of its exclusive right to navigate the Cowlitz River by steam as granted by the Territorial Legislature in 1863." The courts ruled the legislative act void, the injunction was dropped, and both boats chugged up the river. Passengers on the two steamboats during this war enjoyed rates reduced to as little as 25 cents for passage, but the pleasure was short-lived. Neither service could make a profit, and both companies drowned in the competition.

Settlers barely had time to enjoy the luxury of the boats before being forced to ship goods by wagon and travel by stage. In 1867-68, to remedy breakdowns of service, the citizens of Cowlitz Landing took matters in their hands and organized their own company, incorporated as Cowlitz Steam Navigation Company. The steamer *Rainier* made its maiden voyage but became beached when it literally hit a snag in the river. It is not known if it made more than infrequent trips after that.

In 1871 J. Kellogg and Company was first to provide regular service on the Cowlitz. It also brought Toledo its name. Joseph Kellogg purchased an acre of land from Augustus and Celeste Rochon for a warehouse a mile and a quarter upriver from the Landing. At a small dinner party celebrating the transaction, Captain Kellogg suggested that Mrs. Rochon name the new

Kellogg Transportation Schedule. 1800s.

The Cowlitz steamboat "Toledo."

town. She looked out the window of her home on the banks of the river and noticed the name of *Toledo* on Kellogg's steamboat. Toledo it became. The Cowlitz post office was moved upriver and renamed Toledo in 1880.

"A most unaccommodating river is the Cowlitz," was a comment heard by many travelers. Steamboat navigation on the Cowlitz was not an exact science by any means. Its shallow depth in the dry season, extreme flooding conditions during the wet season, and wild river currents the rest of the time made navigation a constant challenge. Pilots had to navigate around numerous sandbars; trees and snags periodically floated by to hinder passage. Some winters the Cowlitz was completely frozen over, bringing all river traffic to a halt. A captain once had to hold his ship for a week waiting for the river currents to subside. A Toledo resident commented on the dilemma of the steamers: "When the river is low, she can't get over the bars. When the water is too high, she can't get under the Olequa bridge." (The Olequa bridge was south of Vader; large concrete abutments still exist from a later road which crossed there.)

Many steamboats were specially designed with a shallow draft of two feet to navigate the low water during the dry season. The *Chester* and the *Northwest*, for example, drew only six inches of water. Most steamboats were sternwheelers, single or double-decked. They were bigger than a house: 100-135 feet in length and 20-30 feet in width. A few classier ones offered staterooms for overnight travel. Even though steamboat travel could be unpredictable in terms of regular service, it had to be a journey in heaven compared to overland travel by stage or wagon.

Steamboat "Chester" tied up behind smaller vessels at the dock in Toledo.

The stern-wheeler "Velma" ferried passengers to shallow parts of the Cowlitz River.

History buff George Nikula compiled an account of the journey by steamboat from Portland to Cowlitz during the height of the steamboat era, probably in the 1870s and 1880s. Nikula explains that once steamboat service was established on a regular basis, three round trips were made weekly. The distance was approximately 32 miles from Portland to Monticello, and another 30 miles to Cowlitz Landing. A trip took 24 hours at a cost of $1, and meals on board were 25 cents.

With a toot of a whistle, the steamboats left Portland from the dock at the foot of Yamhill Street at 6 a.m. to steam down the Willamette River to the conflux of the Columbia. The steamers touched at landings at St. Helens, Columbia City, Kalama, Rainier, Cedar Landing, and Monticello. Amid other river traffic, dockside activity, and shoreline scenery, the vastness of the Columbia River must have been a remarkable sight. Sometimes passengers and freight were shifted to a boat with a shallower draft for the balance of the trip up the Cowlitz. The river channel was much narrower after leaving Freeport (located on what is now Third Street in Kelso). Skilled pilots guided the vessels to the deepest part of the river channel, thereby avoiding shallower sandbars. It was quite a contrast to the old days when the first party of settlers carried goods upon their backs to the head of the rapids! The women had often been forced to get out of the Indian canoes to wade and assist the men in getting the boats over the rapids. Steamboats navigated the rugged river with comparative ease.

Along the way boats picked up cords of firewood to burn as fuel. As they glided to landings at farms and settlements, they picked up pigs, sheep, cream, and bags of grain and potatoes. They dropped off flour made at the grist mill, parts for farm equipment, and maybe a harness or two. Occasionally a farmer flagged down the boat with a red cloth and as a courtesy the steamers always stopped. Pilots eased the boats until the bow touched bottom along a shallow area on the river edge where a team of horses and a wagon waited with produce to be shipped to market.

On the last lap of the 24-hour trip, as the Cowlitz River became more narrow and shallow, boats rounded a big bend in the river to their final destination at Cowlitz Landing. People clustered on the dock to greet the passengers. The journey had taken one day as advertised, an amazing improvement over the ten days the first settlers took from the mouth of the river to the Landing. Of course this trip in early summer was in ideal conditions.

After a night in a rough hotel, the passengers faced the next sixty miles of the journey to Olympia. If a stage was available, travelers paid $20 for the jolting twelve-hour trip over the Military Road. They could rent a team of horses and a wagon to carry their own freight, or they could hire pack horses and walk. Even so the trip was markedly different from that faced by the first settlers in the Simmons party who chopped down trees to get through and built sleds along the way to transport their goods.

The last regularly scheduled steamboat was the *Chester*, whose last run was in March of 1918, while the last actual trip was by the steamer *Oregona* a month later. Several of the vessels moved on to Alaska where they worked the rivers for a few more decades.

According to research by Dr. Wayne Galvin, the demise of the steamboats had nothing to do with access to the railroad. Shipping rates by rail were actually higher than river shipping. The major cause was the influx of automobiles and trucks for transport and an auto bridge across the Columbia River. The heyday of the steamboats lasted five decades, from the end of the Civil War to World War I when more efficient modes of transportation replaced the handsome old boats which plied the waters of the Cowlitz.

Headed out from the Koontz Hotel, Toledo, 1895.

Toledo-Winlock-Knab Stage Line, Ed Wing owner and driver, circa 1906.

Chapter 7

Trails to Rails

In the saga of nation-wide railroading, Lewis County has another claim to being first. The first section of transcontinental line in the northern part of the continent was the 105-mile stretch of the Northern Pacific Railroad (NP) from Kalama to Tacoma through Lewis County. As the land opened from trails to rails, a new era of development began, for many of the towns of "the Mother of Counties" owe their beginnings to the advent of the Iron Horse.

Simon Plamondon and the Hudson's Bay trappers were harvesting beaver pelts along the streams of the future Lewis County in 1825 when the world's first railroad chugged into operation in England. By the time Isaac Stevens was appointed as the first governor of Washington Territory in 1853, "railroad fever" had produced 9,000 miles of track on the East Coast. Stevens, in addition to being the governor and negotiating Indian treaties, was charged with completing surveys for railroads into the new territory.

A West Point graduate engineer, Stevens was perhaps better qualified for the task than that of negotiating the Indian treaties. His task was a mighty one. The assignment required the Stevens party to examine the passes of several mountain ranges, the geography and meteorology of the whole region, the avenues of trade of the Columbia and Missouri Rivers, and the receptiveness of the Indian tribes. Remarkably, Stevens' task was accomplished in about a year, and significantly to Lewis County history, it showed that the valleys of the Columbia and Cowlitz offered a favorable route from Fort Vancouver. The information from the surveys proved to be invaluable in the pool of knowledge about the West and to its future growth. The final report was submitted to Congress in June of 1854, but it took the Civil War to solidify the need to unite the western states by a major railroad system.

Ellsbury survey crew marking the Centralia/Gray's Harbor right of way for the railroad which opened in 1888.

President Abraham Lincoln signed the Pacific Railroad Act in 1862 providing for the construction of the Central Pacific Railroad from California and the Union Pacific from Omaha, Nebraska. The act also authorized vast land grants to the railroads in exchange for their efforts. Two years later in 1864 Lincoln signed another charter for the Northern Pacific Railroad, with the land grant equal to an area roughly fifteen times the size of Connecticut, including vast chunks of Washington Territory.

The Northern Pacific needed some time to get financing squared away and determine exact routes. The terminus of the NP would definitely be in the Puget Sound area, but to ensure the large land grants in Oregon were under NP's domain, the track would have to go through Portland.

The NP needed more money to build the rail line through the Rocky Mountains to its terminus in Portland, Oregon. Its president John Gregory Smith and financier Jay Cooke decided to first construct a rail line from the Columbia River north through Lewis County to a still undefined point on Puget Sound. They hoped to generate enough revenue from passengers and freight on this north-south rail line to help finance their east-west share of the transcontinental railroad.

For this reason Lewis County had train service long before the transcontinental track was complete across the northern part of the continent.

The Minnetonka was Northern Pacific's first locomotive purchased in 1870. It was 27 1/2 feet long and weighed 12 tons, 1/38th as much as a modern diesel locomotive. It was shipped from the east coast around the horn of South America to Kalama to begin construction of the Washington rail line.

Early in 1871 the Northern Pacific granted F.E. Canda and Company a contract for the construction of track from the Columbia River to Puget Sound. The line was to leave the Columbia at the mouth of the Cowlitz River north of Kalama and extend up the valley of the Cowlitz. A virtual army of workers was hired to assure its completion. Captain W.C. Walker supervised the work of about 2,000 Chinese laborers hired from San Francisco. Wages were $2 per day for unskilled labor, $2.50 to $3 for mechanics, and $70 a month for foremen. Most of the material and equipment were shipped from the East Coast around Cape Horn, pushing expenses to the limit.

With NP's first locomotive, the charming Minnetonka, leading the construction, the first rail was laid on March 19, 1871. By June of that year the horde of workers had a thousand tons of rails in place. The first 25 miles were completed by the time of October rains. An additional contract had been let in August for clearing another 40 miles. During the spring and summer of 1872, work was delayed by the lack of a bridge north of the Cowlitz crossing near Pumphrey's Landing, three miles south of Vader. When the bridge was completed that fall, the line went in quickly through settlements which would be known as Olequa, Little Falls, Ainslie, Winlock, Napavine, Newaukum, Chehalis, Centralia, Bucoda and all the way to Tenino. Excitement buzzed in the air as railroad workers swarmed by previously isolated homesteads, buying mounds of fresh produce raised by the settlers.

China Creek, the stream that flows through Centralia — the often flooded and much maligned "ditch" — was supposedly named during this time. Local legend claims that Chinese laborers had a work

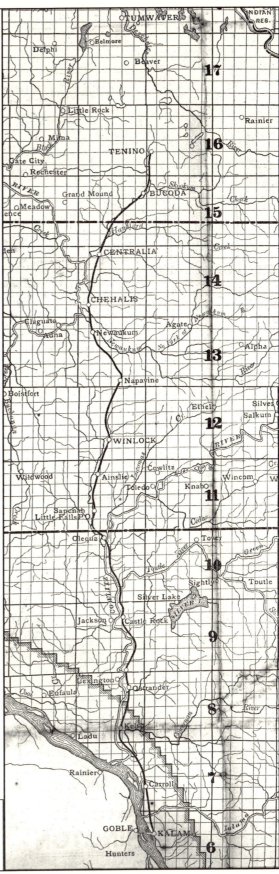

The Northern Pacific rail line reached north from Kalama to Tenino offering an alternative to river travel and difficult trails. Most towns on this map are for reference and were established after the railroad was finished in 1873.

Construction of Northern Pacific Railroad through the Napavine "cut," 1872.

camp there for a short time, hence the name China Creek. (Many of the Chinese workers, discriminated against in their pursuit of other endeavors, later went into "acceptable" businesses such as laundries and saloons in Seattle. Local stories also tell of Chinese people working a gold mine near Centralia.)

It was too soon to predict a "happily-ever-after" ending for the Northern Pacific. The year of 1873 started with a disaster; a heavy landslide blocked the line for two miles near Pumphrey's Landing and the Cowlitz River bridge, halting the trains for nearly four months and requiring a major sluicing operation to clear it.

At last Tacoma was announced as the terminus, to the grief of Seattle and Olympia. But the line still had not been laid to the city, so in May of 1873, a thousand workers set out north from Tenino. By late October the track was within four miles of Tacoma. By then Jay Cooke & Company, a partner of Northern Pacific, had closed its doors in a calamitous financial failure that shook the nation.

So near but so far. A lack of iron caused a work suspension, and the railroad just ran out of money. Angry workmen seized the Clover Creek bridge near Tacoma demanding $73,000 in back pay. Through various financial maneuvers, enough money and iron were scraped up to lay the final track into Tacoma on December 27, 1873, just 24 hours before its charter deadline. The railroad

A Northern Pacific Railroad workman in the Napavine "cut," 1872.

was in business through Lewis County ... barely.

Following the panic of 1873, the Northern Pacific went into bankruptcy, and the business was limited to a single train each direction daily. During this time many Centerville (Centralia) residents earned their sole income by cutting wood for the steam engines. After several years, the financial moguls of the world regained their strength and the Northern Pacific resumed its construction across the nation.

The German-born entrepreneur Henry Villard who had been buying up steamboat operations on the Columbia, including the Oregon Railway & Navigation Company, gained control of the Northern Pacific in 1881. He hired large gangs of Chinese workers to push through the line on the western end of the transcontinental railroad and Irish and Swedes on the eastern end. The final spike was at last driven to connect the east-west lines of the NP in 1883 at Gold Creek, Montana.

The segment from Portland to Kalama was connected in an unusual way; a large transport ferry named *Tacoma* hauled trains across the Columbia River from Goble, Oregon, to Kalama.

By then the little town of Centerville had a brand new depot, the only one between Kalama and Tacoma. When the townsfolk learned that a true dignitary — Henry Villard, the new president of the Northern Pacific — was coming through on the train, they proudly constructed a big arch of welcome, festooned with fir boughs for the celebration. Everyone donned their Sunday best, and very likely speeches were prepared for the big moment. Villard's train appeared...then disappeared...without stopping! The citizenry was highly indignant but saved a photograph as a memento of the (non-)occasion.

Stragglers remain after the ill-fated Henry Villard celebration in Centerville (Centralia), 1883.

The Land Called Lewis

Centralia's new railroad station, 1912.

Centralia quickly became a railroad hub, just as George Washington had hoped. The first depot was replaced with a small red building at the end of Third Street called "Noah's Ark" because of its design. Then a depot large enough for thousands of travelers was built in 1912. Centralia's population rose to 5,500 in 1889, the year of statehood. A large roundhouse built in 1913 had twenty stalls. It was used primarily by the Northern Pacific, which initially used coal and the Union Pacific which used coal from Tono, then fuel oil, for its steam engines. Employed were 27 car men on the rip track (the maintenance area) and 40 men in the roundhouse. By 1914, 44 passenger trains and 17 freight trains passed through Centralia daily. The town fairly

Centralia's roundhouse and a portion of the rip track in the snow, 1915.

burst with lively railroaders who spent their money freely at the sporting houses of ill repute and the saloons, "tieing" one on. The historic Olympic Club, still complete with its original fixtures a century later, opened its doors and spigots to the thirsty.

As for Chehalis (originally Saundersville), nothing reveals more about the spunk and determination of its citizens than the story of how they enticed the Northern Pacific Railroad depot to their town. Initially the railroad decided to locate the train station in Newaukum, located two miles south of Chehalis on the west side of the Newaukum River. An early railroad map shows Grand Prairie and Newaukum but not Chehalis, Winlock, or Centralia. The Northern Pacific wanted a gift of land as an economic benefit in exchange for the privilege of stopping at the little town.

Eliza Saunders Barrett, shrewd businesswoman that she was, had second thoughts about the donation of 40 acres to the cause and upped the price of the land. In retaliation NP officials platted 40 acres at Newaukum, two miles to the south. It was a classic case of poor planning because the only way to climb the steep Newaukum Hill was on the railroad track itself and across a trestle. It was an impossible spot for shipping freight.

William F. West and other local citizens approached railroad official General J.W. Sprague with a proposal for a stop in Chehalis, not knowing that he had purchased property at Newaukum and laid out a town site with the intention of selling it back at inflated prices. Sprague refused to even consider a stop at Chehalis instead of Newaukum. The frustrated townspeople told him they were submitting their plan to higher authorities in the NP. Sprague haughtily put the proposal in his pocket and refused to return it!

Upset at the inaccessibility of the planned depot and the insulting behavior of railroad officials, the citizens dug in their heels. Local legend claims that John T. Alexander gave a conductor a $20 gold piece to unload a shipment of freight in Chehalis. Soon the citizenry learned that trains were required to stop when waved down by red flags. Quickly they persuaded Eliza Barrett to part with a few lots, and several farmers put up a warehouse for grain storage.

"So the folks at Saunders' Bottom got themselves some red bunting and flagged down the train every time it came through. Finally the railroad decided it was cheaper to use a warehouse the folks had thoughtfully provided at that location than to start a competing town on the hill," writes Bill Speidel in *The Wet Side of the Mountains*.

The argument Chehalis had with the railroad was not over by any means. The people of Chehalis wanted the county seat now that Claquato had been bypassed by the train, and besides, the courthouse built so ambitiously by Lewis Hawkins Davis had been used for commissioners' meetings only three times a year.

"Oh, no," the railroad officials said. "Newaukum will be the county seat."

Chehalis won again; however, the next round went to the railroad. When the branch line went in to South Bend, the railroad wheedled a generous donation of land near the site of the Chehalis depot to install a promised roundhouse. The railroad hauled in a turntable to demonstrate good intentions, according to William West in his memoirs. Once the land was gifted to the railroad, the turntable disappeared, never to return.

Chehalis soon had its first depot, a wooden structure matched in such detail to Centralia's that the buildings came to be called the "Twin Depots." By then the steady growth of Chehalis and its status as a center of commerce led to the need for a new depot. Despite delays and disputes,

The Northern Pacific Railroad Chehalis Depot, 1913. In 1975 it became the Lewis County Historical Museum.

the new brick depot was completed in 1912. It was dedicated at a banquet for 200 people, hosted by William F. West, on January 23, 1913.

The old grievances with the railroad lay dormant for almost sixty years, until the railroad, by then the Burlington Northern, announced plans to close the Chehalis depot in 1972. When that generation of Chehalis citizens approached railroad officials with a proposal to convert the building into a museum, the railroad was adamant in its determination to demolish the building.

Frustrated citizens led by James Backman succeeded in placing the building on the National Register of Historic Places and waged a three-year war to preserve the depot with the help of U.S. Senators Warren Magnuson and Henry Jackson. Finally in 1975 Burlington Northern agreed to lease the building to the county. Community fundraising eventually brought the desired $50,000 for renovations needed to convert the building to the Lewis County Historical Museum. It remains a proud statement to the heritage of the area.

Chapter 8

Railroad Boom Years

By 1888 the railroads were flourishing to the point that investors had big plans to stretch their reach everywhere. In Eastern Lewis County, settlers strained to locate claims where the railroad would surely pass through the Big Bottom Country. Although the Union Pacific actually staked out a proposed line from Yakima, nothing ever came of it, and the brief spate of settlement ended in disappointment.

Two items appeared in the newspapers in 1888:

"Three well-known Chehalis businessmen are interested in a new railroad to be known as Pacific-Chehalis-and Eastern. D.C. Millett, Frances Donahoe, and William Urquhart are among the incorporators. Centralia and Chehalis are to have another railroad. Officials from the Portland, Port Angeles, and Victoria Railroad Co. were in the Twin Cities advising the business men that the line would pass through here from Portland to Port Angeles."

There is no documentation that either of the railroads actually materialized.

What did happen was that three other major railroads made Lewis County a part of their route: James Hill's Great Northern, the Union Pacific, and the Chicago, Milwaukee and St. Paul Railway, more commonly known as the Milwaukee Road. Vader and Longview had five railroads with the construction of the Longview, Portland & Northern in 1925.

The years of 1906-1913 were wild with the growth of the different lines. In Eastern Lewis County the Tacoma & Eastern Railway (T&E) reached Mineral in 1906, instantly creating a boom in timber and mining. The residents of Morton struggled for four years, meeting the Mineral trains with wagons to carry supplies over the divide of the Nisqually and Tilton River basins. In 1910 the T&E ended Morton's isolation and encouraged its growth by opening up a market for the timber and mining industries.

Milwaukee engine 1277 at Mineral, April 1941.

In 1890 the Portland & Puget Sound Railway had tried unsuccessfully to establish a Portland-Seattle extension, which was halted for financial reasons. However, in 1906 a historic joint venture began when the fierce railroad competitors forged an agreement for construction of the Portland-Seattle line. On the drawing boards were plans for the line to pass through Winlock, Adna, and Pleasant Valley to Centralia. Instead in 1910 the Union Pacific, Great Northern and Milwaukee Road agreed to share portions of NP's tracks, and Union Pacific initiated its run between the two large Northwest cities.

Competition was still intense. In 1925 the main lines worked out a "pool agreement," whereby all passenger revenue was thrown into one pot and apportioned back to each road based on its average earnings for the past five years. This agreement reduced the number of passenger trains from thirteen to five daily each way.

As if it weren't confusing enough to have so many lines, railroad history is muddled by different companies' ownership of some segments of track with their own operating rules and schedules. Spurs and branch lines were often constructed under different names and only later was it apparent who actually controlled the purse strings. The Union Pacific laid a 5.8-mile branch line from Wabash, two miles north of Centralia, to UP coal mines at Tono in 1909. The Oregon & Washington Railroad put in 52.9 miles of track for the Grays Harbor Branch from Centralia to Aberdeen in 1910, the same year that the joint venture went into effect. Construction crews met from each end on July 4, 1910, giving Independence Valley its name.

In 1911 when the company reorganized as the Oregon-Washington Railroad & Navigation Company (known locally as the "O-Dub"), it completed another 3.6 miles of line to Hoquiam and a spur to Montesano in 1912-13. The line absorbed all Union Pacific subsidiaries. However Milwaukee Road owned the line which ran from Helsing Junction in Independence Valley to Maytown via Rochester.

The Milwaukee Railroad, completed as the sixth transcontinental line in 1911, came into the area under the name of the Willapa Harbor and Puget Sound Railroad to Raymond/South Bend in 1913. Its line ran parallel to those of the Northern Pacific and parallel to Highway 6 to Dryad, crossing the NP line into downtown Doty. Later it shared major portions of the NP's Raymond line. By 1914 the NP double track line was completed from Tenino to Tacoma via the shores of Puget Sound.

To say that the impact of railroads on

Approaching Doty, the Milwaukee line from Chehalis provided an avenue for economic development.

the entire region was phenomenal is an understatement. The serene wilderness boomed like multiple fireworks on the Fourth of July. Most importantly, the link between the rails and timber was forged.

Railroad Ties to Timber

A branch line was the dawning of the first railroad tie to timber. It turned out to be a bonanza for investors.

The Northern Pacific opened its South Bend branch line to Willapa Harbor in Pacific County on June 1, 1893. The line was about 57 miles in length, terminating at South Bend. At one time it ran four daily passenger trains and had 29 stops, most at the small mill towns which dotted the Chehalis and Willapa River valleys. The "Y" visible from the Interstate 5 railroad overpass in Chehalis was a significant point where the branch line headed west off the mainline. Its stops included Claquato, Littell, Syverson, Adna, Bunker, Long's Crossing, Ceres, Meskill, Mays, Dryad, Doty, Apex, Pe Ell, McCormick, Reynolds, Walville, Lester, Pluvius, Frances, Globe, Lebam, Trap Creek, Holcomb, Menlo, Willapa, Raymond, and South Bend. The list did not include the stops made for cows on the tracks, blown down trees, or washouts caused by high water from the Willapa or Chehalis Rivers.

Every two miles on the route to South Bend a lumber mill shot up like new

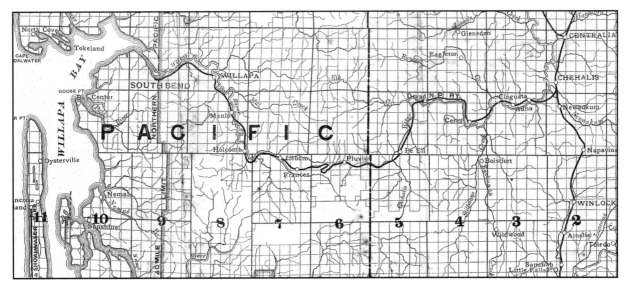

The Northern Pacific line from South Bend to Chehalis, 1893.

growth. Trains ran west six days a week for many years, and massive amounts of logs and lumber were shipped on the branch line.

One of the stops was Meskill, ten miles northeast of Pe Ell. Meskill was the site of a prison work camp for prisoners from Walla Walla Penitentiary. As a traditional "hard rock" camp, the convicts worked a rock pile and operated a crushing plant, the end product of which was loaded on the trains for use as ballast on roads and tracks.

The trains quickly initiated a new way of life. Two passenger trains ran every day

Northern Pacific Depot, Pe Ell, circa 1905. Trains opened up timberland for the lumber industry and a new way of life for previously isolated communities.

including Sunday, and for many years two freight trains also operated. In contrast to the rough roads and long wagon trips, the train service was fairly prompt and gave ease of travel for everyone wanting to come to the Twin Cities. Folks could travel to Sunday dinner or a ball game in another community a dozen miles away. Special trains took brass band and baseball teams, sometimes using up to 14 cars for players and their fans. There were special runs for circuses and dignitary visits, and passenger service made trips to Moclips for special excursions to the beach for as many as 1,500 passengers. For jaunts to Raymond and South Bend, an extra engine was needed to boost the train over the hump at Pluvius, the high point on the track about three miles west of the Lewis County line.

Once a special train ran from Chehalis to Pe Ell with a home talent troupe of Chehalis young people who occupied two coaches and who had their own baggage car. The boys brass band from Chehalis played on every platform to advertise their pending performance. The group played at the Thrash Opera House in Pe Ell to a full house. With short travel spans between stops, conductors couldn't pick up all the tickets, and inevitably free riders—and freeloaders—hopped aboard. These non-paying passengers got off the end of one car as the conductor entered and climbed back through another doorway as he left. The railroad won the great ticket battle, however. West of Chehalis the train screeched to a stop on a long trestle near Claquato and another spot between Pe Ell and McCormick on a long bridge over the Chehalis River. Passengers who attempted to get off a car in either place fell into the river. It was easier to buy a ticket.

The arrival of the train was exciting business in those early days. People came to the depots just to see the train arrive, and if the train was an hour late, it was a hardship on those who made daily visits to the depot. In Dryad, an engineer pulled in on time, and a number of townspeople thought they would take up a collection to show appreciation to the engineer for good work. The trainman was very apologetic that he could not accept the gift. He was on the train that was due the day before!

The NP provided the equipment for a hometown jaunt headed from Chehalis in a different direction. In March of 1888, the following item appeared in the *Chehalis Bee Nugget*: "A number of couples of the younger set of Chehalis went to Napavine to attend a dance. Their mode of transportation was a hand car used on the Northern Pacific railroad tracks. Everything went fine until the trip home. Coming down the steep grade they lost control of the car, and it jumped the tracks injuring a number of the passengers."

A hand-pump car, connected to a flat car and a hand-powered velocipede, used by loggers in the Salzer Valley, 1910.

The regular passenger service to Willapa Harbor lasted until March 19, 1954, and the freight trains ended service in 1994 when the tracks were ripped out.

Railroad Boom Years

Doty Lumber & Shingle Co. No. 3 locomotive used between 1900 and 1910.

plains, railroads were the logical solution to the problematic muddy terrain in timber country at a time when the demand, and price, soared.

Laying out and constructing the railroads over mountains and across streams might have stopped the weak at heart, but the mills needed logs, and the operators "aimed" rather than platted their way into the stands of timber with a fierce determination. Most lines did not

Hometown Trains

The main lines provided the backbone of industrial development in Lewis County, and the muscle and meat came from numerous local and logging railroads. Such railroads became symbols of ingenuity for logging operations in the West. In Lewis County railroad spurs tickled the sides of nearly every major drainage from Morton to McCormick, from Vader to Independence Valley.

The book *Logging Railroads of the West* (1961) lists 128 logging railroads, including parent companies, in the Lewis County area. Their prime began in the early 1900s; some such as Weyerhaeuser's Chehalis Western ran until the 1990s. Before the advent of trucks, railroad historian Harold Borovec of Chehalis ex-

Washington State Fire Association rail-truck on a massive trestle.

Rails built on pilings over soft ground didn't always work as planned.

woods. "A trip on a logging road was reminiscent of Evangelist Billy Sunday's Ford, according to a logging joke of the '20s, because it shook the devil out of you," according to author Kramer Adams in *Glory Days of Logging*. The main goal was to get the logs to mills in the most economical way possible, and wooden tracks were common, despite giving passengers a stomach-lurching ride. Eventually steel rails became the norm. Workers from the large mills at Walville and McCormick, west of Pe Ell, took "loceys" and handcars to get to Pe Ell on Saturday night to indulge in sins of the flesh and quench their mighty thirst in numerous saloons.

exceed a three percent grade, opening up to the woods with a straight, level shot. High intricate trestles and bridges criss-crossed the ravines and creeks in what would be environmental nightmares a century later. Logs were laid in cross patterns like Tinker Toys for fill; for example, S.S. Somerville's entire roadbed at Napavine in 1910 was built on pilings one to six feet above ground.

Some logging railroads became common carriers, allowing other companies to use their track to compete for access to isolated areas. By the 1930s most of the accessible timber had been logged off and the high costs of construction deterred further expansion. Several modern county roads owe their origin to railroad grades, and hunters and woodsmen often stumble on decaying trestles and straight mounded trails in remote, unlikely areas, far from civilization.

In the glory days of logging, hundreds of loggers hopped the "locey" to get to and from the

As the railroads pushed the growth of

Walville Lumber Co. "locey" ready to take workers to Pe Ell for a Saturday night on the town.

Centralia-Chehalis trolleys stopping at the S.W. Washington Fair, 1913.

the towns and cities, the era of the street car was also born. In Centralia the very earliest street car was an old wood- or coal-burning locomotive secured to a rustic passenger car. Passengers paid a nickel to ride within the reaches of the town, which at that time was not a very long ride. This first endeavor was not highly successful; the engine burned up and was not replaced. In fact, the name of the streetcar company was forgotten by those few people who even remembered its existence.

During the boom years the cities of Centralia and Chehalis felt the need to be connected by rails. In 1910 the Washington-Oregon Corporation established an electric street car system, named the Twin City Railroad Company, which was powered by a coal-operated generating plant on Coal Creek. This plant, an early predecessor of Puget Sound Power and Light Company, burned "hog fuel" (wood chips) hauled to the burner by rail from local mills. The Washington-Oregon Corporation also furnished power for numerous local communities and several in Oregon.

The trolley had seven miles of standard gauge track, running east of the former Pacific Highway along the base of the hill. The car route crossed the mainline tracks on an inclined, timbered overpass structure just north of the Southwest Washington Fairgrounds.

In Centralia it ran almost the full length of Tower Avenue, turning west on Third Street where it ended after a few blocks. The Chehalis route ran down National Avenue, shifting over onto Pacific Avenue by the depot. It continued along Pacific to 11th Street sharing Cowlitz, Chehalis & Cascade track before reversing direction back to Centralia. According to a corporate advertisement, the trolley offered "modern rolling stock equipment, efficient, and courteous service and a maximum of fourteen miles for 25 cents." It operated in the twin cities until 1929.

The company was a precursor to a local railroad that held a warm spot in the hearts of many railroaders, passengers and woods workers from the early days. The Cowlitz, Chehalis & Cascade Railroad (CC & C) started and ended as a common carrier, although log hauling was a major part of its revenue. In fact, it owed its origin to the trolley line from Chehalis to Centralia. Stockholders from the Union Pacific, the Great Northern, the Milwaukee Road and Northern Pacific formed the company after eyeing the timber resources of the Newaukum River Valley. The arrangement worked well, for the local train advertised connections to the four major lines. It was managed by its president and general manager, W.E. Brown, and in its early days it hauled trees logged within the city limits of Chehalis. By 1918 rails had extended 18 miles out, crossing and re-crossing the Newaukum River three times. As farm settlement superseded logging, the line pushed farther east into the timber country.

In 1922 the CC & C stopped at stations and sidings in Chehalis, Spenser, Oeschli (pronounced "Oxley"), Pier's, Forest, Klaus, Guerrier's Mill, Doty's Logging Spur, Onalaska, Divide, International Mill, Lacamas, and Zandecki. Remembering their names is a challenge, much less locating the stops themselves.

The owners of the little line had big visions of a 170-mile main line through White Pass to Yakima; its promotional brochure of 1922 boasted of access to 25 billion board feet of timber and a huge untapped vein of anthracite coal in Eastern Lewis County.

The brochure also promoted the dairy industry and the two large milk processing plants in Chehalis which it did indeed serve. As it turned out, the CC & C had to be content with its 32-mile run, after its extension through Salkum, Mayfield and up Winston Creek. Nevertheless, it puffed happily along for many years, hauling empty cars to be loaded in the woods and returned to the 11 mills located near its rails in the 1920s. On its two daily trips, it often brought in 50 to 60 carloads of lumber and logs. For a time passengers from outlying towns enjoyed the convenience of daily service powered by gas cars into the city center of Chehalis. Woods and mill workers hopped aboard the trains for daily and weekend transportation to and from home. When passenger service ceased, the CC & C became the solid workhorse of the woods in the area, pushing its spurs up many major drainages.

The Cowlitz, Chehalis and Cascade trestle on the Cowlitz River. This site was later chosen as the site of Mayfield Dam built in 1963.

To reach the large stands of Douglas fir and western red cedar of East Winston Creek, the CC & C faced a major hurdle: a deep canyon of the Cowlitz River 200 to 300 feet below the surface of the surrounding land. How could the line build a cost effective bridge which was safe and easy to maintain? An engineer from the Milwaukee Road, C.N. Sweet, accomplished an engineering feat of crossing a chasm of the river west of Mossyrock. Old-growth logs 120 feet long were set in concrete as a foundation for a trestle that was 400 feet long, some 200 feet above the canyon of the Cowlitz. The bridge took 200,000 board feet of timber to complete. So strong was the structure that it withstood the rampaging flood of the Cowlitz in 1933 with only minor repairs needed. The location was such a logical one that it was chosen as the site of the Mayfield Dam which was built in 1963.

The CC & C made its last run in May, 1955 but one remnant of its past glories lives on. Baldwin Steam Locomotive #15, affectionately called the "Old Lady" by her crew, was donated to the city of Chehalis and set up in Recreation Park where she was admired by park visitors for years. Then Steve Hendricks and Bill Peterson and a group concerned with a lack of local tourist attractions decided to recommission her. After many volunteer hours, the "Old Lady" later became part of the Chehalis-Centralia Railroad Association, fired up on summer weekends by Harold Borovec and other volunteers to make a nostalgic nine-mile run west of Chehalis.

Napavine had its favorite railroad, too. In the early 1890s Hamilton Pitcher built a sawmill one mile east of town at a time when Napavine was said to be the largest shipping point between Tacoma and Kalama. He and his wife had arrived with nothing but a sack of flour, good health, and determination to get ahead. In 1911 the Pitchers sold their property to the Emery-Nelson Lumber Company and lived in prosperity. Mr. Pitcher bought a Heisler locomotive to be used in logging and named her "Susie" after his daughter born in Napavine; on the side next to her name was painted a large white pitcher. The cheerful whistle of the "Susie" signaled the arrival of the logging train and its crews from the woods, alerting families to get supper on the table. Later two more engines joined "Susie" in hauling logs to the large Emery-Nelson mill.

The Newaukum Valley Railroad ran from Onalaska to Napavine from about 1915 to 1943 under the ownership of the Carlisle Company of Onalaska. As construction was beginning on their mill in 1910, the Carlisle family began cutting ties

Cowlitz, Chehalis and Cascade engine #15 "Old Lady" on display at 13th Street in Chehalis, 1983. After refurbishing in 1989, it lived on, alive and well, taking railroad buffs and tourists on nostalgic summertime rides.

The Land Called Lewis

Napavine Depot circa 1910. Partly hidden behind the depot is Frosty's Tavern. The Urquhart store is at the right edge of the photo.

for a railroad connecting to the four main lines at Napavine. The Newaukum Valley Railroad ran parallel to the south of what is now the route of Highway 508, once known as the River Highway. A 1936 official guide to railways lists its stops on the 10-mile run between the two towns as Gaylord, Dale, and Harding. When the mill closed in 1943, the Newaukum Valley had five steam locomotives, two of which had been acquired in 1940.

One hometown line, now nearly forgotten, was quite unusual. The Longview, Portland & Northern Railway Company, (LP & N) started in 1924, served logging operations by electricity. Generated in Longview by a waste wood burner, the electricity was used in logging and yarding in the woods near Ryderwood. The Long Bell Lumber Company had been informed by NP, the Great Northern and Union Pacific that its log trains were not welcome on the mainline tracks because a spill might block the Rocky Point tunnel. The company put in a $6 million railway that operated on the west bank of the Cowlitz River from Kelso to Olequa. It was so successful that the four main railroad lines bought it out in June of 1931. It was destroyed by the 1933 flood, and logs were then moved over the original NP line via the Rocky Point tunnel.

The line extended from the Long Bell mill in Longview, arcing in and out of Lewis County, to the logging town of Ryderwood. It assisted in harvesting substantial amounts of timber in Lewis County working north of Ryderwood into the Boistfort Valley. In 1954 the track was dismantled from the woods to Vader Junction, but for many years the LP & N performed switching operations for the mainlines in Longview. Ryderwood, originally a Long Bell timber town, became a senior citizen village during the mid-1950s.

The link between rails and timber continued for nearly six decades. The decline of the railroads came with better economic conditions, and simply changing times.

On March 2, 1970, the merging of the Chicago, Burlington and Quincy Railroad, the Great Northern, Northern Pacific, and the Spokane Portland and Seattle Railroad formed the Burlington Northern. Gone were the branch lines, logging spurs, and stops at the small towns which the trains had birthed.

A fitting quote for the demise of the old-time railroads comes from James L. Ehernberger and Francis G. Gschwind's book, *Smoke Along the Columbia*. Referring to the steam locomotives of the Oregon-Washington Railroad & Navigation Company, the authors write, "One by one, they have headed for the final terminal and entered the last great Roundhouse of memories, where their fires have been banked for the endless night of oblivion."

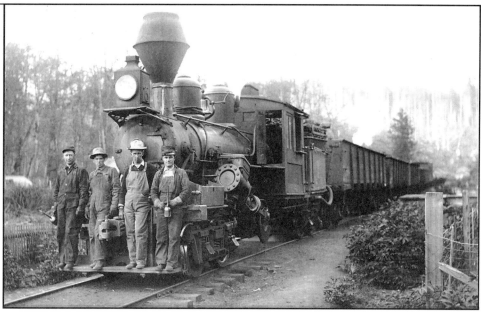
A typical small country railroad train used to haul coal, near Centralia.

Sommerville Mill train, Napavine, circa 1905. (Also spelled Somerville and Summerville.)

Chapter 9

The Towns Came

After the arrival of the early homesteaders, a second wave of people came during the time frame from the end of the Civil War and through the railroad era of the 1870s-1890s. Many Lewis County towns owe not only their existence but their names to the Northern Pacific Railroad whose officials wielded considerable weight in such matters.

Chehalis

The railroad provided the town of Chehalis with the crucial connection it needed for development. Schuyler and Eliza Saunders (Barrett) had established the first post office in their home on May 8, 1858, naming it Saunders Prairie.

But their settlement had attracted few others due to the soggy nature of the land. Although the Saunders tried in vain to discourage the moniker "Saunders Bottom" by insisting on the names of Saunders Prairie and Saundersville, the nickname persisted for obvious reasons. Streets were mud tracks often axle deep to the horse-drawn wagons, and of course, the city government had no money for road improvements. Despite gravel and rock poured onto tracks to help them hold up under traffic, the rock gradually worked its way to bottom. The worst spots were corduroyed with small wooden poles at first, and later, refined to planking with sawn lumber and eventually bricked, concrete paved or oiled. Market Street, for example, was first planked in August of 1889, bricked in 1907, and paved with concrete in 1912.

Market Street, Chehalis planked streets during Teddy Roosevelt's visit to the McKinley Stump, May 22, 1903.

The railroad era helped usher in the name Chehalis on September 23, 1870. As the Indian word for the "shining sands" at the mouth of the river at Westport, it is also the name of the local Indian tribe and the river by which it resided.

In the Saunders' time the post office was set up in the home of Judge Obadiah B. McFadden, who came in 1858 as the Chief Justice of Washington Territory. During his life, McFadden had a distinguished career

Early city streets posed a challenge in wet weather.

as a territorial justice and a territorial delegate to the United States Congress. The handsome log home McFadden had built on Chehalis Avenue is on the National Historic Register as the oldest inhabited house in Lewis County.

William F. West is considered to be the "Father of Chehalis" because of his role in promoting the urban ambitions of the settlement. West and his family arrived in 1864, and when the railroad came through, he persuaded the trains to stop in Chehalis instead of Newaukum. He also brought about the change of the county seat from Claquato to his town, despite opposition from the Northern Pacific representatives who felt it should be at Newaukum.

William F. West is considered to be the "Father of Chehalis."

West labored endlessly to clear the thick forests off the land to establish a farm. When he was able to find a market in Olympia for his wheat, oats, peas, bacon, and eggs, his farm prospered. In a comfortable financial position, he then devoted his life to civic projects, including the construction of the first school in 1876. In 1947 his son and wife, Mr. and Mrs. W.F. West, donated land for a new high school, which became necessary after the earthquake of 1949 damaged the old one. The name of Chehalis High School was changed in 1957 to W.F. West High School.

W. F. "Bill" West, at his St. Helens Hotel office.

The rise of the businesses in Chehalis began in the 1880s with the formation of the first bank and other enterprises. N.B. Coffman owned a big safe, the only place in town where gold coins could be kept securely. When County Treasurer William Urquhart came to him with $7,000 of county money, he wanted a deposit book and a check book. Thus in 1889 began the first bank, the First National Bank of Chehalis, subsequently called Coffman, Dobson & Company. Later many development efforts in the community were headed by Coffman, Dobson, West, Urquhart, Francis Donahoe and Daniel Caldwell Millett.

If it were possible to zip back to Chehalis in 1892 via time machine, one would see a flurry of activity. About 2,500 souls called the little town their home. Residents had electric lights, bonds were approved for water and sewer, and three miles of planked streets graced the city center. It was the center of commerce for settlers from small settlements and farms throughout the county including Eastern Lewis County, whose hearty pioneers journeyed six days to get supplies.

N. B. Coffman and Margaret Wimp Coffman, 1880.

The Land Called Lewis

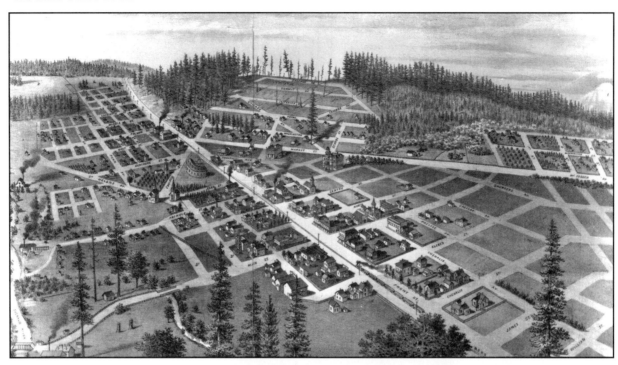

Artist drawing of Chehalis looking north, showing the downtown centered on the railroad tracks, circa 1890.

One night in March of 1892, fire broke out in a jewelry store on Main Street, destroying it and several buildings. The heat striking Mrs. Eliza Barrett's new brick building was so intense that labels on the bottles in the drug store were damaged and $2,000 worth of windows broken. A bucket brigade fought the fire. Tragically a second fire nearly razed the rest of the town center along the railroad tracks less than two months later, leveling about 30 buildings in four blocks. A pumper from Centralia was loaded on a flat car and connected with the water from Dillenbaugh Creek, but the damage had been done in only two hours. Arson was suspected as the cause for both fires.

In a dramatic relocation, a building boom started concurrently six blocks to the north on Market Street. The stunning new

The St. Helens Hotel. On the right is the "camp" of Ezra Meeker on the city hall lawn during his tour through the area, 1906.

St. Helens Hotel, operated by William F. West, Jr., towered as a waypoint for weary travelers by horseback or coach on the town's main road which bypassed the buildings and property of Eliza Barrett.

Eliza Barrett, Founding Mother

Eliza Tynan Saunders Barrett (1826-1900) was Lewis County's first businesswoman and the founding mother of Chehalis. An original settler, landowner, and developer, Eliza Barrett controlled the growth and development of early Chehalis at a time when society's constraints discouraged women from doing such things. Her rocky personal life, cautious business dealings, and fiery disposition spiced up not only the conversations but the history of the town.

As a young woman, Eliza Tynan immigrated from Ireland to Fort Vancouver where she was working as a waitress when she met Schuyler Stuart Saunders. Saunders had first come from New York in search of his wife and two daughters who had surreptitiously joined a Mormon wagon train to the West. Unable to find them, he went back to New York to learn that his wife was dead. He returned to Oregon Territory and married the spunky little Irish girl.

In 1851 the Saunders staked a donation land claim of 640 acres, signed by President Andrew Jackson, on the land that is now the site of Chehalis. By an error in surveying, the land was an acre short and subsequently some streets on Chehalis hills are oddly laid out. During the Indian War of 1855-56, as the Saunders sought refuge in the Claquato blockhouse, their cabin and barn on Market Street was burned and their stock killed.

When Saunders died in 1860, Eliza was left with four sons and a substantial interest in the platted lots of the little town. A 1991 article by Brenda O'Connor, then director of the Lewis County Historical Museum, notes that Eliza married three more times. Her second husband, by whom she had one daughter, went out to look for a cow one evening and never returned. Her third marriage ended in divorce from her imbibing saloon-keeper husband who was convicted of selling liquor to the Indians. The two children from that marriage "trampled on her toes (when they were little); and when they grew up trampled on her heart."

To the dismay of the male business owners in the community, she was particularly cautious about selling her property, and with reason, for she was often cheated. In his memoirs William F. West decried her reluctance to sell land, blaming her for the slow increase in population of the town. Her fourth husband, John Barrett, bragged that he would marry her and the town lots would be freed for development. She was not so easily bamboozled; the property remained in her name, and she divorced Barrett for charging her $25 to sign some legal papers.

Eliza Tynan Saunders Barrett, pioneer business woman of Chehalis.

Shrewdly and slowly Eliza Barrett sold her land, platting small parcels at a time and developing two by herself. Although she could not read nor write, her interest in cultural events led her to construct the Tynan Opera House. She is credited with building the city's first Catholic Church in 1889 and a Catholic boarding school for girls in 1895. She was particularly interested in developing business in the vicinity of Main Street in Chehalis. After a large bank appeared on Market Street, in a counter move she erected a large brick building on Main Street opposite the present Lewis County courthouse. She made sure a new, competing bank occupied the corner room of her building; various businesses moved into other rooms and the upstairs portion became a hotel — an unwelcome rival to the new St. Helens Hotel. The building was later used as the county courthouse until the new one was built.

After the suspicious fire of 1892 razed many of Eliza Barrett's buildings, the town relocated on Market Street, away from her property. The colorful and peppery Eliza Saunders Barrett died in 1900. She was buried in the Fern Hill Cemetery in Chehalis with a final indignity from the town she had helped to found. Her name is misspelled on her headstone. It reads "Barrette," not Barrett.

Eliza Barrett's new office building and later courthouse, looking northwest. In the foreground is Main Street. The building's main entrance was on Chehalis Avenue, circa 1891.

Centralia

Meanwhile, George Washington's little town of Centerville (Centralia) was no longer a village but a small city after the railroad arrived. Where the railroad crossed land that had once been called "Black George Prairie," two stores and a hotel were built at the intersection of Tower and Main streets. According to *Centralia: The First Fifty Years*, the population grew to 75 by 1880. The name of Centralia was adopted in 1883, and by 1886, the population rose to 325. In 1889 a boom in the town's "Golden Era" increased the numbers from 700 to 3,200. The *Centralia News* issued a promotional newspaper in 1891,

Centralia seen from Seminary Hill, July 4, 1885.

Corner of Tower and Main, looking north on Tower. The State Bank of Centralia is on the left, circa 1890.

sent all over the United States. Its goal was to attract 100,000 residents within a few years.

The goal did not seem unrealistic at the time. Centralia would soon be the hub of five railroads. Coal mines were being developed and more than ten lumber companies and at least as many shingle mills rumbled into operation. Timber resources right around the city were so profuse that a shortage of logs was inconceivable. The Centralia Furniture Manufacturing Company operated with the latest in equipment, and the Centralia Iron and Brass Factory, the only company west of Chicago to manufacture shelf hardware, worked its employees 18 hours a day and still lagged six weeks behind in its orders. The American Pump Manufacturing Company literally pumped out 100 double-action devices a week, while two brick yards stacked up profits from their product.

New additions were platted as the price of real estate skyrocketed. One hundred buildings were under construction at one time, and municipal improvements included a sewer system, waterworks, telephone service and a street car line. Two large schools and a seminary were built. There was even talk of locating the state capitol in Centralia.

The boom led to bust in 1893 when a severe financial panic gripped the country. Banks failed, almost all the businesses collapsed, and many of the new buildings were never completed. The new residents packed up their belongings and straggled out of town, while the new mansions built in the north end of town could be purchased for the price of the hardware in them. George Washington came to the rescue of his town; he sent to Portland for rice, flour, and sugar by the ton. He bought lard and bacon from Dobson's Packing Plant in

Chehalis to feed the townspeople, and even furnished shoes for those who needed them. Centralia was a virtual ghost town for six years.

This, too, passed, and by the time of his death in 1905, George Washington had watched Centralia recover. During the time of 1907 to 1915, the core of Centralia's downtown built up. A class project by Centralia College students in 1994 entitled "Looking Back" reveals that in one year's time between 1908 and 1909, twelve new buildings were constructed, and assessed property valuation more than doubled. In 1910 Centralia was the only city between Tacoma and Portland with paved streets and a sewage system.

Clyde Berlin, the only licensed aviator in the Pacific Northwest, poses at the fairgrounds during the Centralia festival, May 30, 1912. Miss Jeannette Salick holds one of the bottles of champagne used during the festival.

Centralia City Commissioners, 1912.

Such a city as this was cause for celebration! The Hub City Festival in May 1912 celebrated the construction of three new and important buildings: the Carnegie Library, the depot, and the Dumon Building which housed the post office near the corner of Main and Pearl. For a full week Centralians celebrated their successes. Topping off the event was Centralia's first pilot, Clyde Berlin, who flew over the city to drop a bottle of champagne on each of the new buildings. His aim was not as accurate as expected; he hit one building, the depot, which was probably just as well, for the bottle broke several tiles on the new roof.

Winlock

Winlock owes its inception to the railroad, and in fact, became the first incorporated city in the county in 1873 as the railroad began service. A railroad construction camp was located on the site, known as "Lee's Camp," named for the contractor. The camp soon caught the eye of one Dr. C.C. Pagett, who had originally distinguished himself in the Indian War, practiced medicine where Shelton now stands, and served as President of the Territorial Council. When he realized the potential of Lee's Camp for shipping grain from Cowlitz and Grand Prairies, he bought eighty acres from the Northern Pacific land grant on the eastern side of the present line. He platted a town at about the same time that Jack Nealy claimed land on the other side of the track. These early claims make up the present town site of Winlock.

Pagett wrote to his friend in Olympia, General Winlock W. Miller, asking for suggestions for a name for the new town. Miller wrote back suggesting the name "Winlock" after numerous members of his family. "If however you should fancy the name, and adopt it, I will agree to give a nice bell to the church or schoolhouse, that is built in the town." And so it was that the town got it name officially on February 2, 1872, and that Winlock's first school, "a suitable, commodious and substantial schoolhouse," had a shiny big bell shipped from San Francisco in 1882. The school expanded in 1887 to offer two years of high school, "a splendid modern school house (occupying) a slightly position in the western part of town." In its first two-year graduating class in 1898 was Charles Metsker, the originator of Metsker maps.

Winlock School with 123 students, July, 1889.

According to unpublished documents in the Lewis County Museum, Jack Nealy was known as one of Winlock's most interesting characters. He rode to Washington by horseback from Georgia, and later fathered 12 children. He once argued so vociferously with a man named Frank Frost that Frost bit Nealy's nose. Locals claimed it was the worst case of Frost bite they'd ever seen! Nealy was once arrested for racing his horse up and down the street. When the judge asked him how fast he was going, Nealy proclaimed loudly, "About a mile a minute." The judge said, "Now, Mr. Nealy, you know you were not going a mile a minute." Jack, quick with his tongue as well as his horse,

The hillside of Winlock with the railroad along the bottom of the photograph.

responded, "Say now, Teddy old boy, who was riding that horse, you or me?"

Winlock's boom began in the 1880s with the completion of the transcontinental route to Portland and train emigrations. Illustrative of the overnight arrival of the second wave of settlers was the "Colony" that arrived in Winlock by train in 1884. A group of 43 people from Newport, Tennessee, chartered a railroad car to Kalama only to find that the only hotel there had burned to the ground. As they waited for the river steamer to transport the train across the river, they sought the advice of a conductor who wired ahead to see if Winlock could accommodate them. Indeed it could. The new settlers rented the hotel for a month for the entire group. When the Fourth of July rolled around, they hosted a gala affair with a lavish picnic, singing by numerous groups, a speech by Dr. Pagett, and a Grand Ball complete with live music in their quarters.

By 1887 when a number of additions were platted in the fledgling town, lots sold like proverbial hotcakes during a period of remarkable expansion. It was estimated that Winlock in that year received more emigrants than any other town in the county. In the fall of 1887 the Chehalis *Bee Nugget* reported that not only had the population doubled within the year, but so had the numbers of residences, businesses, and values of property. The first phone line in the county—connecting Winlock and Toledo—was installed in that year as well. In 1890 Winlock's population was just 300 souls short of that of the county seat of Chehalis (877 vs. 1157), and the town succeeded in getting its bid to be the county seat on the ballot. The measure was defeated at the time a branch line of the railroad from Chehalis to South Bend was being constructed. By 1910 the population was equal to that of Chehalis, but by 1920 the population had dropped back to around 850 where it remained for decades.

A large two-story hall in Winlock became the social center of town in the 1890s — and the scene of a battle between saints and sinners. The Protestant churches of the time forbade their members to smoke, drink, play cards, or dance. Prominent citizens were said to have been dropped from church rolls for dancing at the hall.

By 1904 Winlock had a hospital and in addition to the usual round of businesses, the town also tooted its own horn with a sixteen-piece cornet brass band.

Winlock Commercial Hotel and Drug Store, built in 1890 and burned in 1911.

Napavine

Napavine's first post office began in 1873 as a result of the new railroad track; its first mill was opened by Northern Pacific (NP) to make railroad ties. What was probably Napavine's second store was set up by the railroad. It was an odd arrangement indicative of the early segregation of Chinese workers, or conceivably as a way to deal with language barriers. The store was a tent divided in the center with a white man to wait on white customers and a Chinese man to wait on the 300 Chinese workers camped nearby to work on the NP grading.

Napavine was a perfect example of the

Sommerville Brothers Mill buildings, Napavine.

railroad's impact as it reached the timber-rich resources in the drainages and on the hillsides of the area. Within five or six years, Napavine boasted a phenomenal number of mills: six sawmills, a shingle mill, and two factories making decorative wood columns. For support services, to these were added a general repair shop, two shoe shops, four general stores, two meat markets, two saloons, a drug store, a doctor's office and other businesses. Its peak of population occurred between 1900 and 1925 when 1,500 people resided within the town and about as many in outlying areas. As the numbers of mills declined during the Depression, the population decreased and remained stable at under 500 throughout the 20th century.

Early Napavine businesses, circa 1895.

Adna

The town of Adna and areas surrounding it carried several names. In 1864 the family of Joel Fay had settled west of Adna where Deep Creek empties into Bunker Creek, and the area was known as Fayette. It was established as a post office in 1880 by Henry S. Stearns. (Stearns deservedly earns a spot in local history. He arrived at Claquato with the Davis family before its beginnings and became the county's first surveyor, county auditor and county superintendent of schools, all at the same time!)

The Adna area had the melodious name of "Willaway" coined when a settler's wife frequently said, "Where there's a will, there's a way." This post office started in 1892. The NP folks didn't like the name because it was too similar to nearby Willapa and therefore confusing. Someone chose the name "Pomona" for the Roman goddess of fruit trees, but that didn't work either since there was another Pomona east of the Cascades. So in 1894 it became Adna. Although some people maintain the name was a misspelling of Edna, railroad histories refer to a railroad official who was responsible for the name.

Vader

Several other towns owe their beginnings directly to the railroad, as well. Along the line in south Lewis County, the town of Vader was originally named Little Falls for the falls on Olequa Creek. However, railroad officials recognized it only by Sopenah because of confusion with a town of Little Falls in Minnesota. One night an undersized shack was deposited from a flatcar, inscribed with "Sopenah," to the chagrin of townsfolk who couldn't even buy a ticket to Little Falls and refused to accept Sopenah as a name. Finally, the issue was resolved in a special meeting with a railroad official who suggested residents choose a name of a local resident. Martin Vader was given the honor. Local legend

Adna from the hillside looking south, 1911.

The Towns Came

The new Northern Pacific train station in Little Falls (later Vader) with the railroad's Sopenah sign.

says that he resented the honor and moved to Florida, but the story has been debunked. Mr. Vader was ill at the time and passed away in 1935 in the veterans hospital near Fort Lewis. His grave can be seen in the Little Falls Cemetery.

becoming a manufacturing center. Peter Breuse and Sons built a sawmill and an adjoining sash and door factory capable of turning out 100 doors per day, shipped out on steamboats.

The Breuse family erected a building three stories high for a flour and grist mill

Toledo

Toledo's rise during the 1880s and '90s can be attributed only indirectly to trains, for its claim to prosperity came because of its location on the Cowlitz River and steamboats. In 1887 Toledo at the head of navigation on the Cowlitz River showed promise of

Toledo, 1886, from 2nd Street looking south, with the Cowlitz River upper left.

in full production by 1891. During July of 1893 an organization known as the Cowlitz River Milling Company took over the flour mill and added machinery capable of producing 75 barrels of flour a day. The farmers of the area brought in so much wheat that the mill was compelled to run day and night, and in spite of the double shifts, a backload of a week was stacked up. An evaporating plant in Toledo prepared dried potatoes for the Alaska trade during the Klondike gold rush. A furniture factory fashioned beautifully grained furniture from the native woods prior to 1890, and at one time pleasure launches were built there for the Cowlitz River sportsmen.

The year of 1892 was a red-letter year for Toledo — or perhaps a red wagon bridge year, for that was when its red wagon bridge was constructed. At a cost of $20,000, it was the longest bridge in Lewis County with a total span of 841 feet. Eadonia, across the river from Toledo, fell victim to the bridge for now its residents could cross the river to do their buying in Toledo. The muddy quagmires in Toledo's intersections became intolerable. The property owners installed sidewalks and thus earned the "Gem City of the Cowlitz" the reputation of being one of the prettiest towns in the area. The town had kerosene street lamps and its own water system at the dawn of the new century. The culture of Toledo was complete when the Odd Fellows Lodge adapted its lower floor for an opera house, the center of entertainment for many years. It hosted minstrel shows, medicine shows, small time road companies, and later the first moving pictures.

Toledo has long been subject to the whims of the capricious Cowlitz River. Cowlitz Landing, that famous stepping-off point in the history of Washington where Simon Plamondon first set foot, was flooded in 1896, never to be used again as a major landing. A sizable flood in 1906 severely damaged the old red wagon bridge and changed the course of the river. In 1933 flooding was so severe that many people lost fields of potatoes.

Bridge No. 6 across the Cowlitz River at Toledo.

Although Toledo did not owe its initial rise to the railroads, its lack of growth occurred from not having them. Toledo residents had always hoped that the Union Pacific or the Milwaukee Road would build through their town, for the seven miles to the railroad at Winlock was prohibitive for shipping. There was no inducement for people or industry to locate in the area, and the town's growth spurt sputtered out about 1912.

Morton

Morton also owed its growth to the reaches of the railroad. When the Tacoma and Eastern Railroad entered the town in 1910, Morton became a small city in its own right. Its first post office was established in 1889, the year of statehood, and later in 1913 local citizens filed for incorporation. Its downtown core was razed by a disastrous fire in 1924, an event that served as a marker in time for businesses. After the fire most of the new buildings were constructed to be fireproof. As the demand for railroad ties was filled by small operations located on nearly every hillside, Morton boomed and boasted of having the longest tie dock in the world.

Other Towns

The railroad determined whether towns survived or died. Claquato, which had been the county seat, lost out when the railroad came through Chehalis. Other settlements in the vicinity came and went too.

The post office of Gleneden was established in 1871 on Lincoln Creek about 13 miles northwest of Centralia, gaining enough prominence to appear on maps for several decades. In the same vicinity Meadow Brook also offered mail service for a short time. Mail service was discontinued and routed to Rochester in 1907. Had they been on the railroad line, both settlements may have prospered as Centralia and Chehalis did.

The destiny of Lewis County towns was determined not just by the trains but by the next development that charted their course for the 20th century. The forests of the land lay waiting.

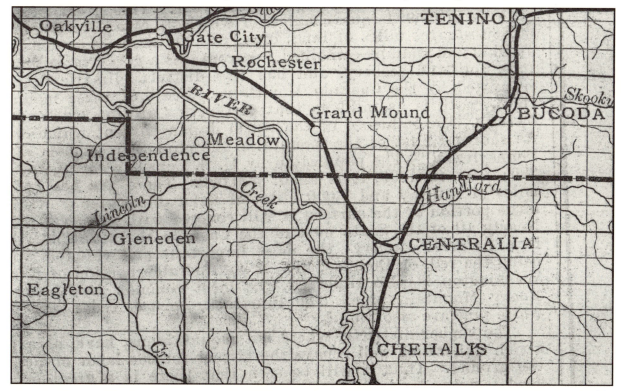

Chapter 10

The East End

The scenic, diverse areas of Eastern Lewis County and the Big Bottom Country of the Cowlitz River were given a nod in early recorded history, but settlement came much later. The early history of East County is so recent, in fact, that it is still possible to interview second or third generation pioneers, as recorded in local historian LaVonne M. Sparkman's series of books.

Although it's debatable, many people agree that Eastern Lewis County begins at Mossyrock and extends to White Pass at the crest of the Cascades. The Big Bottom Country refers to the Cowlitz River valley bottom land about two to five miles wide and thirty miles long, resplendent in the surrounding scenery of towering mountains. Isolated from the beginning, this area of Lewis County still feels the sting of being a geographic and social stepchild, removed by distance and neglected by the more populous Centralia-Chehalis area. Yet it has its own unique story, a richness of history enhanced by its very isolation.

Of its early history, we know that Simon Plamondon was probably one of the first white men to see the Big Bottom Country of Randle when he traveled there with the Cowlitz Indians around 1820. Other Hudson's Bay trappers set up a small trading post at the mouth of Surrey Creek in the 1830s, teaching the Indians a few basic techniques in agriculture which resulted in the clearing of some of the land. When the Americans arrived, the Indians shared their seed and grain.

In 1854 (some sources say 1852) miner William Packwood and James Longmire prospected for coal in the Skate Creek drainage, traveling up the Nisqually River through Longmire, and searched for a route across the Cascades. They earned the title as the discoverers of the area. Packwood was a settler in Thurston County whose name appears in early histories. The name of the town of Packwood now honors the pioneer miner who never actually lived there but maintained a mining claim in the area. His pack trains were a familiar sight on the mountain trails.

An official survey likely followed the initial discovery, for the Tilton River and its three major forks were named for the first surveyor general of Washington Territory, James Tilton. Mineral Lake was charted in 1857 as Goldsboro Lake.

The land was virtually untouched until the 1880s, but by 1891 post offices had sprouted like the ubiquitous vine maples. First, in 1886 came the Vance post office across the river from Randle and named for a Senator from South Carolina; and Osborn, whose location seemed to follow whoever agreed to be postmaster. In 1890 Morton's post office was named after Levi P. Morton, the Vice-President of the United States under President Harrison.

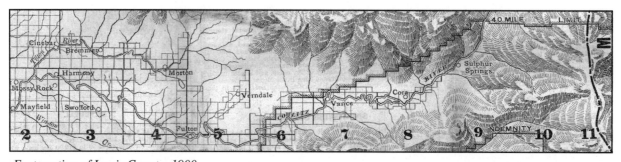

East portion of Lewis County, 1900.

Almost simultaneously post offices became official at Bremer, nine miles northwest of Morton on the Tilton River; Verndale, near Glenoma; Sulphur Springs, three miles southeast of Packwood (changed later to Lewis for a man who planned to place dozens of dams on the Cowlitz River in the early 1900s); Cora, between Randle and Packwood; Swofford, southeast of Mossyrock; Harmony, three and a half miles north of Mossyrock; and Ferry, six and half miles southwest of Mossyrock. Alpha, 19 miles southeast of Chehalis, was started at the same time. Within a year or so, several others opened up mail service: Fulton, 12 miles southeast of Morton; Wilson, nine miles south of Mayfield; and Cinebar and Mineral, the only familiar names a century later. Mineral claims to have the smallest post office in the United States, an eight-foot square cubicle maintained as a curiosity by the Mineral Lake Lions Club.

Mineral claims to have the smallest post office.

A 1954 report prepared by a history committee of the Packwood Community Study Program and included in *Postmarked Washington Lewis and Cowlitz Counties* described the early days of mail delivery in the Packwood area. "Each family had a small sack of oil cloth or canvas which was hung on a post near the road. The mail carrier picked up these sacks daily and took them to the post office where the respective mail was placed in them by the postmaster. The carrier tied the locked sack containing the through mail behind his saddle. The individual sacks, which were to be delivered along the way, he hung on the saddle horn." For a few years each man was expected to take his turn delivering mail by horseback. Getting the mail was a vital connection to the world from the isolation of the rugged wilderness.

Nearly fifty years after the "Black Robes" had established St. Frances Xavier Mission in 1838 near the Cowlitz Landing, a few settlers were tenuously making their way up the rugged Cowlitz River to homestead. The claims of those who did settle were on shaky ground as well, for settlers had no title to their claims until surveys were completed in the Morton area in 1881 and the Big Bottom in 1889. Encouraged by the hope of a railroad, they endured pioneer hardships which had been nearly forgotten by then. Some were convinced that a separate county would be formed to give them more political clout.

Three possible routes led into the East County area from the west side of the Cascades, two of them requiring a hard week's

Horses from the Chehalis mail run were stabled at this farm of Thomas I. Blankenship in Riffe, 1906. Noah Blankenship's house is in the distance.

walk from Chehalis. One was from Tacoma and Elbe, another from Chehalis and the Tilton River, and a third, partly an Indian trail, from Chehalis through the Klickitat Prairie near Mossyrock — all of them passable only by human foot or a really tough horse. The trails were so poorly marked that people often became lost trying to relocate the route.

Levi Adrian Davis, his brothers, and sons relocated in the Big Bottom Country in the mid-1880s. They were descendents of Lewis Hawkins Davis, the founder of Claquato and builder of parts of the Military Road some 30 years before. Claquato had already witnessed its own rise and fall after being bypassed by the railroad after which the family set out on another pioneer venture.

The Davis ranch was eight miles east of Vance across the river from Randle. It was a large strip of land with "the finest views of the mountains from any point in the valley," according to a newspaper interview in 1890. The article further reported that Davis' "health and the health of his wife is better than it had previously been for several years." At that time the only wagon in the entire valley belonged to the Davises who brought it in pieces by pony— a commentary on the treacherous state of the trails. L.A. Davis established the Cora post office at the family home in 1886, naming it after his (healthy) wife Cora. In modern times a bridge known by the locals as the Cora Bridge crosses the Cowlitz River east of Randle, dividing the Randle and Packwood country.

An early Cora bridge collapsed from the weight of a truck crossing the bridge in 1943.

L. A. Davis, a settler in the East End, 1891.

To reach their future homestead site in Morton in 1884, Henry Clay Temple and his adolescent son Gus walked up the old Indian trail from Cowlitz Landing and along the Klickitat Prairie near Mossyrock. The Temples had been one of the first families to homestead in the Puyallup Valley. After building a cabin in the Davis Lake Valley, they walked out to Chehalis along the Tilton River, now known as Bear Canyon on State Highway 508. This became the major route for East County residents when they went into Chehalis for supplies once or twice a year. They passed through the settlements of Alpha and Bremer on their way. Eventually a horse trail three feet wide was cut out to Centerville (Centralia), and later enlarged to a wagon trail so that the settlers took turns going in every month or so for supplies.

The East End

Eastern Lewis County house built with split cedar.

Ethel post office, 1925.

In the early days before lumber mills, homes were made of logs or split cedar with puncheon floors split out of logs and hewn smooth, and furniture was all constructed by hand.

Morton residents did not have the luxury of rich river bottom land like their neighbors in the Big Bottom country had. Instead of crops, they raised livestock which they drove to market in Chehalis, a three-week round trip.

The Temple family brought the first cook stove to Morton. Because the roads were not passable with a wagon at the time, the stove was tied to a sling between two ponies. A third pony carried the extra pieces of lids and doors. When the week-long journey of 40 miles was over, everyone from miles around came to celebrate Independence Day by having bread baked in a real oven. For those who didn't have an oven, a reflector oven or a Dutch oven served almost as well.

Life in those dark, heavy woods had its own terrors. Joseph Moorhead had barely finished his cabin when he came home one day to an uninvited dinner guest — a seven-foot cougar inside the cabin, attracted to the bacon hanging from the ceiling. Wolves and bears were a nagging threat to livestock, while a wave of consumption (tuberculosis) nearly

Early settlers in the East End endured primitive conditions.

wiped out many families soon after they settled in the Randle area. Swarms of fleas were a constant irritation. The woods themselves were so dense, that as LaVonne Sparkman so aptly titled one of her books, "The trees were so thick, there was *Nowhere To Look But Up.*"

German-born William Joerk (York) came to settle near Randle in 1883; he had the distinction of owning the first cow and calf, and later the first pigs. Mr. York, figuring that the prairie land must be less fertile if it grew no trees, spent years hacking bitterly away at the vine maple covering his claim. Ironically, a vine maple whacked him in the stomach and killed him in 1914. Other settlers joined Joerk and his brother Herman to boost the population to seven by 1885. The first family to arrive was the Chilcoats who arrived by horseback; Mrs. Chilcoat was the first woman to settle in the Randle area.

Mineral Trading Co., owner Frederick Jonas, circa 1900.

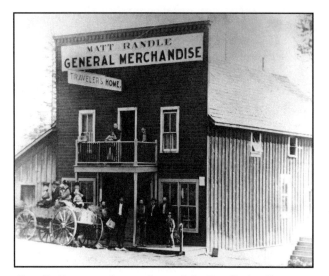
Randle Store run by members of the Randle family.

Most of East County's residents were bachelors, numbering at least 80 or so, who spent a few months on their claims and worked "outside" the rest of the time. When the community of Morton decided to have a big oyster stew supper, there was concern that with so many hungry bachelors coming, there might not be enough food, Lavonne Sparkman writes. One enterprising male solved the problem; pepper was sprinkled so generously in the stew, no one returned for seconds! Where the oysters came from is cause for speculation.

The Mineral area was settled almost exclusively at first by Swedes. One of the first settlers, Emil Ahlstrand, often said that when he arrived all he could understand were the dogs and the chickens. The children at Mineral's first school spoke only Swedish and had to learn English before they tackled the three Rs.

In an interesting example of emigration in the United States, the settlement of Riffe and Glenoma occurred in the first part of the 20th century when an entire clan moved from the Southern Appalachian

Mountains to the Cascade foothills in the areas of Mossyrock, Riffe, and Verndale, later known as Glenoma or "Little Kentucky." The group was sired by five blood-related men discontented with the poverty in Virginia, West Virginia, and Kentucky. Some came first to Grays Harbor to work as loggers, and then moved their families to Eastern Lewis County in about 1910-1917.

The originator of the movement was Floyd Riffe, who with his wife Armedia (Blankenship) came from West Virginia to the area east of Mossyrock before the turn of the century. In the early 1890s Floyd Riffe, an ordained Baptist minister, wrote to several railroad companies to inquire about the best train fare for members of the Primitive Baptist Church. Sixty people made up of eighteen families, many of them with eleven and twelve children, boarded a train in Greenbriar, West Virginia, on Sept. 19, 1893, and arrived at Chehalis Sept. 27, 1893. Riffe purchased 160 acres where the community carrying his name was later located.

In early 1894 he split cedar boards and purchased 2x4s from a small sawmill in Mossyrock to construct a two-story home for his family. He and his followers cleared the land by burning large old-growth fir trees, boring holes and stuffing them full of pitch. When the trees toppled over after four or five days of burning, they were cut into bolts six feet long and split into boards for construction. Floyd Riffe established the Riffe Post Office on Sept. 20, 1898, on the banks of the Cowlitz River nine miles east of Mossyrock. The Riffe Star Route mail delivery continued through the 1960s.

Riffe's community met a sad demise under the waters of Mossyrock Dam. An article in the *Daily Chronicle* of June 18, 1966, read "The Valley was Gouged Out: Riffe Community Exists No More." Homes were leveled into piles of junk, brush was burned and timber cleared as long-time residents with heavy hearts moved elsewhere. After considerable controversy, the lake behind the dam, originally named

Riffe Baptist Church congregation holding a baptism in the Cowlitz River, 1912.

Thomas I. Blankenship and son Arthur Blankenship with their horse "Coffee" at Riffe, 1906.

Davisson, was officially changed to Riffe to honor the hearty pioneer from West Virginia who led so many people to Lewis County. The names of Stiltner, Blankenship, Clevinger and Clevenger are prominent in the history and development of Eastern Lewis County, and the descendants of the original settlers are numerous enough to create a small city.

One of the most poignant stories to emerge in the history of Lewis County comes from the James Randle family, for whom Randle was named. May Randle McMahan was 13 years old in 1887 when she trudged over the winding Indian trail from Mossyrock to her father's new ten-by-ten foot cabin. Their first winter was a vicious one with three-foot drifts of snow. The family had no amenities such as a stove or sewing machine and for three months had no mail delivery until an Indian brought it in on snowshoes.

The following excerpts of her story told in 1930 are taken from LaVonne Sparkman and Irma Boyer's book, *Where the Big Bottom Begins, Randle History* (1995).

"I was the only girl within twenty miles. Of course, there were no schools, nor churches, no stores, or post offices, just a poor trail through the rushes, brush, and woods between these homesteads...

"The next winter I had the most terrible toothache in my back teeth. I could neither eat or sleep as I should... In the month of March, Father went to Mossyrock after some cows...I went along to get my teeth out, as we had heard there was a man nine miles below there who had a pair of forceps. I rode the nine miles alone. He broke one tooth off and all to pieces and left the roots in. I came back home with it in that condition and suffered every minute of the way.

"Dode Doss helped Father take the cows back. It took three days. I led the pack horses, one of which had only been packed a few times. They were a way ahead with the cattle. The wild, foolish pony got scared as we were going through a slough in a swampy place...To make matters worse, my horse balked and I could not make it go at all. It was pouring rain with snow mixed in and with the horses splashing water all over me, I was... getting so cold and numb that I could hardly stay on. I tried to call for help, but they could not hear. I was so long out of sight that Father came back to see what was the matter...

"I was almost frozen and could not stand up when he got me off the horse...We went on to find a place to stay all night. We had to stay with two or three bachelors in a one-room shack. I had no clothes to change, so slept in my cold underwear. I didn't even catch cold, but suffered until the next February with toothache, then went to Tacoma and kept house for Father while he worked in the mill and I went to school. While I was there, of course, I had my teeth out...

"My ambition from childhood was to get a good education and to make something of myself, and because I could not and because of the awful loneliness, I used to cry myself to sleep almost every night.

Through the day, when I had time I would go into woods and lie down to think and cry. I had no childhood days."

When a young man named Jim McMahan homesteaded across the river from the Randles, May became friends with him and married him when she was barely 17. "I didn't want to marry so young, but I was just desperate. I thought if I got married, then I would know I could not go to school any more; that I would have to take care of my home and help make a home."

During her lifetime, May Randle McMahan helped to start a little school, then a little log church. She lived to see both grow into solid community entities.

"I am proud to know that I have had a part in helping to develop this little part of the world from a wilderness to a beautiful little valley, blest with all the blessings of civilization. Good homes, good roads, good people, schools, churches, etc...We old timers will soon be gone and I hope to a better land. We trust our children and grandchildren will appreciate and enjoy the heritage we leave them."

May Randle McMahan and Jim McMahan, 1949.

Garland Ward had the first car in the area and is seen crossing the Randle Bridge, circa 1911. Photo courtesy of Tami (DeRossett) Moorcroft.

Chapter 11

Timber!

Rugged men in hickory shirts and stagged-off pants, red suspenders and ubiquitous caulked ("cork") boots are deeply imbedded in the history of Lewis County. With their tin hats and chain saws and a lingo all their own, the loggers of the Northwest were, and are, a colorful, hearty breed with a distinct culture. Their work represented the challenge of meeting face-

Loggers in hickory shirts, staged-off pants, red suspenders and caulked books in front of Yeoman Lumber Co.'s donkey engine near Pe Ell, circa 1921.

on the danger of giants much bigger than they were. They were drawn to feats of fortitude, rascality, and hard-drinking. Their livelihood stood for the honor of hard work and money well-earned, of a means to support one's family, of pride in the quality of their product.

Before logging came into conflict with environmental concerns, the logger and his family carried themselves with pride, for they were meeting the needs of a nation and a world hungry for wood. The timber was viewed as being theirs for the taking and an inexhaustible resource. The timber industry and those who earned their livelihood in the woods and mills account for a major piece of Lewis County history. In the past, timber and agriculture have accounted for 80 percent of the jobs in this rural area.

The influx of population and the arrival of railroads in the late 1800s led directly to the woods of the land called Lewis. The Cowlitz and Chehalis Indians were the first ones to cut timber for long houses, shelters, and canoes. They were followed by the French Canadians of the Hudson's Bay Company on Cowlitz Prairie who set up a sawmill and cut timber for their outbuildings.

To the first American settlers, timber was more of an impediment than an incentive to settlement, but soon the amazing timber resource of the new land stood on its own as an enticement. The first pioneers brought crude tools to convert the trees into their homes. They used wood for block houses during the Indian War, made cradles for their children, and fashioned furniture before there

Mack's Log & Timber Company men stand in the roots of a huge tree at Camp #2, near Elma, 1908.

was any to buy. Mostly, though, they wanted the big trees to be out of their way and simply burned them up to clear the land. For building homes, they went to commercial sources when possible. Michael T. Simmons, one of the first settlers to travel north of the Columbia, established an "up and down" mill in 1847 at Tumwater, then known as New Market, and settlers from Lewis County were among his first customers. Within a decade, there were 16 sawmills on Puget Sound, including the Pope and Talbot operation with its fleet of sailing ships journeying the Seven Seas with Northwest wood.

Green Gold

The intent of the land grants to the railroads was to stimulate settlement and develop resources. After the Northern Pacific Railway acquired over seven million acres in the Washington Territory, it wasn't long before Midwest timber barons' eyes boggled at the timbered hillsides. The nation was growing; new towns in the East and Midwest needed building materials. Their holdings exhausted in Minnesota and Wisconsin, many lumbermen shipped their machinery around the Horn on sailing vessels to set up shop in the new land. Soon the banks of all principal rivers were dotted with mills. By the 1890s there was a general complaint about the scarcity of lumber for building, though new mills were going up everywhere and previous ones were running night and day. The rush for timberlands extended throughout Washington. Among the entrepreneurs who recognized the possibilities was a man named Fredrick Weyerhaeuser.

The huge size of trees is shown by this fallen giant in the Salzer Valley, east of Centralia, 1902.

In 1899 Weyerhaeuser purchased almost a million acres of Washington timberland from Northern Pacific for six dollars an acre. Then, more than half a million acres of Lewis County's timberland was owned by the Weyerhaeuser Company. Encompassing timberland with some of the world's richest forest soils, Weyerhaeuser's McDonald tree farm extends west from Interstate 5 to Frances and from Oakville south to Winlock. Its Vail tree farm stretches east from I-5 to Morton, and from Tenino south to the Cowlitz River.

The profusion and height of timber was a source of awe to those who came here in the early days. Legend has it that the trees of the Northwest were so tall at one time that it took Paul Bunyan *two days* to see the tops. He looked as far as he could in one day and started from that point the next morning!

Legend aside, a special edition of the *Centralia Daily News* in 1891 boasted that "a mile square will have upon it from ten to twenty millions (board feet) of lumber...The Chehalis River borders the city on the south and southwest and is used for logging by the numerous mills on its banks. The amount of timber available above the city is variously estimated at between two hundred and three hundred billions; an amount which finite mind can scarcely grasp without illustration. In boards a foot wide, this would reach about sixteen times around the world." While such publications were prone to hyperbole, the amount of timber was indeed impressive.

Commercial logging began along the rivers with teams of oxen straining to haul the giant logs over greased skid roads. For decades, oxen (which were actually strong cattle) were the sole "horsepower." Like

Levi Smith using oxen to log in back of the Winlock School, 1887.

thick forests. Ox-hauling was inefficient at more than a mile from waterways, and at the rate of harvest, the timber near water was being rapidly depleted.

One reminder of oxen logging remains in use today in the jargon of the woods. A "bull buck" or "bull of the woods" is the person with the most responsibility in a logging operation.

Finley Hays, retired editor of the publication, *Loggers World*, explained that "Many times horses as well as men were hurt at the business of logging. Sled loads of logs being pulled downhill would overrun the horses and injure or kill them. To keep this from happening sometimes a 'rough lock' would be put on one or both of the sled runners. Or another piece of line would be fastened to the back of the sled and a couple of turns taken around a stump. Thus a man holding the line could keep the sled from running over the horses. The teams were both well-trained and fast. They knew that the way to stay out of trouble was to turn aside when a sled load of logs threatened them and just let the load go by."

the men, they had Sundays off and were often turned loose to browse at will in the camps and settlements. When horse teams were introduced by the Simpson Company in Mason County, the idea was ridiculed at first because horses were thought to be too fragile, too long-legged and too expensive to feed. Change has never come easily to loggers, but after several years of balking at the idea, they discovered that 16- or 18-horse teams were much better suited to handle large loads for long distances in the

Skid roads in Lewis County were similar to this elaborate skid road in Carnation, WA, circa 1910.

One story is told about the days of horse logging, recounted in the *West Coast and Puget Sound Lumberman* in February of 1902. The story was about Jim Gilchrist, the boss of the Salzer Valley Lumber Company outside of Centralia. One day his crew had a big six-horse team attached to a seven-foot fir log which had been pulled to the top of a long grade of well-greased skids extending down to the water. Gilchrist figured the

95

team could keep out of the way of the log and gave the driver the go-ahead. The log moved easily and pretty soon picked up speed down the steep grade. The driver realized his team was in danger of being squashed by the runaway log; the only choice was to run. Down the long grade they galloped, chains and gear flapping and jangling. "Over the rough skids, muddy and dangerous, they raced, the log at times almost on the heels of the team. A stumble and all would be lost, but on they went, thundering and splashing down and on to the level, till the chain tightened and the great dumb brutes knew they were saved and slackened their fearful pace."

Guerrier's Logging Company's horse team on the Newaukum Middle Fork, circa 1920.

In 1881 came an invention which signaled what one observer called, "the conversion of logging oxen into steaks and hamburgers." John Dolbeer invented the steam-powered donkey engine in California. Basically a steam-powered winch, the donkey consisted of a vertical boiler and single cylinder. It operated a drum or windlass to yard the felled logs out of the woods by winding the cable around a "Gypsy" or spool, much like a fishing reel. Then a horse pulled the end of the cable into the woods to pick up the next log. The steam donkeys were fast and cheap to operate, and soon Washington had three times more of the new beasts than Oregon and California combined. By 1904 the size of the donkey engines had doubled. The Salzer Valley Lumber Company purchased one of the largest ones in the state for its logging camp. Its main drum contained a quarter mile of cable and half a mile of haul back. With a 14-by-9-foot bed and 120 horsepower, it would have been mounted either on a 75-foot hand-built sled or railroad car to be moved into the woods.

Washington Iron Works steam donkey, circa 1915. The donkey engines revolutionized early logging.

The steam donkey was soon joined by another beast of burden, the locomotive. Logging railroads eventually reached into nearly every drainage in Lewis County. Probably the loggers' favorite puffer belly was the Shay, according to an article in the Centennial edition of the *Daily Chronicle* in 1953.

The Shay locomotive of an unidentified logging company, circa 1900.

The Shay was a steam-geared contraption that could go anywhere loggers could climb "with the sure footedness of a Tibetan yak. She spanned ravines on wooden trestles assembled with more faith than engineering know-how. She stuck to mountainsides like flypaper and turned corners as sharp as a logger's ax. Old-timers used to swear that the Shay could turn so sharply that the headlight often shone over the engineer's shoulder. The Shay looked like an accident, but she was one of the best logging locomotives and one of the primary movers of logs from the forests to the mills in the glory days of logging." Those who were committed to Climax engines, competitor to the Shay, could well have expressed the same degree of loyalty. The era of the "locey" (locomotive) was in its prime from the early 1900s until about 1940 when trucks came into use. However, the Weyerhaeuser Company shipped logs by rail to South Bay in Olympia from the Pe Ell area until 1985 and from the Vail area until 1990. The logs were rafted to the company's big mill in Everett.

Typically, the companies that set up the numerous mills also set up logging camps out in the woods. At first the conditions were deplorable; men slept on straw on the ground without the benefits of hot meals or hot showers. They worked ten-hour days, six and a half days a week. Woods work was very dangerous. If someone were hurt or killed, he was hauled off behind a rock to wait until the day's work was done and the locey came to pick everyone up. At the end of a workday one local logger found out that his brother had been killed in the woods that morning and left to lie by the trail all day; such was the grim reality of life and death in the woods.

Local cemeteries all have tree-shaped gravestones for woodsmen killed on the

Lincoln Creek Logging Company crew. A note on the back of the photograph says that just before this picture was taken a man was thrown off the boom to his death (note the boom line extending across the top of the photograph).

job, and many died as very young men. Because of the often cold, damp working conditions and the unhealthy camps, others died young of pneumonia and other illnesses. It wasn't until the labor unions became militant in the 'teens and '20s that lumbermen — quite surprised that loggers would want hot showers, of all things — granted woods workers an 8-hour work day and improved the condition of the logging camps.

Finley Hays explains that loggers from the Puget Sound, Columbia River, Oregon, and Grays Harbor (Lewis County loggers identified with this group) were distinctive. Each group had its own language and methods for doing things, and each thought its own way was the best. Single men often made up the bulk of work force as "tramp loggers" they moved from one camp to another often with only the slightest provocation, such as one character nicknamed "One Paycheck Jack." The work in the woods and the camps was held together by the "home guards," the stable, family men who were well-paid and loyal.

Camp McDonald, a Weyerhaeuser logging camp, operated in the Boistfort Valley for many years. Finley Hays shares this story about a die-hard logging boss who ran Camp McDonald. At his funeral, he was being packed out from the church to the hearse in his casket. "He raised up in his casket and barked, 'Lay off two of these pall bearers, tell the scaler to tighten up on the scale and tell the cook to butter the hard tack on the smooth side.' Then he closed the lid and lay down to rest, satisfied with his last order."

Shingle Bolt Drivers

The settlers of Eastern Lewis County in the 1880s had a cash flow problem. There were simply very few ways to get money, although they met their most basic needs and ate well enough from subsistence farming. One woods product represented real money in their pockets. Their first cash crop? Cedar. Certainly there were plenty of cedars, rising like giant sentinels from every drainage, blocking out the sun, and stunting every effort at farming. The big problem was how to market the unwieldy beasts to meet a rising demand for cedar bolts (chunks of wood to be cut later into shakes for roofs). The river had always been the obvious solution to transportation needs, and so it was that the upper Cowlitz River became the avenue for transporting cedar bolts from Cispus Creek to market.

The shingle bolt drivers felled western red cedar during the winter when there was a lull in farming and the rivers were raging with icy water. With massive trunks too wide to cut near the ground, the men axed notches in the trees where they inserted springboards many feet off the ground. They chopped wedge-shaped undercuts with precision to make the tree fall exactly where they wanted it. From a rope attached to one of the fallers, they hauled up a "misery whip," a two-man crosscut saw. "As they sawed, they drove steel wedges into the cut with sledge hammers," explained LaVonne Sparkman in a 1992 article in *True West* magazine. "With bulg-

Loggers took risks to climb to great heights so their saws would reach through to fall the giant cedar trees of the Northwest.

ing muscles and sweat pouring even on a winter day, they toiled until the tree fell — right where they planned."

They measured the felled trees into exact lengths of four feet, six inches required by the mill, and then they bucked up (sawed) the bolts and branded them with an unheated iron so the mill would know whom to pay. Horses dragged the bolts, two cord loads at a time, on 16-foot

Dave White's shingle bolt crew, circa 1930.

sleds to holding ponds. In steep areas the men slid the bolts down long log chutes. The storage ponds and splash dams held the logs until high water in the spring when the spillway planks were jerked out and the logs were floated down the river. Ten strong men had the miserable task of driving the bolts for a three-week, seventy-mile trip down the Cowlitz. Some owners made the drive, others were hired for a dollar a day. They spent days upon days in frigid water, with their only extra insulation being heavy woolen socks and black woolen underwear.

Ed Cooper, one of Morton's pioneers, was on a drive in 1907. His most prized possessions were two pairs of wool socks hand knit by an Indian woman who wove in some of her long hair for strength. "They were so good that the other men pestered him to sell the socks, but no price was high enough," LaVonne Sparkman writes.

When the bolts finally reached the mill in Kelso, a year might lapse before the owners were paid their two dollars a cord, but only after the bolts were made into shingles. After the old-growth cedar was harvested from most of the homesteads, the bolt drivers moved to unsettled areas for their supply. Eventually a mill was built in Morton and the harvest of the cedar was no longer dependent on the long, cold trip of the shingle bolt drives down the Cowlitz River.

Shingle bolts floating down the Chehalis River in Centralia, 1907.

From the Hills to the Mills

The vast numbers of lumber and manufacturing mills in Lewis County would make a history book unto itself, for thousands of people have earned their livelihoods in the Lewis County lumber industry throughout the years. A Lewis County Historical Museum file contains references of at least fourteen mills in the era from 1887 to 1891, and at one time there were 29 mills between Chehalis and South Bend. Small sawmills and tie mills popped up on nearly every hillside in Eastern Lewis County. Of the many mills, those discussed here are representative of county history. While the mill history is an ongoing story, its zenith was between the years of 1890 and start of the Depression in about 1930.

The lumbermen from Wisconsin, Michigan, and Minnesota who relocated here in the 1880s and 1890s often had enough financial backing to purchase thousands of acres of timberland, as well as planing mills and circular saws. Nearly all the mill operations put in large holding ponds for log storage and listed their assets in terms of board feet in the water as well as standing timber. Others used existing waterways; Mineral Lake, for example, once stored millions of board feet of logs, and anyone who swam in the lake contracted a severe rash from the cedar. Employees often numbered in the hundreds, and settlements cropped up around the mill for the workers and their families; a post office, school, company store, a church and a saloon rounded out the mill towns. Significantly, the key to every successful operation was access to the railroad and to the thick stands of virgin timber.

Joe Zeek tending logs on the Snow mill pond, Littell, 1922.

The launch belonging to August Ahlstrand and Johann Carlson shown on Mineral Lake, was used to tow logs across the lake to the Mineral saw mill.

Brown Brothers Lumber Company, Napavine, circa 1910.

Many of the products produced by the mills would be anachronisms if not antiques today. The wood products industry has produced everything from broom handles and bows, to pre-cut houses dating back to the 1920s, to vast numbers of railroad ties in Eastern Lewis County. For example, the Nudd and Taylor Eave & Gutter Factory (located in Centralia at the site of the outdoor swimming pool on North Pearl Street) manufactured 15 different kinds of wooden eaves and gutters. The Frank D. Harms Sash and Door Factory, circa 1901, made porch columns and pickets, fashionable for turn-of-the-century homes. Andrew Johnson of Winlock made ships knees, which were braces for support used in wooden ships and for braces in mills. In 1915 the Chehalis Furniture and Manufacturing Company produced an 80-page catalog of "The Chehalis Line," featuring ivory enamel furniture, "turned out in dressing tables, dressers, chiffoniers, beds, stands, chairs, etc." The furniture was made of ash or western maple. The mills supplied railroads with car timbers and ties for the tracks. The mainstay of many large mills was the manufacturing of crossarms for the telegraph and telephone lines leaping across the nation.

And of course, the mills have turned out billions of board feet of lumber, plywood, veneer, and building materials for hundreds of thousands of buildings worldwide.

To manufacture shingles the large cutoff saw on the left cuts the cedar log into a shingle length such as the length between the carriage operator and Henry Brooks on the right. The Chester Snow Log and Shingle Company, Littell, 1920.

Timber!

Centralia Millwork & Supply Company fire, June 11, 1921. Fires were the worst enemy of mills in Lewis County.

One four-letter word was the common and worst enemy of all the mills: FIRE. Nearly every mill burned at least once and sometimes even four or five times. In fact, mills which *didn't* burn were almost the exception. Errant sparks in tinder-dry buildings led to catastrophic losses. Some mills were insured; others weren't. The limited fire protection equipment either malfunctioned or proved to be inadequate. A sampling of headlines from old newspapers read as follows: "Flames Devour Mill at Napavine/Big Blaze Levels Buildings/Somerville Brothers Will Rebuild" (July 1, 1910) "Macomber & Urquhart Mill four miles from Chehalis Total Loss" (August 3, 1912). And later in Randle: "Jennings shake mill destroyed by fire after fuel tanks explode" (August 18, 1982).

The old mills that didn't burn were dismantled and hauled off; consequently, few mill sites are even recognizable now.

Because of access to the railroad, Centralia had some of the first mills. The H.H. Martin Lumber Company, known as one of the "biggest little mills" on the Pacific Coast, dated back to the 1880s when Centralia was known as Centerville. Timberland owned by the Martins was far enough from the mill that logs were driven down the Big Hanaford Creek and Skookumchuck Rivers. The company did its logging during the summer and fall, and in 1900 had millions of board feet of logs in the water. The plant covered 23 acres, including two dams, booms for holding logs, and its own blacksmith and carpentry shop.

A fire at the Palmer Lumber and Manufacturing Company on State Street, Chehalis, July 25, 1939.

The competitor of the Martin mill in the 1890s (if one can consider competition to be an open market with billions of board feet available for the taking) was the Tower Lumber and Manufacturing Company, owned by Charlemagne Tower for whom Tower Avenue in Centralia is named. Because the railroad had a monopoly on shipping costs, every attempt was made to reduce weight. This mill introduced the Sturdevant dry kiln to the milling process whereby the weight of the lumber (Douglas fir) was reduced to less than half, "an important factor in shipping to great treeless middle west," according to the *Centralia Daily News* Special Edition of 1891. "Twelve cars each holding 10,000 feet are pushed into the kiln ...and if pressed for time, lumber is ready for shipment in three days." The seasoning process for wet lumber had been six to ten months; the process "cooked" it and dried the pitch.

Both local and Eastern capitalists provided the backing for the Eastern Railway & Lumber Company in 1903. Absorbing the estate of Charlemagne Tower, the Atkinson Lumber Company, and the Ballard and Bond Lumber Company (which had supplied lumber for the first mile of plank road between Centralia and Chehalis in 1893), Eastern was to become Centralia's largest, and indeed one of the Northwest's, most significant mill operations. The name of its president, F. B. Hubbard, crops up in reference to dozens of investments and business dealings. He was an original founder of the local Elks Lodge, and his name is linked with the Centralia Armistice Day Tragedy of 1919; his nephew, Dale Hubbard, was one of the shooting victims. Sam Agnew, the second superintendent, came to signify generations of Lewis County businesses.

The first task of Eastern Railway & Lumber Company was to construct a

Eastern Railway & Lumber Co. mill yards on the east side of the railroad mainline in Centralia. Note the streak of a steam locomotive passing through the photograph.

railroad ten miles out of town into the dense timber with a branch line to the Kopiah coal mines. The company purchased the bankrupt H.H. Martin Lumber Company and operated it under the name of Western Crossarm and Manufacturing Company and later as the Western Lumber Company. At their peak the Eastern and Western mills, combined with logging camps, employed about 1,000 people.

The history of Eastern Railway & Lumber Company and the story of the colorful and penurious Sam Agnew are difficult to separate. Agnew came to Centralia near the turn of the century in the days of logging by ox-team and delivery of finished lumber by horse-drawn wagons. He started out with the company almost from its beginning, owning a little stock and gradually acquiring more. Working the business from the ground up, he was a yard foreman and woods superintendent. After F.B. Hubbard left the company, Sam became general manager with a controlling interest. In the 1920s the city of Centralia appealed to Sam Agnew to supply its power, and large generators from the mills kept the lights on for ten years until a hydroelectric plant on the Nisqually River came into usage.

In August of 1939, fire struck the Eastern mill in a huge conflagration that burned in the memories of all who saw it. Within a couple years Sam and his son Jay Agnew formed a new company known as S.A. Agnew Lumber Co. and started up operations in the Western Mill. With 225 employees, this was to be the last of Centralia's large mills. Agnew Lumber was set up in 1947 as a local outlet in retail and wholesale trade.

Sam Agnew died in 1965 at the age of 86, one of the Northwest's last lumber kings. The mill was dismantled in 1966, and the Agnew Lumber company closed in 1990, spanning the 20th century. Hundreds of bidders swarmed in as the veneer mill and equipment went on the auction block in 1991.

Another local firm, the Lincoln Creek Lumber Company, has been a family operated business since 1903 when father and son, William and Byrd Thompson, set up a mill in Galvin. With its own company houses and logging camps, the company logged virtually all over the Lincoln Creek drainage. Although the mill went bankrupt in the early 1930s, a small retail business survived in Galvin before moving in 1947 to its present location on Harrison Avenue in Centralia. The company bought out Palmer Lumber Company in Chehalis in 1939, which had been one of largest door manufacturers on the Pacific coast at the turn of the century. When World War II dawned, the company, now named West Coast Mills, had a contract with the U.S. Army for pre-fabricated barracks shipped wherever the war effort demanded. The business shifted to prefabricated houses in the 1950s as the nation demanded post-war housing. The family business has continued into the 21st century under the management of Bob Thompson.

Lincoln Creek Lumber Co. steam donkey in Galvin, 1925.

The Land Called Lewis

Sommerville Mill, Napavine, 1900.

Napavine and Winlock: Boom Towns

Meanwhile, Napavine, said to be the largest shipping point between Tacoma and Kalama in the boom years, grew into one of the largest lumber mill areas in the county. At the turn of the century there were eight mills with three more added almost overnight.

Hamilton Pitcher had built a sawmill in the 1890s near an especially valuable stand of timber through which the Military Road extended. The Pitcher mill was sold profitably in 1911 to a new firm, Emery and Nelson, incorporated specifically to take over Pitcher's lumber manufacturing business. Under Walter W. Emery's shrewd management and Herman H. Nelson's hands-on knowledge of logging, the firm prospered, and in 1913 the two partners replaced the old mill with a modern structure. Its porch column factory was hugely profitable, shipping out a carload per week.

Emery & Nelson was considered to be a family oriented firm with lifelong employees, including a contingency of Japanese laborers, and a commitment to the community. Many of the woods and mill employees owned small farms nearby. When World War I rolled around, about 140 men were employed at an annual payroll of $200,000.

Enduring a century of changes, Hemphill-O'Neill Lumber Company, Inc. of Chehalis was started in 1947 to sell the output of 150 local portable mills and handle lumber sales for the Holman Lumber Company in Napavine and Woodproducts Corporation in Chehalis. The Woodproducts Corporation had a rich, 60-year history of its own. It evolved from the companies of Coal Creek, Harm and Brown, Twin City Associated Shingle, Owen and Tufts, and Lloyd Owen and Sons.

The Holman mill had been started by Archie Flock and purchased in the late 1950s by Walter Holman, who added a

Browns Coal Creek Lumber Co. from 1905 until 1929 at the north end of Chehalis. It was bought by Winston Lumber and Timber, becoming Hemphill-O'Neill Lumber Co. through 1985, then Columbia Harbor Lumber Co.

milling plant in Tenino to finish the rough lumber from Napavine. Hemphill-O'Neill purchased the Holman mills and timber in 1962, the Woodproducts Corporation in 1966, and the Date mill and timberland from Henry Date in 1976. As a result of modernization in 1969 and 1977, Hemphill-O'Neill was the seventh largest privately owned producer in North America. Some 300 employees produced a phenomenal 100 million board feet of lumber per year in 1977. According to Bob O'Neill, the loss of raw material to the Asian market and fierce competition for logs on the domestic front caused the milling operations to close down in 1982.

Winlock's first mill was built by David Ainslie four miles south of town. He borrowed money for the mill, a railroad, hotel, and store, and established the Ainslie post office one mile south of Winlock in 1887. In the early 1890s the mill employed 100 workers. Just as Ainslie was preparing to develop a bank, the panic of 1892 struck and three of the company principals supposedly defrauded the company of a considerable sum of money. A Tacoma furniture manufacturer named F.E. Doernbecher who operated for a short time nearby, was lured to Chehalis instead, and Ainslie ceased to exist.

The history of Winlock's timber industry is tied to the Veness name. Winlock was a village of less than 150 persons when J.A. "Jack" Veness arrived in 1892, writes Dr. Wayne W. Galvin in *The Timber Baron of Winlock*. "It was a rough and ready mill town of wooden bunkhouses, lumbermen's and mill workers' shanties, and mill sheds....There were plank sidewalks and dirt or, more often, mud streets. The biggest structures were the Northern Pacific Railroad station and a large barn in the meadow just across the tracks where the mill oxen were run up at night and on weekends. Winlock had one redeeming factor, however; surrounding it on every side was an untouched virgin forest of trees that rose 100 to 200 feet to the first limb."

Jack Veness promptly bought into the largest existing mill, the Prescott & Furber mill, which had originally been an oxen operation started by Andrew Miller and Eugene Finch on land purchased from Jack

Veness Lumber Co. office, later Cattermole Funeral Home, in Winlock. Note the school in the background.

Nealy, the original settler. The mill became the Prescott, Veness and Company and later the J.A. Veness Lumber Company when Veness became the sole owner in 1892. Soon the company built two mills which were the largest in Lewis County with ponds and fourteen cottages. The company furnished the planks for Winlock's first puncheon road in 1895. In 1905 the Veness mill shipped out 1,000 railroad carloads of lumber.

In 1907 Veness sold one mill to M.T. O'Connell who expanded it further. The O'Connell mill burned in 1911 with flames that could be seen for miles, consuming the greater portion of Winlock's business district and the Northern Pacific depot. Jack and his son Fred continued in the mill business with Fred as key player in the holdings of the J.A. Veness Lumber Co., the Oregon-Kalama Lumber Co., the F.E. Veness and Capitol mills and a logging railroad company, the Winlock & Toledo Logging and Railroad Company constructed to open a line to a large stand of timber near Toledo. When Jack died unexpectedly in 1925, Galvin writes, family squabbles and lawsuits stripped Fred Veness of his businesses and his home. However, he preserved his dignity and loyalty to Winlock, working at a variety of businesses until his death in 1953.

Another mill owner, J.H. England constructed a large modern mill in 1915 which survived the Depression and operated until it also burned, on April 20, 1951. Despite his setbacks England, a colorful character, retired with more than $1 million, having entered Winlock in 1900 with 20 cents in his pocket.

Besides fire, another consistent problem for early mill owners was the lack of railroad cars for shipping their products to the East Coast. With no cars available, the term "backlog" took on its true meaning as mills stockpiled orders for shipment. J.A. Veness, who became a state legislator, opposed a bill fining the railroads for every day of delay, but he no doubt helped draw attention to the problem. (He also predicted in 1908 that the government would take over construction of highways in the U.S. and solve the ever-recurring problem of bad roads in Lewis County; he was right.) The lack of cars along with fluctuations in the lumber industry, Finley Hays notes, led directly to the formation of the West Coast Lumberman's Association as a united force in the industry.

Mills Galore in the Pe Ell Area

Today as one travels on Highway 6 from Chehalis to South Bend, the imagination has to stretch to picture a mill almost every two miles. Pe Ell was always a logging center. The *Pe Ell Examiner*, its first newspaper, touted it as "Nature's Paradise, Man's Opportunity." A booklet published by the Pe Ell Commercial Club in 1911 boasted of three large saw mills and three shingle mills. The town also had a broom handle factory using alder and maple. The Commercial Club claimed that two billion feet of timber lay contiguous to the town, and in view of its exceptional soil, that may not have been an exaggeration.

Many operations starting small grew into substantial businesses. The six Mueller brothers of Pe Ell, for example, came with their widowed mother to Willapa Bay in 1888 and met an old friend known as "Rock Creek" Meyer, so nicknamed because of his homestead site. Meyer advised the boys to join him as there were plenty more homesteads to be had in the area. The only drawback — they were all covered with large Douglas fir. The brothers made the trip over a rough trail, and three of them homesteaded and made real farms. The brothers built a sawmill immediately, using water power from the falls in Rock Creek a mile above Pe Ell. It was a crude, homemade affair, but later in 1892 just as the Northern Pacific was building through Pe Ell, they bought a turbine which they placed in the falls to create power. Oddly enough, their friend Meyer lost his homestead on Rock Creek when the land turned out to be railroad property. In 1902 the Muellers sold their operation to McCormick Lumber Company.

Between Pe Ell and the Pacific County line is the McCormick Road near the former site of the huge McCormick mill and

Mueller Brothers mill, Pe Ell, circa 1900, later bought by McCormick Lumber Company.

McCormick mill and residential area, 1905. Nothing remains of the town once located west of Pe Ell.

the town of the same name. Harry McCormick was the first postmaster in 1899; the post office closed 30 years later when mail was routed to Pe Ell.

A little farther down the road to the west was the mill site of Reynolds, which began business in January of 1888 and shut down in 1904. Its owner, J.W. Reynolds, later opened a mill in Napavine. And straddling the county line was the booming settlement of Walville where a post office operated from 1903 to 1936.

A 1901 newspaper article stated that: "The center of the cross arm industry in Washington is undoubtedly at McCormick, midway between the town of Chehalis and the town of South Bend, where the salt waters of the Pacific Ocean meet the rails. Here are the saw mills of McCormick, the Davie & Reynolds Lumber Co, and Mueller & Co. Telegraph and Telephone Cross Arms." The local fir was ideal for the cross arms of Western Union's telegraph poles; it was straight, light, solid, and durable.

The 1911 obituary for Harry McCormick tells the story of an enterprising and highly regarded lumberman. At one time a lineman for the Northern Pacific, he opened a small cross arm factory in Centralia. With F.B. Hubbard, who was then employed by Western Union Telegraph Company, and C.A. Doty, he organized the McCormick Lumber Company in 1897 at the railroad site known as Pluvius on the South Bend branch of the Northern Pacific.

In 1903 McCormick probably purchased what the *Centralia News* called "the last standing lot of first-class timber left in a bunch in the county." McCormick owned "4,200 acres of heavy timber...which has never yet had an ax into it." The article indicated that in 1903 it was becoming more of a struggle to get standing timber.

McCormick sold his Rock Creek sawmill to the firm of Walworth & Neville of Chicago, dealers in cross arms, that same year. As an indication of the large demand for cross arms, Walworth & Neville owned other factories for the product at Port Blakely, Washington; Minnesota; Michigan;

and Virginia. From the Walworth & Neville Company came the name "Walville" for the mill and settlement that rapidly grew to a population of a thousand people, including about 200 Japanese workers. At first, the residents of Walville had sent their children to school at nearby Reynolds. When it closed, Walville then ended up with the distinction of having two schools. Because schools were funded strictly within county boundaries, Walville had one in Lewis County and another in Pacific County. The county road to the logging community was approved in 1906.

The McCormick mill burns, July 5, 1909.

McCormick's mill burned to the ground in 1909, destroying the entire plant. At an estimated loss of $250,000-300,000, it was the third fire in five years and put 300 out of work.

Other towns laid claim to being as among the biggest and the best. Dryad, in western Lewis County about 17 miles west of Chehalis, hosted a large mill on the Northern Pacific line from Chehalis to Raymond. Originally named "Salal" for the profuse evergreen shrub, the railroad decided instead that it would be named "Dryad," meaning "nymph of the woods." As far back as 1885, Leudinghaus Brothers and Mitchell instigated a steam planing plant beside the Chehalis River in Dryad. A news item on Feb. 17, 1899, noted that the Leudinghaus Brothers reportedly sold their shingle mill at Pe Ell. Their properties at that time included two shingle mills at Lebam, another the east side of Lebam, and still another at Frances. In its prime, Dryad had four shingle mills and one large sawmill, and even a large concert hall. The Leudinghaus firm sold out to Shaffer Brothers of Montesano which once had over 100 employees logging up Bunker Creek and the Klaber-Wildwood area. The Dryad mill burned in 1931.

Doty, its neighbor, boasted of one of the largest mills in the county, the Doty and Stoddard mill —started in 1889 by C.A. Doty. By 1900 Doty had cut a large hole in the forest and built up a little village in a year and a half. By 1906 the mill was enlarged and its capacity increased. After thirty years the facility and the rest of the standing timber was also sold to Shaffer Brothers.

The fall of the many large mills occurred almost as quickly as their rise. Because so many of the mill owners had made substantial investments in timberland, there was no income to sustain the operations after the land was logged. Many owners simply could not pay taxes on their holdings during the Depression, and the bubble of the boom years quietly burst and faded into history.

Kosmos: The Logging Town that Drowned

One Lewis County lumbering operation now under the water of Riffe Lake was Kosmos, located southeast of Morton in Eastern Lewis County. Logging, as well as settlement, occurred much later in East County than in the rest of the area, although operations in Mineral at the turn of the century had supplied Tacoma mills with logs when the Tacoma and Eastern Railroad opened up access to the timber. The idea for the Kosmos Logging Company started when Jack Southerland was superintendent of various CCC camps in the Cowlitz and Cispus drainages in the years of 1934-36. In 1936 he formed the Kosmos Logging Company and built a road from Kosmos Corners to a railroad landing south of Morton. A source of great jest was Jack's "pea gravel" on the road from Morton to Kosmos, made up of rocks from twelve inches to three feet in diameter.

Kosmos Timber truck (Kenworth model 588) loaded with 30,000 board feet of timber.

At first Kosmos loggers worked one of two shifts per day, and loaded trucks which roared out of the woods from dawn to dusk. When the construction of a railroad started in August of 1937, trucking was discontinued. By the time a bridge was built crossing the Cowlitz River, 120 men

Kosmos Logging Company locomotives and crew, 1932.

Kosmos at the top, circa 1965. Champion Logging Company is at the bottom. The old highway runs left to right at the top. All of this area later was buried under the waters of Riffe Lake created by the Mossyrock Dam.

were employed. With a logging railroad of nine locomotives on 90 miles of grade, the operation extended to a point about half way between Kosmos and Randle on the north side of the Cowlitz. The maximum production for the outfit was 128 train carloads on any day. But that wasn't all; also located at Kosmos was a veneer plant and a salvage sawmill, producing 30 million board feet per year and employing over 400 people in manufacturing and logging operations. In 1953 the owner was United States Plywood Corporation from New York.

Kosmos residents were active in PTA and the Glenoma School, and the Kosmos Garden Club won a national award for its flowers in 1950. According to LaVonne Sparkman's book about Kosmos, *From Homestead to Lakebed*, the residents of the town were moved out and the site inundated with the water of Riffe Lake in 1969.

Unfortunately, not everything was cleared out. During low water large, underground storage tanks posing environmental hazards were discovered and cleaned up in 1992. Periodically when the level of the reservoir is low, curiosity-seekers can explore the ghostly remains of the town.

Meanwhile, nearby Morton had its claim to fame in the world of logging; it supposedly had the longest tie dock in the world during the days when railroad ties were in big demand.

—

Even more significant to modern technology is Morton's claim to being the birthplace of the well-known Peterbuilt truck. T.A. "Al" Petterman (note the extra "t" in his name) came to Morton during the depression to harvest logs from Cottler's Rock for mills in Tacoma, providing a greatly appreciated payroll for the Morton area. The innovative Petterman, notes Lavonne

Sparkman, would contribute a great deal more to the trucking world. He began buying Army surplus trucks and modifying them, particularly working on the brakes so they would hold better on the steep hillsides and devising a roller so that the loads would give a little on sharp corners. After a few years in Morton, Peterman bought a factory near Oakland, California, to produce the quality trucks known as Peterbuilt.

Logging and lumbering took on a new face at the end of 20th century. After World War II, loggers slowly abandoned their "misery whips," the crosscut saws, for gasoline-operated chain saws. Logging railroads were replaced by the grumbling roar of more economical, diesel-operated trucks. Helicopter logging allowed the harvest of trees from steep hillsides without ecological damage. As before, small "gypo" (independent) operations, as well as large companies, earned their livelihood in the woods, despite the recession of the 1980s and federal legislation intended to protect the endangered spotted owl.

The rich forests of Lewis County have indeed proven to be a renewable resource as third and fourth growth trees are being harvested. A new forest industry has been developed with numerous Christmas tree farms, while the Weyerhaeuser Company has perfected nursery stocks for replanting with stronger strains ideally suited for the local climate and soils. With the legal requirement that all forest lands must be replanted within two years of logging, one can see thousands of acres of new growth

Loggers stand in awe of new logging equipment, circa 1940.

rising to meet the needs of the next generation. The forests of Eastern Lewis County in the area of Mt. Rainier have become a recreation area for hundreds of thousands of people from around the world as trees are viewed as living entities and a vital link with our natural heritage.

Chapter 12

Mill Town: Onalaska

In 1909 a shiny new Oldsmobile, among the first cars seen in the area, pulled into a timber-laden homestead carrying the Carlisle family. The prosperous passengers were a father, son and the son's new bride. They were about to launch a new business enterprise that would create the town of Onalaska in Lewis County

A history compiled by Alberta (Berg) Hamilton for the Onalaska Parent-Teachers Organization Cook Book in 1975 entitled "Remembrances and Recipes" provides a homey, well-documented story of Onalaska's past. Along with compiled recipes and local lore, Mrs. Hamilton wrote that two post offices operated in the area for several years for early homesteaders. Rankin (1882-1885) was located about a mile southwest of the present Onalaska, and Webster (1900-1905) was three miles to the east in a farmhouse. For the most part people in the area journeyed by wagon from their farms to Alpha or the closest post office for their mail.

The senior William Carlisle and his son William A. Carlisle, 25, had first come in 1899 to look for timber and a possible mill site at the homestead of the Graves family. The two came from Carlisle, Washington, on the coast between Aloha and Copalis Crossing in Grays Harbor County where they operated a large mill. They purchased the Onalaska land in 1902, but construction did not begin until 1914.

Unlike the austere beginnings of many Lewis County newlyweds of the time, the young Carlisles had an impressive dowry. Local lore says they had a million dollars as a gift from the bride's father and a million dollar interest in the prospective new mill from the Carlisle side of the family. They even had laborers; they brought with them many of the workers from their Grays Harbor operation which had burned. From a small mill hauled by wagon from Littell, they cut lumber for some tiny houses.

W. A. Carlisle's home, Onalaska, built in 1915.

The elder Carlisle named the new place Onalaska, which was not original in the least; he had already named his mill sites Onalaska, Wisconsin; Onalaska, Arkansas; and Onalaska, Texas. Apparently it was a name that pleased him! Supposedly the first reference comes from a poem written by Thomas Campbell in 1851, *"...And waft across the waves' tumultous roar; The wolf's long howl from Oonalaska's shore."* The word is said to have come from the Aleut language, "Al-ay-ek-sa" meaning "great land."

The Carlisles distributed brochures in the East that said, "Come to a country of year-round warm climate, rich vegetation where cattle graze out all winter, and blackberries grow on every stump." (The irony of the latter statement will not be lost on any property owner who wages a perennial war on blackberries.) Local accounts say that by 1913 more than 1,000 workers had poured in, and the town was platted. Orderly streets were laid over the hub-deep wagon tracks through the timber. In 1914 a

The Carlisle-Pennell Lumber Company, left and Onalaska is on the right. Hwy. 508 crosses the bottom, 1930.

planer, dry kiln and big saw mill were erected. They were just off the trail leading into Onalaska in the area known as "Milt Graves Opening" because it was the only opening where one could see out through trees so thick "it was a veritable tunnel." Nearby was the 76-acre holding pond now known as Carlisle Lake.

The mill shipped its first lumber out on November 15, 1915, and it was fully operational in 1916. Onalaska's first post office was established February 3, 1915, in the company's store, according to *Postmarked Washington Lewis and Cowlitz Counties.* Its first postmaster was none other than the energetic and ever-present mill proprietor, the senior William Carlisle.

The mill, then named the Carlisle-Pennell Lumber Co., was considered to be the largest inland mill in the world.

Among its thousand employees were Greeks, Swedes, and Japanese, each group with its own cookhouse and bunkhouse. The Swedes stacked all the lumber off the green chain while George Ohatta had the contract to furnish men, usually Japanese, for the green chain. In a term acceptable for the times, the Japanese lived in the part of town known as "Jap Town." Three large annexes and a large cookhouse provided room and board for 250 other employees.

According to the blueprints adopted by a planning committee, Mr. Carlisle constructed 225 houses of four, five and six rooms of the finest lumber and "quite modern" construction. "But they all looked alike and were painted a dull gray," observed Mrs. Hamilton. They were next to the permanent residences of company officials which were a variety of shapes and colors. Most of these homes are still residences in Onalaska today, as is Mr. Carlisle's big home.

With the first school overflowing, the Onalaska Union High School was moved to the upstairs of the I.O.O.F. Lodge Hall, known as Swede Hall. Adding to the settlement was the new Community Presbyterian Church.

The original 225 houses were not enough to house everyone. "Those without a place to live picked up slabs cut from the logs at the mill, pieces of tin, and anything that would suffice to build with...and soon the area (south of Highway 508) was spotted with little slab shanties thrown up for emergency shelters. Hence, this lower part of town has always been known as Slab Town," explained Mrs. Hamilton.

The Carlisles developed the essential railroad connection to the four main lines at Napavine with the Newaukum Valley Railroad south of what is now the route of Highway 508, once known as the River Highway. The Cowlitz, Chehalis and Cascade Railroad (CC & C) was connected to haul logs to the Onalaska mill. At one time the CC & C offered a passenger service to Chehalis. No ordinary passenger train, this. It resembled a large truck with seats, pulled by a gas car, and was known as the "Galloping Goose."

By the time the big mill was in operation and producing 250,000

CC&C engine hauling lumber from Onalaska.

board feet a day, lumber was readily available for the construction of new businesses. A handsome boardwalk soon fronted a drug store, a large company store, an ice plant, a butcher shop, a tailor shop, dry cleaners, and a J.C. Penney store. A theater and new grade school were added. (A new elementary building was constructed in 1918 on land donated by the Carlisle family.) The Graham Land Co. was organized

The Galloping Goose on the CC&C rail line. A truck chassis with a passenger cab, it ran between Chehalis and Onalaska from 1912 to 1925.

to sell real estate, primarily logged-off "stump ranches" at $40 an acre. The little stump ranches turned into dairy farms, and milk was collected daily by the Carnation Milk Company in Chehalis or later the Borden Milk Company in Toledo.

The development and progress of Onalaska grew steadily until about 1928 and the start of the Depression. Even in the months following the onset of the Depression when mills everywhere had closed due to the decline in the world market, the Carlisle mill continued to run. When its wage was at its lowest point — minimum wages at the time were 28 cents an hour — and the lowest operating time was 30 hours a week, the company cut all the rents in town by half.

Nevertheless, trouble was brewing. By January of 1934, 355 of the 411 workers had joined the 4 L Union, the Loyal Legion of Loggers and Lumbermen. Wages were increased to 42.5 cents an hour, but many unskilled laborers did not benefit. In 1934 the American Federation of Labor came in to organize the Loggers and Sawmill Workers Union, soon followed by the Sawmill and Timber Workers Union.

On May 3, 1935, about ninety men stopped work, and a strike was on. The mill closed the next day. It reopened temporarily under "scab" labor a few months later, but basically the strike lasted three long years. When the mill shut down, the town had no lights. The company attempted to evict families from the mill houses, but Mrs. Carlisle put her foot down and refused to allow it. People on the stump ranches gaffed and canned salmon to supplement what they could raise on their farms. Food vouchers were issued and people went to the cookhouse for "Bean Tickets" as they called them. Many moved out to try to get work elsewhere. It was a miserable time.

The Carlisle mill reopened in 1938 and operated until 1942, but it never regained its strength. It had torn up tracks to the woods which had to be re-laid, and it had mortgaged its timber holdings which were taken over by the Weyerhaeuser Company. Basically, it had no lumber. The mill was sold for scrap and in the process of its being dismantled, a spark from a torch ignited a fire which burned the remains to the ground. In its ashes lay the death of a lumber mill.

When news was released that Onalaska's business was over, its occupants spread through Washington and Oregon to new homes. Their houses were sold but many were not left there; they were mounted on wheels or truck beds and move out one by one in a drawn out funeral march, wrote one observer.

The mill's tombstone is the tall smokestack at the edge of Onalaska, paying tribute to the past glories of a prosperous mill town.

The Carlisle smokestack remained as the marker of the mill, Onalaska.

Chapter 13

Tragedy in Centralia

Intense passion lies at the root of most significant historical events. People mark tragic moments in the framework of their lives at the time and by the ways the power of the event alters the course of history and thus, their own lives. The date of November 11, 1919, and Centralia in Lewis County, Washington, are linked by the events referred to as the "Centralia Tragedy" or the "Centralia Massacre."

While the events of that day are referred to by some as a massacre, the word isn't nearly broad enough to describe the long-lasting effects of murders of young veterans in the street, a lynching, possible false imprisonment, and conspiracy. Nor does it describe the complicated build-up of passion from the two sides that clashed in an Armistice parade on North Tower in Centralia that fall day. There is no single word to explain generations of bitterness and secrecy buried in the psyche of Lewis County.

Understanding the event that earned Centralia a footnote in most American history books requires a look at the international climate of the times. World War I intensified feelings of patriotism, fear of communism, and intolerance for dissent, explains Northwest history professor, Dr. James Vosper. On the other hand, years of tension between labor and large business owners were sparked by poor working conditions, resulting in strikes and violence in the Northwest and the nation. "The success of the Communist Bolshevik Revolution in Russia (in 1917) and the extreme rhetoric of the era were all ingredients in what historians term 'the Red Scare.' The Centralia incident is to be understood in that context," Vosper explains.

Centralia 4th of July parade on North Tower, 1920. North Tower was the site of the Centralia Tragedy eight months before this photograph was taken.

The Industrial Workers of the World (I.W.W.), also known as the Wobblies, was founded by socialist and labor leaders in 1905 to demand better conditions and wages for workers. Directed by Big Bill Haywood who took over the leadership in 1908, the Marxist-based group turned to a revolutionary doctrine and guerrilla tactics to change the system. Throughout the Pacific Northwest, the I.W.W. recruited in logging camps, lumber mills, and mines, stirring unrest.

An I.W.W.-related dispute in Northern Washington in 1916 known as the "Everett Massacre" left seven dead. While few workers were actually card-carrying members in the radical movement, many probably had a gut level sympathy for its defiant style and maybe even agreed with some of the issues. In retrospect, Vosper observes, the Wobblies brought about a significant change in workers' rights, but their language and tactics inflamed many business people and alienated the larger community at the time.

The first spark of trouble began in May of 1918 when a local mob vandalized an I.W.W. hall in Centralia during a patriotic parade. Wobblies were beaten and run out of town. In June a partially blind news vendor was assaulted and dumped by a roadside in a neighboring county for selling pro-labor newspapers. When the Wobblies re-established a hall on North Tower Avenue in 1919, passions heated to a boil. Members of the community vowed to destroy the site; I.W.W. members were determined to defend it.

When rumors circulated of a raid set for the first Armistice Day (now Veterans Day) — Nov. 11, 1919 — local Wobblies took the advice of attorney Elmer Smith that they had a right to defend their property. "They even posted snipers on Seminary Hill and at least one in a hotel across and down the street from the hall," according to Vosper.

The tragic day started with a patriotic parade on that Armistice Day in honor of veterans of World War I. The parade was designed so that the Centralia unit of the American Legion passed the I.W.W. hall twice.

Armistice Day parade in Centralia, 1919, just before it ended in tragedy.

Who fired the first shot? No one knows for sure. When the unit halted in front of the hall, either some Legionnaires broke ranks toward the hall or as others claimed, I.W.W. gunmen opened fire first. Within moments three young Centralia war veterans lay dead or dying and others were wounded in the bloodied street. Warren Grimm, Arthur McElfresh and Ben Casagranda had survived the Great War only to be cut down on the streets of their hometown. Furious Legionnaires forced

Angry residents tore lumber from the front and interior of the I.W.W. Hall on North Tower after the Centralia Tragedy on Nov. 11, 1919. Photograph courtesy of The Walter P. Reuther Library, Wayne State University.

their way into the hall. Several Wobblies quickly surrendered. One armed Wobbly ran to the bank of the Skookumchuck River with the Legionnaires in hot pursuit. The gunman fired and mortally wounded a fourth veteran, Dale Hubbard. The shooter was captured and taken to the city jail where the other Wobblies were already incarcerated.

The gunman was Wesley Everest—a veteran of the war himself.

The violence of the day was far from over. At about 7 p.m. the power went out in Centralia. Several unlit automobiles crept through the darkness to the jail. A group of men burst in and dragged Wesley Everest out. He was beaten, allegedly maimed, and driven to the Mellen Street bridge over the Chehalis River where he was hanged and his body riddled by bullets. Until its replacement, the bridge was known for decades as "hangman's bridge."

Mellen Street Bridge, 1919, the site of hanging of Wesley Everest. Orland Steele pulls Vernon, Lloyd and Glenn Treat on a sled on the frozen Chehalis River.

Armed soldiers force I.W.W. members to bury Wesley Everest who was lynched in the Centralia Tragedy of 1919. His grave is in the Sticklin-Greenwood Memorial Park, Centralia.

The National Guard arrived in Centralia shortly thereafter to restore order. The American Legion nevertheless acted as an extra-legal posse for several days—and the tragedy surged on with disastrous aftershocks. A posse member was shot dead in pursuit of an I.W.W. member, making the death toll six. Rumors have never been proven that a second Wobbly gunman was killed by mob action. Wobblies claimed that two of their members were never seen again after Nov. 11, 1919.

Eleven I.W.W. members or associates were put on trial in 1920 at the Grays Harbor County Courthouse in Montesano, an event presided over by Thurston County Judge John M. Wilson. An army unit camped on the grounds; some people speculated that the presence of the armed soldiers intimidated the jury into its verdicts. Guilty of second degree murder: O.C. Bland, Britt Smith, James McInerney, Ray Becker, Bert Bland, Eugene Barnett, and John Lamb. The jury found Loren Roberts guilty but insane. Acquitted were attorney Elmer Smith and Mike Shee-

I.W.W. members on trial: (top row) Loren Roberts, James McInerney, Britt Smith, O. C. Bland, Bert Faulkner and Ray Becker (bottom row) Mike Sheehan, John Lamb, Eugene Barnett, Bert Bland and Elmer Smith. Photograph courtesy of The Walter P. Reuther Library, Wayne State University.

han, and charges against Bert Faulkner had already been dropped. Judge Wilson imposed sentences of 25 to 40 years on the convicted. Those who had lynched Wesley Everest were never brought to trial.

Neither side was ever satisfied with the outcome.

Of the eight men sent to prison: McInerney died in 1930; six were released in the early 1930s. The last, Ray Becker, left prison in 1939. The American Legion also raised funds to create a statue, "The Sentinel," as a tribute to their four fallen comrades. It still stands in George Washington Park in downtown Centralia. For a few years it attracted distinguished visitors such as President Warren Harding, Vice President Charles Dawes, and Gen. Ferdinand Foch.

However, changing times and the reactions of labor groups and others placed accountability on the community and the local Legion post for the tragic events of that day. Even former jurors supported a move to release the jailed men. Distinguished visits to the statue became rare.

History's ironies present themselves in strange ways. To break the shroud of secrecy and blame, labor groups joined together in 1997 to create a mural in commemoration of the tragedy. It is on the Antique Mall Building across the street from Washington Park. Even that particular effort to present a civic tribute, however, resulted in vitriolic arguments and name-calling among labor groups. In November when the nation observes Veterans Day and Centralia mourns its own tragic day in history, the Sentinel that honors the slain veterans can be seen through the leafless trees standing guard near the stark mural commemorating the labor movement and the demise of Wesley Everest.

"A lesson for today would seem to be that a bitter harvest comes when sown in angry passion and cultivated by harsh rhetoric and intolerance," observes Dr. Vosper. "May we pause and reflect."

The unveiling of The Sentinel in Washington Park, Centralia on November 11, 1924.

Chapter 14

Lodes of Ore

Today's passersby would not look at the Centralia-Chehalis area and think of mining towns, but in the early 1900s entire communities thrived on coal—local, easily accessible seams of the black fuel. The coal beds cover nearly 9,000 acres and drew two different eras of mining.

At the peak of the first one, from 1906 to 1920, thirty-four mines, some surface and some underground, operated in the Twin Cities area.

Many of those mines were just northwest of Centralia in and near the Hanaford Valley, where the long-forgotten towns of Kopiah, Mendota and Tono thrived and then died when the coal boom was over.

But by the early 1970s, the dairy pastures of the Hanaford Valley once again gave way to coal mining. Instead of handheld shovels, dynamite and coal carts, the valley yielded more of its seemingly unlimited supply of coal to machines so gargantuan that their parts had to be shipped in by rail or truck and assembled on site.

The modern mining era, which lasted for almost four decades, was necessary to feed the power-producing Centralia Steam-Electric Plant, an operation that has dominated the valley.

While huge strip-mining machines did the job until late 2006, the biggest machines of the original coal-mining days were the railroad's steam engines, which served to transport the coal to local residents. They also created a demand for coal when the locomotives switched from wood to coal as their source of power.

Getting the coal to the customers was at first problematic. N.B. Kelsey was hunting bears on his homestead in 1878 when he discovered coal, but it wasn't until six years later that he stumbled across veins two and a half miles from Centralia, close enough to be transported to town. He graded and corduroyed a wagon road to his "By-Jo" mine at a cost to the city of $2,000.

The entire town of Centralia celebrated the first arrival of Kelsey's coal in 1888. The two wagon loads rumbled in to the jubilant tunes of a brass band and the whole citizenry of about 2,000 people waving flags and cheering. One excited businessman offered to pay a whopping $20 for the honor of purchasing the first ton, but the parties settled on the more reasonable amount of $4.50 a ton instead.

Kelsey later sold the 400 acres where the vein was located, and in 1890 the Tacoma, Olympia & Chehalis Valley Railroad (TO & CV) extended a line to what was to become the Florence Mine. Soon people in Centralia and Chehalis were burning the product, and orders flowed in from Seattle, Tacoma, Castle Rock, and the Grays Harbor area. The first commercial coal producing

The Monarch mine in Kopiah, 1918. Nothing remains of this mining town which was located nine miles east of Centralia.

An elevated coal bunker in north Centralia supplied locomotive coal cars through gravity feed. The tower supplied water to make steam.

and shipping mine opened, and serious mining began in 1906 at Kopiah, nine miles east of Centralia on an extension of the TO & CV line. Its owner, L.C. Wilson, became known as the father of the coal industry when the Wilson Coal Co. and the town of Kopiah became synonymous. During its first year, the Wilson mine shipped out 50,000 tons which was more than any other mine in the state had produced up until then. Because it contained a better grade of coal than other local mines, the Wilson mine found a ready market for its product.

The *Daily Chronicle* reported in 1909, "It is less than three years since the opening of the Wilson mine, yet Kopiah boasts of a school, stores, daily mail, hotel and electric lights, religious services, and comfortable homes for workmen with the best paid labor of any company in the country." Its success was short-lived; a slump in the economy in 1907 cut the demand for coal, and the mine closed in 1914 due to competition from other coal fields in the state.

L.C. Wilson had overcome the misconception that the coal here was not "commercial," and by doing so encouraged other mining development. Near Kopiah despite the hard times, another mine, the Monarch, opened in 1907 on 9,000 acres leased from the Eastern Railway and Lumber Company, and the town of Mendota sprouted. Illustrating the later dependency of railroads on the coal industry, Mendota backers spent $175,000 just to build a standard gauge railroad from Centralia. The Mendota Coal and Coke Company spent an additional $200,000 for the development of the Monarch mine itself. It hired between 150 and 200 employees at a monthly payroll of $14,000 and an annual wage of about $800 per worker.

In 1914 Mendota consisted of sixty dwellings with running water piped into many of them, a hotel large enough for a hundred guests in its dining room alone, and the usual general store, post office, and school. Its streets were laid out, sidewalks built, and four-inch fire hydrants were placed in front of each home. The Mendota mine lasted until the mid-1920s when an underground fire forced its closure.

Mendota coal mine, rail yard and hotel, 1914.

Tono miners, circa 1907. Miners' lamps burned lard oil, a combination of lard and kerosene. After 1912 carbide lamps were used.

The mine at Tono across the county line in Thurston County, on the other hand, operated for nearly seventy years. Its post office opened in 1907 when the Hurn post office, two miles away in Lewis County, was moved. The name of "Tono" may have been a shortening of "ton of coal" written on receipts. Union Pacific Railroad owned the Black Prince Mine in Tono, using its coal for locomotives as far away as Eastern Oregon. It ceased operations by that name in 1949 when the Martin Brothers bought it, renamed it the Stoker Coal Company, and continued to mine it until the 1970s. The Tono post office functioned until 1932 when the mail was routed to Centralia.

Other mines poured out coal at a remarkable rate too. Smaller mines in Salzer Valley and many shafts from Coal Creek supplied coal directly to local customers. A coal-fired power plant on Coal Creek created power for street cars in the Twin Cities and standby power for Centralia. The Chehalis Coal Company located a mile and a half northeast of Chehalis hauled out 100 tons a day in 1915. Millions of tons of coal lay under its holdings in eleven known distinct veins varying in thickness from four to fourteen feet.

The product was marketed from Portland to Tacoma and shipped out on the four major railroads. The Superior Coal Mining Company on Coal Creek had an extensive operation for coal delivery on National Avenue in Chehalis with the main street running underneath a trestle.

The Superior Coal Company at the approximate site of the later Chamber Way railway overpass in Chehalis, circa 1920. The street passes under the coal trestle. The Liederkrandtz Hall is in the upper right corner. (See next page.)

Lodes of Ore

Liederkrandtz Hall, social center of Chehalis, circa 1920.

Superior Coal Company, Chehalis. Gangway, 2nd level.

Superior Coal Company mine shaft, Chehalis. The photograph is straight, the mine shaft is tilted.

A familiar landmark was the Liederkrantz Hall in north Chehalis which was a community center for coal mine families and others of German and Swiss descent.

The Crescent Coal Company operated between Littell and Claquato from about 1897 to 1912 with a rather spotted history. It was owned by at least four different companies, and a couple of its many investors landed in jail for selling property they did not own.

The Foron at Fords Prairie Mine operated from 1911 to 1934 when a fire in the processing plant closed it for two years. It was later known as the Monarch Mine, although the first mine by that name was at Mendota. Two other coal mines operated until 1976, the Black Prince Mine, eight miles northeast of Centralia, and the Martins' mine at Tono.

During the time when "Coal was King" in northern Lewis and southern Thurston counties, timber and railroading were prominent as well. The railroad link enabled people from one community to visit another for entertainment and merrymaking. In 1967 long-time miner Bert E. Jones recalled in a *Daily Chronicle* interview that Tono was a town "unaffected by prohibition." Residents enjoyed basket socials and dances featuring the schottische, fox trot, and square dance. "Most interesting to me," he said, "was the blend of nationalities (of the miners themselves) and how well everyone worked together. They were loyal to the industry..." Jones also recalled the stubborn but clever mules that hauled the black yield out of the pits.

The Imperial Powder Company at Coal Creek east of Chehalis, manufactured explosive powder for blasting in coal mines all over Washington State. It employed girls at low wages in the packing house to wrap powder for shipment to local mines.

On Nov. 1, 1911 a fire broke out in the packing house. Two girls escaped through the doors but seven girls went to save their coats and were overcome by fumes before they could escape.

The burning powder could not be extinguished and consumed six buildings before dying out. The bodies of the young girls were burned beyond recognition. They were Bertha Hagle, age 17; Bertha Crown, age 16; Tilly Rosbach, age 18; Sadie Westfall, age 16; Vera Mulford, age 14; Eva Gilmore, age 17, and Ethel Tharp, age 20.

The Imperial Powder Company paid $50 for each death. The money paid for caskets and a cement border around their common grave plot in the Pioneer Greenwood Cemetery on Jackson Highway in south Chehalis.

Virtually nothing remains of the towns of Kopiah, Mendota, or Tono. In fact, the entire landscape has been radically altered by strip mining, removing all traces of the former once-thriving towns.

Other Lodes

"Gold fever" struck full force in Mayfield in Lewis County around 1909. Although early showings of gold had turned up on Coal Creek, in an area south of Chehalis, and on Thrash Creek, eleven miles south of Pe Ell, it took the arrest of a Mossyrock man for insanity before anyone paid attention to the claim of gold around Mayfield. Daniel Shaner of Mossyrock was hauled off to Chehalis to be tried for insanity when he first announced a discovery of gold near Mayfield in 1885. He defended himself and was released. Despite being a distinguished Civil War veteran who had served as President Lincoln's bodyguard and helped to carry the assassinated President from Ford's Theater, Shaner was not believed for fourteen years.

A copy of The Daily Nugget photo shows the girls who died in the Imperial Powder Company fire, 1911.

Interior of Lang's gold mine in the Spirit Lake area of Mt. St. Helens, 1912.

New Consolidated Mercury Mining Company plant at Morton, 1930.

Then the little town of Mayfield, according to the *Centralia News Examiner* in 1909, was suddenly "destined to become one of the most important gold mining camps in the United States." The *Daily Chronicle* predicted that "there would be the greatest stampede of gold seekers imaginable," and "Eastern Lewis County will become the greatest mining camp of the Northwest." Three tunnels were driven in cliffs of the Cowlitz River canyon to a depth of 125 feet with an impressive showing of gold, and local residents abandoned their crops to scour the hills and creeks. While publicity about the anticipated gold rush was prolific, little note was made of its failure. Whether the gold or its promoters "petered out" is not known.

In Eastern Lewis County, mining was yet another story. The town of Mineral got its name for obvious reasons: coal, arsenic, and cinnabar. Even if some of the minerals didn't exist, they were still sought by hopeful prospectors who clustered in the hills in numerous cabins and tents in the 1890s.

Two early settlements called Mineral City and Contact City cropped up from a reputed silver strike in 1892. It seems that a minister turned prospector dug up what he thought was a vein of silver, and although it was actually a deposit of arsenic, he sold stock religiously to those who rushed there seeking silver instead of salvation. When the strikes failed to pan out, so did the "cities"; the last remains of the settlements were washed away in a flood in 1902. The arsenic discovered by the good reverend was mined successfully until the 1920s when it was produced cheaper as a by-product of metal smelting.

Meanwhile, Mineral, with a bustling population of 1,600, had three coal mines. The mine at the nearby community of Ladd had several gondolas toting out forty tons of coal each day, to be shipped to Tacoma and Seattle for powering ocean-going ships.

When the Tacoma Eastern Railroad right-of-way was being constructed into Morton in 1910, a vein of cinnabar was discovered. Within a few years, Morton was considered to be the mercury capital of the United States, producing more than any other deposit in the world. Along the same vein, the neighboring town of Cinebar got its name from the metal found in the surrounding hills. The only problem was that a bad speller among postal officials in Washington, D.C., changed the spelling when the post office was chartered, and the community's name remains a misspelling for cinnabar, the red ore of mercury.

An estimated nine million tons of coal had been mined from the Lewis County area before 1971. Between 1905 and 1920 as much as 300,000 tons a year were mined for use by the railroads and for heating. By the 1930s as oil became more prominent and coal fields in other states were more competitive, the production in Lewis County declined. During World War II the production increased to 150,000 tons a year but steadily dropped as railroads changed to other sources of fuel. The picture changed in the late 1950s when exploration began for coal as an energy source for steam-produced electricity.

An announcement in January of 1967 broke the news: a major steam plant and coal mine would open in the Hanaford Valley. The coal beds covering nearly 9,000 acres and dating back 60 million years were to be developed into a significant power source. And so, for the second time in the civilized history of Lewis County, a major coal-mining era was launched.

The Washington Irrigation and Development Co. (WIDCO), a subsidiary of Washington Water Power Company, opened its operation in 1971 at the Centralia Coal Mine to provide coal for the Centralia Steam-Electric Plant nearby. Mining that was once a mere hen-scratching had turned into big business: monster trucks of 150 tons with 17-foot tall tires began to growl into a pit some 300 feet deep. Several monolithic dragline shovels with booms the length of a football field could scoop out enough coal-laden earth to fill two bedrooms in a single bucket. The previous production figure of 300,000 tons of coal per year became 300,000 tons per month. In 1990 PacifiCorp became sole owner of the mine, making the Centralia

The WIDCO dragline bucket, 1977.

The huge scale of surface coal mining for electricity generation is shown by the size of a mine truck next to a school bus seen from an upper story of the TransAlta electric generating plant, Centralia, 2002.

Mining Company its subsidiary, and owner of 47 percent of the Centralia Steam-Electric Plant. In 1994 the 100 millionth ton of coal was hauled out of what had become one of the top twenty coal mines in the nation.

Environmental concerns that never crossed the minds of the first miners have topped the list of priorities for mining companies. The cost to produce electricity is lowest in the nation among thermal-based utilities, a fact that is in itself an environmental plus.

As early as 1974, WIDCO received its first Environmental Excellence award presented to mine workers for a land reclamation project replacing topsoil and contouring land that had been opened to a depth of 300 feet. PacifiCorps received the U.S. Department of Interior award for excellence in surface mining reclamation in 1994 and the 1995 Environmental Restoration Award from the Association of Washington Businesses for a wildlife habitat management program near the Skookumchuck dam and land reclamation. The landscape that was once a yawning pit has been transformed into rolling fields of grass and Douglas fir seedlings. The mine has developed deep lakes, marshes, and seasonal wetlands to provide waterfowl nesting sites and recreational opportunities.

In 2000 a Canadian Corporation, TransAlta, purchased both the Centralia electric generation plant and the adjacent coal mine. By 2006, the cost of mining the lower grade Centralia coal became prohibitive, and the TransAlta mine was closed in favor of bringing in better quality coal by rail from other U.S. mines for processing at the steam-electric plant.

Will there be a third coal boom in the Hanaford Valley's future? Changing times and technology could make it happen.

Chapter 15

Crops and Hops

The crops of Lewis County have come in a variety of stripes, and looking back, some of the stories related to agriculture are quite curious if not outright entertaining. One of the more amusing illustrations of local creativity occurred around Thanksgiving time, probably in the late 1890s, when some folks from Randle decided to herd a flock of turkeys all the way to Tacoma. The idea was to avoid butchering the birds so they could be sold live. Turkeys are not known to be the world's brightest beasts, but they had enough sense to flock to the trees to avoid the fate of becoming Thanksgiving dinner, arguably exhibiting more intelligence than their human caretakers. After weeks of frustration en route, the turkey herders finally gave up when they reached Spanaway and butchered their crop on the spot. At least they weren't alone in their endeavor; an unnamed Mossyrock settler once herded his flock to Chehalis. However, there is no record that anyone ever tried turkey herding more than once.

Most of the first settlers in early Lewis County were farmers. They had to be. Farming was simply the best insurance against starving. The first farm that proved to the world that the Northwest was viable farm land was the prosperous British-owned Cowlitz Farm near Toledo, developed by the Hudson's Bay Company and its offshoot company, the Puget Sound Agricultural Company. American settlers arrived thereafter with a few cows and promptly put in gardens, orchards, and fields of grain. From all over the county, they herded pigs, sheep, cattle — and turkeys — to markets in Centralia, Chehalis, Morton, and Tacoma in drives that took weeks at a time.

With the dawning of the steamboat trade on the Cowlitz River, the farmers had access to a market for what they produced. They raised great quantities of hay and grain on the productive prairies and shipped it to Portland via river boats. In August of 1884 the crop on the Cowlitz prairie alone was estimated as 50,000 bushels of wheat and in 1885 the yield was 125,000 bushels. Wheat, oats, and barley were primary crops in those days; however, wheat produced here was soft and not competitive with the quality of harder grains grown in drier climates.

Loading produce on river boats near Toledo, circa 1885.

Once the prairies were taken by donation land claims, other settlers were forced to choose forest land. It was a second choice; farming was a priority, and clearing out the huge trees was an awesome task. To get rid of the stumps, sometimes eight to ten feet in diameter, the farmers packed the roots with pitch and burned them for days. Later they used dynamite. Once cleared, the land was constantly subject to takeover by vine maple and brush. After the era of logging had taken the old-growth timber

The John Krebs stump ranch on Pleasant Hill, south of Adna, showing shocks of hay.

from the land, a new crop of farmers came to buy it for a low price, and the "stump ranches" of the 1920s and '30s became commonplace. In spite of the challenge of clearing the forests and although cash was not always plentiful, agriculture was an economic mainstay of Lewis County. The variety of its crops throughout the years tells the story of generations of families whose lives have been dependent on the land.

Berries and Fruit

Long before white men even knew there was such a place as the Northwest, Indians were picking huckleberries in Eastern Lewis County. Their trail to the berry patches was so well-used that it was packed down 18 inches deep in places. John Kehoe, a *Chehalis Bee Nugget* correspondent, wrote in 1890 of berry-picking north of present-day Randle: "the ripe fruit hung in clusters along the trail in great profusion… The bushes stretched off for miles on either side of the trail." He was joined in the evening by a crowd of Cowlitz Indians. "They came in a long procession, carrying guns, babies, and baskets. As they approached I recognized them to be my friends and neighbors…The scene was a very animated one; the merry laugh of maids and beaux make glad the desolate mountains… The new arrivals spent the first two days strolling over the mountains, looking for the choicest berry patches and hunting grouse, which are very plentiful here." This was likely the area named Huckleberry Mountain for the extensive Indian summer encampments based around berry-picking.

Strawberries were produced on a commercial basis in Lewis County and vicinity for decades, and moreover, the succulent fruit was a cause for social gatherings. Clearly, this was a natural environment for berries; when the Sidney S. Ford family arrived to settle at Ford's Prairie, they chose land covered with wild strawberries. In 1884 the *Lewis County Bee* described a strawberry expedition to the well-kept farm

Strawberry fields, July 3, 1909. The ladies' hats were intended to keep their skin from tanning.

A truck advertises Washington Fruit Growers Association, "Largest Shippers of Small Fruit in S. W. Wash."

of Lewis H. Davis at Claquato, west of Chehalis. The party, the account relates, "were driven, jolted, and jammed along in dead-axle wagon driven by Johnnie West, whose sympathies were not in the least extended to those who squatted on empty greasy coal-oil boxes." Despite their bruises, the group vowed not to return until the last berry was picked. The writer concludes: "Besides having two baskets and a coal-oil can full...handkerchiefs and aprons were filled with the precious fruit. All that was necessary on reaching home was to put them in bottles, cork and label ready for the shelf. For if we ever saw jam or jell before it was made out of those very berries — jam the jam things to jell anyhow!"

In southern Thurston County the Grand Mound, Rochester, and Littlerock area later was to be known as "Berry Prairie" for having hundreds of acres of strawberries. Berries picked by local residents were taken to a 400- by 90-foot building along a Northern Pacific railroad siding where machines and conveyors fed them into 50-gallon containers for shipment by train. The berry-packing plant was later operated by Emory Coleman until 1950 when the prairie failed to yield good crops. A local barreling plant of the Washington Packers, Inc. was located in Winlock as well.

In the 1920s, '30s, and '40s strawberries were grown on Logan Hill south of Chehalis and in the Middle Fork area of the Newaukum River. The first job for many young people was berry-picking, and entire families camped near the fields for the harvest. Undaunted by long hours of back-wrenching work, many people remember these festive times as one of the happiest periods in their lives, explained long-time resident Margaret McIntire. To celebrate the harvest, strawberry festivals featured large gatherings, box suppers, square dancing, and all the strawberries one could eat.

"The World's Largest Strawberry Shortcake" with Queen Agnes Young at the Annual Farmer's & Merchant's Picnic, Chehalis, July 20, 1928.

The building that became National Fruit Canning Company on State Street in Chehalis, circa 1925.

Lack of crop rotation, better job opportunities for berry-pickers and laws prohibiting child workers brought about the end of the strawberry industry, although the Rochester area was known for many years for its berries.

Opportunities in berry production led to the formation of one of the primary industries of Chehalis. Two young entrepreneurs, William McCaffray, Sr., and Mark Ewald, formed the National Fruit Canning Co. (NFC) in Olympia in 1912. The firm shipped products nation-wide from its base in Seattle, and after World War I, began freezing strawberries in 50-gallon wooden barrels, each with 300 pounds of berries and 150 pounds of sugar, to sell to ice cream and jam manufacturers. In 1928 NFC bought a vegetable-canning and berry-freezing operation in Chehalis, and that same year became one of the first companies in the world to freeze one-pound cups of strawberries for retail trade. When the technique of quick freezing was developed, NFC put in its first fast-freezing tunnel in Chehalis in 1936 and a freezing-tunnel belt in 1958. During the 1950s and '60s NFC processed tons of peas for the national market and operations have continued into the 21st century.

Mossyrock

If one were to choose a town in the area most representative of agriculture, Mossyrock would be the "meat and potatoes" of all the early communities. Mossyrock at "the Heart of Lewis County" was neither a railroad stop nor a mill town; its rich soil of sand, silt, and clay makes it a vital farming community. Early settlers raised cattle, hogs, turkeys, hops, and grain which they took to the railroad at Napavine for shipping or to stock markets in Chehalis. They and their neighbors in Eastern Lewis County dug Oregon grape roots and other plants for medicines. Some folks raised white ducks for down for pillows and quilts; they sold sacks of potatoes and carrots.

The profuse growth of wild blackberries, seen as a pest by many, was a source of capital for G. Ghosn who built a cannery

The Ghosn store and post office in Mossyrock. Sign on left wall of building reads, "Ringling Bros. World's Greatest Show."

at Mayfield around 1916. (Ghosn was from Lebanon and named the community of Ajlune for a Lebanese myth about six kneeling camels.) Soon the locals joined in his endeavor by picking berries for extra income.

Other innovative families figured out other ways to make the most of their farm products. The Huntting family of Silver Creek, for example, devised a fruit dryer for prunes, apples, and pears. When several teenagers of the family reached high school age, they rented an apartment in Winlock to attend the nearest high school. Dried fruit from their father's dryer was bartered in exchange for their supplies. In the 1930s and '40s strawberries and raspberries became an important cash crop, and several filbert orchards produced nuts for shipping. The Neal Aldrich family started the blueberry industry in the '40s.

Flower Bulbs

Tracing their family roots (and bulbs) back to Holland, the DeGoede family chose Mossyrock's fertile soil to start a bulb farm in 1978. During the depressed economic times in the Netherlands after World War II, Henry DeGoede moved to the Mount Vernon area. After 27 years of operating a 20-acre bulb farm in the Skagit Valley, Henry, his wife Hildegarde and their six children chose 300 acres in "the Heart of Lewis County" to start a new operation. The DeGoedes' nursery produces daffodils, iris, and some fifty varieties of tulips of such a high quality that some are exported to the Netherlands. In the spring, the operation is a veritable feast for the eyes as vivid colors flow throughout the valley. The event has inspired the Mossyrock spring tulip festival, Showers of Flowers.

DeGoede bulb farm, April, 1983.

Crops and Hops

Tobacco

Toledo residents had an unusual commercial establishment in the early days. The Duncan Brothers established a cigar factory in 1888 using imported and eastern tobaccos. The brothers had been experimenting with locally grown tobacco, supposedly of a fine quality. A steadily increasing market led the firm to erect a new cigar factory in 1891, though its length of operation is unknown.

Plums and Prunes

The Centralia and Chehalis area was the site of yet another successful crop at the turn of the 20th century: prunes. Some 200 acres of trees were located between Chehalis and Fords Prairie by 1900. Some growers went so far as to have artists' sketches and postcards made of their orchards. This industry failed because drying facilities were not available for the tons of fruit produced. For a time filbert orchards spread throughout the county, as well.

Chickens and Eggs

Agriculture around Winlock in the early days was generally the stump ranch variety because of the logged-off nature of the country. Then came the discovery that the uplands were usable for farming, and what promoters said was unexcelled for orchard and fruit-raising. Some record-breaking crops sprouted up: turnips weighing 12 and 17 pounds and rutabagas weighing 22 pounds. Instead of crops, however, Winlock discovered its own identity with eggs.

The egg industry in Winlock had an inauspicious beginning before the turn of the 20th century when William Warne brought in a flock of about 100 hens and sold eggs to railroad workers. The business died when he did, but the idea of the poultry business was well-hatched by 1910 when John Marcotte came to town as a railroad agent. He had a new bride, a meager income, and a lot of ambition.

M. W. Brun pointing to the oxen plowing on his farm at Newaukum Hill, 1911.

Samson-S-25 Sieve-Grip Tractor signals the end of oxen plowing, circa 1915.

Observing that the ranchers in the area had a few hens but no market for eggs, he journeyed to Grays Harbor and set up an agreement with one of the large logging companies for the sale of eggs, hogs, and veal. Upon his return to Winlock, he announced to the farmers that he'd take all they could produce and pay cash on delivery. They responded by producing more. At first Marcotte did all his own candling, grading and packaging of the eggs at night until he formed the Cowlitz Produce Co. and put a full time person in charge.

A typical poultry barn in the Winlock area, 1940s.

By 1919 when Marcotte shipped the first carload of eggs to New York, his business was bringing in a whopping $80,000 a month. The next year poultry men formed an organization which linked up with Washington Co-op Poultry and Egg Association. Always looking for ways to increase his nest egg, Marcotte established a branch in Olympia in 1922, shipping the eggs to Winlock for processing and distribution. The year of 1922 was the year of the golden egg: a total of 141 carloads were shipped out of Winlock with a value of $700,000!

1929 Egg Day Queen Sylvia Annonen and court. Photo from the Darrah estate, courtesy of Bob/Connie Prevallet.

About that same time Jake Irving started a chick hatchery which burned and was rebuilt with a 40,000-egg incubator. Its capacity increased to 194,000 in 1926, and soon other hatcheries were built by Finnish settlers. In 1937, a man appropriately named Gordon Egbert started the fryer business with a modern quick freeze and storage plant.

The egg and poultry industry has since evolved to fewer and larger producers, and the amount of production has declined from the old days when the Winlock egg was king. The community still celebrates its annual Egg Day in the spring, originated in 1921 with the opening of the Pacific Highway from Olympia to Salem, Oregon. The town's icon, billed as the World's Largest Egg, remains nested in its place of honor in the town center.

Cascara and Mint

A frustrated teacher turned newspaper man played a significant role in one of Lewis County's crops. In 1900 I.P. Callison was at a low ebb in his life. He had given up teaching with the idea of starting a weekly newspaper in Chehalis. When it faltered, he was invited by a stranger in town to become a partner in the cascara business. The stranger had an order in hand for two carloads of cascara bark from the drug manufacturer Parke, Davis & Company. Callison knew that buckthorn trees grew in large groves outside of Chehalis; what he didn't know is that the trees are found only in the Northwest and that the bark, Cascara Sagrada (literally, *sacred bark*), had commercial value as a pharmaceutical ingredient in laxatives.

Using an advance by a local bank Callison and his partner soon began filling the orders for a 60,000 pound shipment. The partner, whose name is lost to history, left town with his share of the proceeds, and Callison offered drug companies all the cascara they could use. When they accepted, Callison set up a receiving station in a feed store where farmers could exchange the bark for hay and grain. Callison's newspaper became a hobby, and he became the world's biggest supplier of cascara. His company was so successful that by 1920 he took his sons Cecil, Clarence, Harry, and later Donald into the firm and changed the company name to I.P. Callison & Sons. For many years local residents including many young people peeled and harvested cascara bark for Callison.

The company expanded its product line in 1941 with the purchase of W.J. Lake & Co. of Portland which had produced

Borden's Milk plant, later I.P. Callison on National Avenue in north Chehalis, circa 1935. Evidence of the 1929 earthquake is visible in the foreground.

peppermint oil. Thus began the mint industry. At first there were limited opportunities for peppermint and spearmint oils in the Northwest until the firm began an intensive marketing effort. By 1966 I.P. Callison & Sons was the only mint processing plant west of the Mississippi.

Dairies

From the earliest days, most people in Lewis County kept a few dairy cows, and as the roads improved and the processing plants began in Chehalis, milk and cream was shipped out. Several milk haulers from Silver Creek, Riffe, and Green Mountain drove teams and wagons full of milk cans and freight into town, as did others throughout the county. Marjorie Aldrich recalled in the 1976 Mossyrock Community History that until more people owned cars, the milk wagon drivers were often met by farmers asking them to buy machinery parts or by women asking them to pick up a few yards of lace, shoes for a child, or even an Easter hat. The haulers obliged by delivering the items on their return trip.

Residents in Eastern Lewis County remember milk checks coming in from the Borden Milk Company in Chehalis. Their checks of $8-10 a month were the sole source of cash income for many families. With 18-20 milk cows per family, they separated cream to sell in 5- or 10-gallon cans.

The Studhalter family at Bremer (west of Morton), for example, took their cream to the Morton depot to be weighed on a spring scale with a movable arm which swung out from the side of a wagon. The cream was stirred with a special utensil before being tested for its butterfat content to determine the price. Eventually "Grade A" dairies operated under tighter restrictions, Mrs. Aldrich observed, forcing many small operations out of business.

1923 Moreland model trucks at the Darigold Creamery in Chehalis.

A typical mixed dairy herd in rural Lewis County. Note split rail fence at left.

Milk cans awaiting the train at the Morton depot.

Cooperative marketing for dairy products began at the turn of the 20th century. Farmers joined together to form the Winlock Cooperative Creamery, the Chehalis Cooperative Creamery, and the Willapa Valley Cheese Association, all small but successful ventures. With World War I came a tremendous demand for whole milk products, followed by a drastic cutback in the postwar period. Dissatisfaction with the prices paid and treatment by the Carnation Milk Products Company in Chehalis led dairymen to boycott the "non-cooperative" plant. Seeking a voice in price-setting, farmers banned together to form the Lewis County Dairy Association. It later took in Pacific County and became the Lewis-Pacific Dairymens' Association.

"The Lewis County Association has a membership of over five hundred and around 6,000 cows represented," wrote the *Chehalis Bee Nugget* on March 4, 1919. Organized and chartered in 1919 to handle the farmers' own dairy products, the Association quickly set out to build its own milk plant, completed in 1921 at a cost of $250,000. By 1923 nearly a million pounds of butter and more than a million pounds of milk powder were shipped out of the county. By 1937 the enterprise included 1,300 members and a cheese factory at Randle. The Dairy Association continued to grow.

Kraft at that time, a company that made cottage cheese and hard cheeses, had started in Chehalis in 1946 and served as a distributor of local dairy products. By 1953, with a membership of 1,600, the Lewis County Association milked a profit of $4 million. Despite a weakness in the butter market when yellow margarine was legalized in Washington, the Association was a prime example of a cooperative success for half a century.

In 1968 the Lewis-Pacific Dairymens' Association, by then with a workforce of 180 employees, merged with the Seattle-based Darigold Company. When the Kraft Company moved away in 1970, its plant was purchased by Darigold and its facilities were modernized. In 1983 a new evaporator-dryer facility was constructed as part of a $13 million expansion project; a giant stainless steel evaporator and crystallizer tanks were enclosed by 65-foot concrete walls. The Darigold Feed mill, built in 1980, was expanded in 1983 and leased to Land O'Lakes. In the first feed-blending system of its type in the Northwest, the computerized feed mill was the tallest building in Chehalis. In 1986 a $6 million expansion

Lewis-Pacific Dairymens' Association trucks.

project doubled production capacity at the dry milk and cheese plant when another milk dryer and evaporator was installed. The man known as "Mr. Darigold," Lloyd Dobyns, retired in 1995.

Toledo's Cheese Day started in 1919 when shippers of the newly organized Cowlitz Valley Cheese Association gathered to receive their first checks, and their wives prepared coffee and

The Farmers and Merchants Picnic prepared "The World's Largest Omelet" at Alexander Park, Chehalis, 1931. The giant frying pan was borrowed from, and returned to Long Beach, WA.

cheese sandwiches. The next year in June of 1920 marked the first official public Cheese Day. Townsfolk erected a dance platform, brought in a carnival, scheduled a community baseball game, and long-winded speakers. They loaded tables with whole cheeses to be cut as needed. Folks arrived by buggy, horseback, and boat. Although the cheese factory left Toledo long ago, the local celebration lives on.

A "modern" Lewis County dairy barn, circa 1950. Dairies were a major industry in the agricultural history of Lewis County.

The business of dairying has changed considerably. Dairymen once milked by hand, separated the milk by "leaning" the cream to go to local creameries, and used the skim milk for home consumption. They hauled milk to market by horse and wagon, Larry Zander wrote in the Bicentennial Edition of *The Daily Chronicle* in 1976, "Gone too are the four- and five-cow dairies that helped provide a livelihood for hundreds in the county… (They have been) replaced by dairies often with more than 100 cows, pipeline milking systems that take the milk directly from the cow's udder to the milk tank and giant bulk tank trucks that haul the milk to distant places…"

Now the herds are larger, the production per cow has steadily increased, and limited herds of purebred dairy cattle graze in the verdant valleys of Lewis County. Along with increased production, the number of farmers has declined. From the dual-purpose family cow of the early settler, many of the once-prosperous dairy farms of the 20th century have closed their doors.

Hops

The loss of the ocean liner *Titanic* in 1912 contributed to the demise of one of Lewis County's most abundant agricultural products.

The crop was hops. For many years, the pastoral Boistfort Valley—significantly also known as the Klaber Valley—was called the "Hops Capital of the World." Hops were raised in the west-central Lewis County area as early as 1888, and in 1897 an entrepreneur named Herman Klaber began buying land from former Donation Land Act claims to raise them. By 1906 he had decided to build a model hops farm. The Boistfort Post Office, after nearly fifty years of carrying that name, was renamed Klaber in 1907. In 1910 some 900 acres of hops were grown in the Klaber Valley, the Cowlitz Prairie, and other parts of Lewis

Herman Klaber, circa 1911, established the hops industry in the Boistfort area.

pickin's" for those days. To house the seasonal influx of harvesters, shacks and tents sprouted everywhere in the valley, some 400 shacks at a time. The opening of many country schools was delayed until children were finished picking hops. Klaber erected twelve dry kilns, six on each side of the field, the large letters on the kilns spelling out K-L-A-B-E-R and he developed an extensive water system from a nearby spring. The cones of the hops were roasted with heat, bleached with sulphur, and then baled and wrapped in burlap for shipment.

The shipping point for all the hops from the Boistfort Valley was the large red depot at Ceres, eleven miles from Chehalis and along the Northern Pacific line from Chehalis to Willapa Harbor. Ceres, named for the Goddess of Grain, was utilized by the Longs, the Blacks, the Whites, and many other farm families to ship their produce. The Boistfort Valley wasn't the only area for "hops crops." Drying kilns were located on Klickitat Prairie near Mossyrock and at Silver Creek; several hop yards County. Herman Klaber had the largest yard in the county with about 140 acres in hops. Hops became a growth industry from 1912 to 1920.

The harvest required as many as 2,000 pickers who were paid a dollar for a 25-bushel box measuring seven feet long by three feet wide and three feet deep. Both native and white residents supplemented their small incomes with cash by picking hops. A good picker could make up to three dollars a day, and that was more than "slim

Pearson Ranch, Oakville. Indians working in the hop fields, circa 1920.

The Klaber hop farm, 1912. Notice the name spelled on the distant kiln stacks.

popped up in the Toledo area; Winlock farmers joined in, and residents of Eastern Lewis County not only grew hops but trekked to other places to camp and pick them.

Not everyone was happy about the hops industry. According to *Daily Chronicle* news stories of the day, some Twin Cities pastors forbade their members to work in the hop yards because the hops were being used to make beer. However, "workers with thin consciences" claimed the hops were earmarked for the manufacture of yeast, an essential ingredient of their daily bread.

The hops were shipped to a worldwide market, prompting Herman Klaber to make a business trip to England in the spring of 1912. It was thought that he also may have been investigating a cure for the mildew fungus that was beginning to show up around the roots of the plants. Whatever the case, Klaber was returning to the U.S. aboard the *Titanic* along with more than 2,500 others when it struck an iceberg on the evening of April 14, 1912. The ship was so severely damaged that it sank in the 12,400-foot-deep Atlantic the following morning.

Klaber perished, along with more than 1,500 other passengers.

Although hops were grown until the 1930s, the Klaber business was mismanaged, the mildew spread, and Prohibition reduced the demand for hops. The "Hops Capital of the World" fizzled into the annals of history.

Hops leaving Klaber farm for market, circa 1912.

Chapter 16

Quest for Power: Dams on the Cowlitz

As World War II ended, the cities of the Northwest thrived, fed by strong industries and increasing population. The city of Tacoma realized the demand for electrical power was certain to increase, and its leaders looked to the Cowlitz River as a source. In 1946 Tacoma City Light acquired water rights and construction permits for a project of two dams that would double its hydroelectric capacity. Optimistically, the 1947 City Light annual report predicted the Cowlitz River power project would be completed in three or four years after its authorization. It took 20 years and a fight as turbulent as the river the power company hoped to harness.

The quest for sources of hydroelectric power in Lewis County was nothing new. The town of Packwood was once known as Lewis, not for the county's name or the Northwest explorer but for a Portland developer who in 1911 proposed hydroelectric dams on the upper Cowlitz River. Chehalis had secured a grant in 1923 for Cowlitz dams which never materialized, and before 1930 Centralia considered the river for municipal power but chose the Nisqually River instead.

From the onset Tacoma City Light faced a bitter, 15-year controversy about its proposal to build two dams on the wild and rugged Cowlitz, a prime fishing area for salmon and steelhead. The proposal meant the demise of the towns of Riffe and Mayfield (the original proposal would not have inundated Kosmos) and the rerouting of 15 miles of state highway. The fight led all the way to the U.S. Supreme Court, not once, but three times. *The Tacoma Times* described sportsmen at one meeting as exhibiting "uncontrolled anger, vitriolic verbal assault. They quivered visibly. They whirled on their feet, arms sweeping wildly, they shouted." Testifying on behalf of the Native Americans in opposition to the dam was Cowlitz tribal member Mary Kiona whose ancestors and family had always lived and fished on the river.

Meanwhile, power was so limited that clocks in Tacoma in 1949 were losing six minutes each day. In 1951 the U.S. Supreme Court upheld Tacoma's right of construction, and in 1955 about 400 workers began construction on the Mayfield Dam. The Cowlitz project stopped dead in its tracks in 1957 when the Washington Supreme Court ruled that it could not condemn and remove a state fish hatchery in its way. That decision was overturned by the U.S. Supreme Court shortly before Independence Day in 1959.

Mayfield Dam construction, November 29, 1961.

Looking west over the old Mayfield Bridge with the new, higher Mayfield Bridge behind it. The old Mayfield bridge still sits below the surface of the reservoir.

The machines again rumbled and employees scrambled to continue the construction of Mayfield Dam. A "cable car for fish" was devised to carry fish safely past the dam. Located where the Cowlitz, Cascade, and Chehalis Railroad bridge had once spanned the river, the dam for the 13.5-mile Mayfield Lake was formally dedicated in 1963. It was named for newspaperman Henry Clay Mayfield who established the community of Mayfield on Winston Creek in 1891.

Mayfield Dam, and behind it Lake Mayfield.

But the Cowlitz River project was only one-third completed. The Mossyrock Dam, 13 miles upstream, would be twice as big and twice as expensive. Along with the dam came Tacoma City Light's commitment to build and maintain two large fish hatcheries, one of which at the time was the world's largest, to compensate for fish losses. Construction began in 1964, and finally on May 16, 1969, the Mossyrock Dam was formally dedicated.

At 605 feet, Mossyrock Dam ranked as the highest in the Pacific Northwest, the fifth highest in the country, and 17th highest in the world. The dam once won a listing in the World Almanac among "Major World Dams" — one of 21 in the U.S. to receive the distinction.

Mossyrock Dam holds water to the height of the Seattle Space Needle.

Fishing on Davisson Lake, later renamed to Riffe Lake, behind the Mossyrock Dam, 1970.

The naming of the body of water behind the dam was still a contentious issue. Instead of being named Riffe Lake to commemorate the early settler Floyd Riffe who was instrumental in bringing so many settlers from West Virginia and Kentucky to Lewis County, the lake was named Davisson, after a Tacoma utilities director — a person whose name had no significance to Lewis County. People in the central part of the county were sick at heart at not having the pioneer name and community perpetuated. John Martin, a newspaper reporter at the time, notes that in February of 1975, Marjorie Aldrich, the Lewis County Historical Society's Names Chairman, wrote resolutions and petitions requesting a name change. She was joined by local Granges; Jim Marvin, publisher of the *Morton Journal*; Harold Cooper, county commissioner; the Riffe family and other

The west end of Riffe Lake and the Mossyrock Dam.

interested citizens. Finally on March 12, 1976, the State Board of Geographic Names was influenced to rename the body of water Riffe Lake, thus restoring the pioneer name to the area. Martin explains that, while the name change "does not restore the homes, birth places of many, the churches or cemeteries, it does commemorate the communities in existence no more."

A third dam, the Cowlitz Falls Project, was constructed in the early 1990s with the dam and power generation facility completed in 1994. Located immediately upstream from Tacoma City Light's dams at the conflux of the Cowlitz and Cispus Rivers, the Cowlitz Falls Project is owned by Lewis County Public Utilities District in cooperation with the Bonneville Power Administration to supply the needs of Lewis County residents and businesses. The 610-acre reservoir behind the dam is appropriately named Lake Scanewa for the historic chief of the Cowlitz Tribe.

The hydroelectric projects have changed the face of the central part of Lewis County. The Cowlitz River, now mostly harnessed, has ceased some of its wild rampages of the past, although in 1995-96 parts of Toledo were flooded by spillage from the dam during heavy rains, and a dozen homes were damaged. The three lakes today bring in thousands of campers, boaters, and recreationalists to enjoy numerous modern campsites.

Chapter 17

The Great Melting Pot

The ethnic makeup of Lewis County is like a serving from the great American melting pot. Most notable are the ethnic settlements representing Finland, Switzerland, Poland, and Japan, with a smattering of African-American and Jewish residents. Germans, Irish, and Scots were also represented. They came with the hope of opportunity, good job prospects, and the possibility of owning their own land.

Finnish people formed substantial communities in Winlock, Independence Valley and Lincoln Creek Valley. Many worked in mines and mills prior to becoming landowners. The Finnish settlers in Winlock arrived quite by mistake when they missed the train. Several from a group working in the coal mines at Carbonado in 1903 decided they wanted to get a little ranch somewhere. Nick Kolenen, Charles Martalla and Henry Pistnen went by train to Chehalis, where they set out on foot to look over the Boistfort Valley.

Though they found good farms, the land was too expensive, and they planned to return to the mine with a negative report. It was closer to walk back over the hill to Winlock to catch the train instead of returning to Chehalis. But, alas, they missed the train and had to stay overnight.

Gertrude and Martha Hilli, Finland, 1916. They were born at Independence Valley, grew up in Finland, and returned to Lewis County to raise families as Gertrude Saari and Martha Nikula.

A mixture of races is represented in these students at the Winlock School, 1925.

The Finnish Lutheran Church at Independence, built in 1909, shown before it was demolished in the 1960s.

In Winlock they learned that logged-off land was cheap. The old Ainslie Lumber Company had 500 acres for sale near the old mill site, which they promptly bought and divided among eight of their compatriots. By word of mouth many other Finnish mine workers heard of available land near Chehalis which was similar to their home country.

The Finns throughout the county engaged in the poultry industry for almost forty years and operated small dairies prior to the decline of the small farm. Forming a cohesive community, they constructed Finnish halls, churches, and many barns. The Finnish Lutheran Church in Independence Valley served the community for many years, as did a small church at Lincoln Creek. Saturday nights were celebrated by firing up the sauna for a good cleansing in hot steam. Joining in on the logging and railroad boom in the early part of the century, they named Helsing Junction, a railroad crossing, after a channel in Finland. High on a pristine hillside of Independence Valley is a quiet little cemetery where many of the early Finnish settlers are buried.

Winlock was once home to a Black settlement of about one hundred people. Dating back to the 1870s, the first teacher in Olequa Territory was a Black man named Dick Powell who traveled to a number of schools in Southwest Washington teaching mainly white children. In 1892 Thomas

"Old Colored Church," Winlock, circa 1926. University of Washington, Special Collections, UW 13566.

Lynch came from Alaska and bought 80 acres one mile north of town from the Northern Pacific Railroad.

The owner of several farms, Lynch acted as the financier for other Black families who came to Winlock. He frequently invited people from Portland to come to Winlock where they could work, obtain financial aid if necessary, and enjoy a "downright friendly atmosphere." Lynch became a leader of the Black community, serving as justice of the peace in 1912 and opening his orchard to World War I settlers who camped there. He also donated land for a Methodist Church on a hill just outside of town. Known by Blacks and their neighbors alike as the "Old Colored Church," at first it was an old shed moved up from the Veness mill by hay wagon. It was enlarged in 1915 and attended by both races with the stipulation that the church must always leave its doors open to Black people.

Another highly regarded family was that of Andy Whiteside in the late 1910s and '20s. Whiteside was a logging hooktender and the only Black man on the Pacific Coast to supervise a logging crew. His wife, Ann Adams Whiteside, answered "a calling from God" that led her from a brush with death in her Southern home to Winlock. She too became a vital part of the community.

Several Blacks worked in nearby hops fields, and most took care of small farms while working away from home. The settlement dissipated as its young people moved to larger cities. When the older members of the community died, there was simply no one left.

A community built along the Military Road near Winlock was established by several Swiss families in the 1880s. Naming their settlement St. Urban after a patron saint, the residents attended a tiny Catholic Church by the same name. The Bremgartners, Wallers, Limmers, and Meiers settled there. The Swiss people in the Chehalis and Frances area built immaculate farms and dairies, much like those in their native Switzerland. Early settlers included the Gisler, Faver, Furrer, and Blaser families. Elsie Blaser Spahr recalled the early days when the Swiss frugally made use of every part of butchered animals for food: they made head cheese, blood soup, boiled tongues and ears, and scrambled eggs and brains.

The Swiss worked hard but played hard too, for they were sociable folks. Many times they danced to the music of a squeeze box accordion and played cards until 6 a.m. when it was time to milk the cows. They generously shared their supply of fermented apple cider, undeterred by Prohibition. Sundays were an occasion for church, visiting, and card parties of Jass (pronounced "Yahss"). In the 1920s Swiss families traveled to Tacoma for dances and schwingfests which are Swiss wrestling matches. An annual Fourth of July festival in Frances still features the traditional Swiss sporting event.

Some of the lumber mills drew in entire communities of Japanese workers. A term that would be considered a racial slur today was a common descriptor then. "Jap Creek" was the drainage area near the Pacific County line that was home to a large number of Japanese who worked in the Walville mill; bits of broken Asian china can be found at the site. The Carlisle mill in Onalaska had numerous Japanese workers, as did the Napavine mills and the Chehalis Lumber Company at Littell. There was also a Greek settlement at the Wisconsin mill at

A Swiss gathering on the Mueller homestead on Rock Creek, west of Pe Ell, circa 1920. John K. Mueller is holding up a Swiss cheese. Photo is courtesy of his son, Louie Muller.

The Land Called Lewis

The Walville mill Asian crew. University of Washington Libraries, Special Collections, C. Kinsey 4536.

Littell, historian Margaret Shields noted.

The introduction of the Japanese to the workplace was not always met with open arms, especially in the early years of mill history. *The Chehalis Bee Nugget* in its June 1, 1906, issue reported that: "About 18 Japs were employed at the Somerville mill (at Napavine) recently and nearly all the old employees at once pulled their stakes and started for new fields where white labor is used." The *Centralia News Examiner* on March 19, 1907, had this item: "The Chehalis River Lumber Co. of this city, employed four Japanese last week. In consequence, all the white men employed in the mill and logging camps walked out, with the exception of one man who was to be boss over the Japs. Many of the strikers have been in the employ of the Chehalis River Lumber Co. for three and four years."

Eventually the Japanese communities were grudgingly accepted, if not integrated, into the mainstream of mill town life. Several local Japanese farmers were highly regarded, and when they were so abruptly sent to internment camps during World War II, residents were ashamed and embarrassed by their ill treatment.

The National Polish Catholic Church, Pe Ell.

1,113 with another 609 in the rural areas. Over a quarter of these, or 417, were Polish with others of German, Austrian, and Swiss descent. Most were not yet American citizens. In the document laden with biases of the times, the unknown writer provided a picture of Pe Ell complete with an analysis of housing, industry, and even a listing of "recreational or amusement agencies… which are detrimental to the morals of the children and young people": two public dance halls, two movie halls, and three pool halls.

One of the first tasks and ultimate conflicts of the immigrants revolved around the establishment of a Polish Catholic Church. Convincing the Catholic Church to provide a Polish-speaking priest was a controversy that lasted from 1893 to 1916, when Rev. F. Barszchowski arrived to provide leadership to his Polish flock. The Polish Catholic Church in Pe Ell is now on the National Register of Historic Places.

Pe Ell, the timber town in the western part of Lewis County, was the chosen home for a substantial number of Polish immigrants. Perhaps their choice can be attributed to Frank Nalewaja who acquired land and partitioned it to sell to his countrymen. By the early 1900s, between 500 and 1,000 "Polanders" struck root in the newly established community.

In a 1924 unpublished document by the Methodist Church, the total inhabitants of the "village" numbered

Vincent Paniczko (1861-1946) from Poland, far right, translated for Polish immigrants who rode the train into Chehalis from Pe Ell. He is next to John Paniczko, (later Panesko) father of the publisher of this book. Prindle Street, Chehalis, 1910.

A small Jewish community in Centralia introduced the Temple Adath Israel as a place of worship. David and Isaac Robinson arrived in 1903, and within a decade there were enough families for Sabbath services every Friday night. During the 1920s the Jewish population increased to nearly 30 families, most of whom were of East European origin, according to Dr. James Vosper in a 1980 radio series entitled "Legacies of the Past." The synagogue at West Locust and South King was constructed in 1930 with funds raised by Gentiles as well as Jews. Many of the Jews were in retail trade, and the reduced business of the Depression forced their exodus from Centralia to larger cities.

Despite the ethnic diversity of the county, there arose groups whose very philosophy opposed it. One group, the Knights of the Ku Klux Klan, sponsored a huge gathering in 1924 at the Southwest Washington Fairgrounds. Attendance, by an account in *The Lewis County Advocate*, August 1, 1924, was variously estimated at 15,000 to 50,000 with some estimates as high as 70,000; a reasonable estimate was that a minimum of 35,000 people poured in via some 8,000 automobiles.

Besides local residents, large delegations came from Portland, Seattle, Tacoma and Olympia, many of whom came merely as curious onlookers. One overcrowded grandstand nearly collapsed. The evening's activities opened with a speech by a Seattle judge entitled "America for Americans," and several hundred new members were initiated. "Members wearing white robes, but faces bared, formed a square around the race track enclosure with a fiery red cross towering above them." A law had been passed forbidding group appearances of masked individuals, so they did show their faces in the darkened arena. The ceremony ended with a lavish display of fireworks. It took three hours for the cars to clear.

The members of the KKK often appeared in Fourth of July parades during the 1920s and early 1930s. Newspaper accounts tell of their appearance in a parade at Vader, and another tells of their providing entertainment at a Christmas party in Mossyrock. The *Chehalis Bee* of Dec. 26, 1928, wrote: "The program includes speaking, singing and the un-masking of the first Klansmen." A local woman sang "Just for Today" and "a splendid number by the Ajlune sextet was enjoyed. There was old time music while candy and nuts were given out to the children by six Klan ladies."

Klu Klux Klan in the Vader parade, 1927. Photo courtesy of the Daily News, Longview.

The activities of the KKK were not always so benign. On March 7, 1927, some 400 people gathered in Mossyrock to witness the burning of a fiery cross and ceremonies led by about 65 Klansmen. A newspaper account of the event said, "The white-clad group appeared very earnest, although a bit weird in the dim light of the fiery cross and a single torch carried by the leader." The cross was located on the highest point of Mossyrock and burned steadily throughout the evening. Another flaming cross burned in Randle in September of the same year, and a newspaper article said, "a Bible was found nearby."

Still another local group known as the Silver Shirts earned notoriety in a feature story in the March 6, 1939, edition of *Life* magazine. Members of the Chehalis group were American Fascists. "Losing their faith in democracy, they bowed to the arrogant Fascist-Communist assertion that America's only choice is between Fascism and Communism." The article noted that the Chehalis residents were "but simple folk of the kind to be found in any American town...groping for something to fight back at in a bewildering, swift-changing world." Among the tenets of the Silver Shirts was the belief that President Roosevelt was three-fourths Jewish and that Washington, D.C., had been turned over to Jews. To counteract the outcry from local residents, *Life* printed a follow-up article two months later on May 15 that showed a different side of Chehalis; pictured were the family of banker N.B. Coffman, log trucks, agricultural scenes, and civic scenes submitted by Chehalis High School students.

The wave of immigrants and ethnic groups continued in the latter part of the 20th century. A group of Pentecostal Russian/Ukrainian refugees joined the community, and in the late 1980s and 1990s the population of Mexican-born residents increased dramatically. In the five years between 1990 and 1995, the number of English-as-a-Second Language school children grew thirteen-fold in the Centralia School District. Just as previous ethnic groups before them, the Hispanic community seeks improved opportunities and better economic conditions. Like other newcomers they have earned their livelihood by working in the woods industry and in agriculture. They too have integrated into the community, broadening the cultural base and the great melting pot with new foods and customs.

Chapter 18

The Great Depression, World War II, and Post-War Times

The boom years when railroading and the lumber industries ruled Lewis County came to a grumbling halt with the Great Depression in 1929. The era of the large mills ended as one after another of these sprawling giants ground to a standstill. Those that burned were not rebuilt. Hardest hit were residents of the mill towns such as Onalaska and Ryderwood whose livelihood depended exclusively on lumber. Some towns, such as McCormick and Walville near Pe Ell, simply disappeared, and the ubiquitous logging railroads cut back their forays into the woods as the demand for lumber declined. Many people drifted away from the mill towns, but others came to settle on land that was more accommodating than the mid-western dust bowl.

Cash was especially scarce. Prices hit rock bottom for nearly everything, but bargains didn't matter much because hardly anyone had the money to buy things. Bread sold for five cents a loaf, a pound of peanut butter was 23 cents, and a pound of bacon, a mere 16 cents. The price of hamburger, 18 cents a pound in 1930, plummeted to a dime, while beef roast could be purchased for 12 cents a pound. There were virtually no jobs to be had.

Hoboes were a common sight, riding into towns on the trains. Usurped from their homes by hard times, the lack of a job, and the dream of better places, the hoboes were usually ordinary men who were down on their luck, although there were a few who were criminals. They set up a shanty town by the brickyard in Chehalis and covered a regular route of houses where they asked for food. When they

The Citizens Unemployment League, Centralia.

found a particularly generous place, they put a mark on the front gate so that the next one would know where the handouts were. A police chief at the time remarked that the hoboes always provided an excellent grapevine for detective work on a crime. He was actually sorry to see the shanties removed and their occupants dispersed in the 1940s.

The Great Depression, World War II, and Post-War Times

Margaret O. Payton, sister of N.B. Coffman, shows fruit grown in her yard, 1919.

Still, people in the Lewis County area did not suffer as their urban countrymen did. The Depression was more of an abstraction to read about in the newspapers, and life simply went on as usual. Local newspapers focused more on daily happenings than hardships.

Because of the agricultural resources, most people raised big gardens and their own beef or pork. Wild game was plentiful, and game wardens looked the other way when poaching provided food for a hungry family. People's needs were simple; long before the era of designer clothing, school children had one outfit for school and one for play. Most families had a car (which could be purchased new for $500-700), but they used it sparingly for a rare trip to town. Recreation consisted of card parties, country dances, or an occasional trip to the movies.

Theaters up until the late 1920s were venues for traveling troupes of vaudeville players. Centralia's Liberty Theater, built before 1920, featured both vaudeville and early silent movies until the luxurious Fox Theater opened in 1930 and captured the market specifically for "talkies." In the depths of the Great

The Fox Theater in Centralia, offered an escape from bad economic news, shown in 1940.

Grand Mound Fruit Growers Cooperative Association, July 24, 1929.

Depression a ticket to the Fox cost 10 cents for children. Tickets to the Onalaska theater were also only a dime but in order to draw customers when there weren't many dimes to be spared, the owner often raffled off groceries or a case of beans with the price of the ticket.

The Depression years were times of camaraderie. Folks helped each other out, and neighbors did neighborly deeds. If someone needed a new barn or if a house burned down, everyone banded together to help. Centralia residents decided to resolve their own relief problems in 1930. They established a fund for the destitute which quickly grew to over $6,000 and provided aid for some 285 families. Benefit parties and donations from businesses included bread, milk, furniture, wood, coal and shoes. Families formed canning clubs where they pooled food, jars, and canning supplies. Seed was distributed in the spring and the county commissioners sponsored a garden. In nearby Thurston County the community of Tenino "minted" wooden money which was accepted as legal tender by local merchants.

The Depression brought in a group of people to Mossyrock "blown out of the dust bowl of Iowa and Nebraska" based on the hope of more productive farmland. Mrs. Marjorie Aldrich of Mossyrock tells of a woman who arrived one fall with everything from socks to dish towels packed in canning jars. When she saw all the apples and blackberries wasting on the ground, she couldn't unpack fast enough to begin canning. Never mind that she couldn't afford sugar for the fruit — that could be added later. She was appalled by the casual lack of interest in using of all of the various resources the land offered.

Orphanages were busy during the 1930s.

"All that wood going to waste! ... Such abundance; such neglect of conservation; people here didn't appreciate what they had," wrote Mrs. Aldrich in the Mossyrock Community History.

About this time and for the next few decades, people from North and South Dakota relocated here, finding the opportunities and the climate more favorable.

To create jobs during the Depression era, the Roosevelt administration set up the Works Progress Administration (later the Works Project Administration). Locally WPA projects included playgrounds, river control, the fairgrounds, Centralia's Borst Park, the Chehalis airfield, Lewis & Clark State Park, several city parks, and the streets. They built important transportation links such as the Centralia-Alpha Road.

A significant force in Eastern Lewis County, the Civilian Conservation Corps (CCCs) was formed to employ young men, many from cities on the East Coast, and to provide an income for their families. With camps at Packwood and Cispus, the CCCs were responsible for developing Rainbow Falls State Park, the campsite at Ohanapecosh in Mt. Rainier National Park, building numerous trails and roads, and falling snags to prevent forest fires.

The Chehalis Airport (Donahoe Field) hanger built by the WPA.

Packwood Civilian Conservation Corps (CCC) camp, circa 1935.

Civilian Conservation Corps Camp at Doty, 1937.

The biggest camp was at Packwood, according to L.E. "Bud" Panco, and consisted of one long officers' quarters, five bunkhouses, and a big recreation room. The remains of the Packwood camp were converted into apartments in use decades later, while one building of the original camp is now part of the Cispus Environmental Center. The CCCs in effect opened up the wilderness for recreation and laid the groundwork for roads that later were used for logging, fire protection and recreation.

Federal land in East County underwent a change during this period; in 1933 the Rainier National Forest Reserve became the Columbia National Forest. The name was changed to the Gifford Pinchot National Forest in 1949.

Moonshiners and Bootleggers

Prohibition was in effect in Washington from 1919 to 1933 but the law did not dampen the spirits of Lewis County moonshiners who made the booze, and bootleggers who sold it. As early as 1910, newspaper accounts tell of illicit production of whiskey that was sold in various parts of the county. In 1913 a Greek cook at McCormick was arrested for operating a "blind pig," a Prohibition term for a tavern. Some 18 barrels of beer and 11 kegs of his liquor were destroyed. During the 1920s, stills popped up everywhere, out of sight of the law, of course. Of all sizes and descriptions, they bubbled and gurgled in chicken houses, barns, attics, basements, cedar-sided shacks deep in the canyons, and under the cover of heavy brush.

Eastern Lewis County was the moonshine capital, certainly of Lewis County and possibly of the whole state. Many of the residents who had relocated from the hills of Kentucky and West Virginia brought their skills for making "white lightnin'" to the upper Cowlitz country, along with their rifles for protection. A party of railroad surveyors in 1910 were mistaken for "revenooers" and threatened with their lives when they stumbled onto some stills of corn whiskey. Later during Prohibition law enforcement officials who chose not to have a 30-30 slug creasing their hats always stopped to visit at one of the small stores on the way into that part of the country. They'd visit an hour or so — just long enough for the local phones to crank out a warning signal.

The files at the Lewis County Historical Museum reveal many curious episodes

Sheriff Edward Deggeller and deputies at the site of a still, 1927.

from the era. One over-eager agent once confiscated a large collection of bottles from under the bed of one East County family. It turned out to be a stock of homemade root beer for Mom and the kids! Locals chuckled over the story for years.

One of the biggest bootlegging enterprises was operated out of a chicken house near Evaline in the Winlock area by some East County entrepreneurs who wanted a central location to transport their product north to the Puget Sound and south to Portland. Chicken houses were not uncommon sites for stills, and sanitation was not a big concern. A 1921 headline in *The Chehalis Bee Nugget* warned that "Moonshine is Poison Stuff," based on the seizure of five stills made from rusty wash tub boilers that were covered with dirt.

Whiskey was usually made of corn mash consisting of a 50-pound sack each of sugar and cracked or ground corn, but it was also made of potatoes, prunes, or other fruit. One confiscated batch made from potatoes was so strong that a match added to a few drops on a piece of wood set a hearty fire.

Hiding the stills was pretty easy, but disposing of the odiferous mash was harder. A moonshiner near Littell thought he had solved the problem by dumping the mash in the creek — until a farmer downriver discovered that his milk cows were coming home tipsy. Moonshiners who made home brew had another challenge because bottles of the stuff could explode like fireworks and alert everyone to their contents. Some bootleggers dropped off their product in gunny sacks in remote areas to be picked up later by the customer,

Harry Truman was known to be an active bootlegger in Chehalis in the 1920s. He is shown on the steps of the Inn at Spirit Lake a few weeks before he and it were buried in the eruption of Mt. St. Helens, 1980.

but one hapless fellow discovered that his brew was in a patch of nettles. Worse yet, after digging it out, he was arrested by deputies on his way home.

When the Volstead Act was nullified in 1933 by the 21st Amendment, the thrill in defying the law was gone. But as late as 1978, East Lewis County was still viewed as one of the state's hotspots for moonshiners, though law enforcement had lost interest long before. As a footnote in history, when Mt. St. Helens erupted in 1980, the blast took with it the colorful character, Harry Truman — who had been an active bootlegger in the Chehalis area in 1920s.

War Years

As the Depression eased in the late 1930s, logging resumed and more jobs became available. But the area was not insulated from worldwide tensions. Life changed considerably for Lewis County residents on December 7, 1941, "the day of infamy" for Americans. When the Japanese bombs were dropped on Pearl Harbor, four servicemen from Lewis County lost their lives. And so began another saga of history in the area. The local National Guard Unit, the 803rd Tank Battalion, had been federalized before the war started and many men had already been taken into service. On Dec. 15, 1941, barely a week after Pearl Harbor, the unit reported to Fort Lewis as the 803rd Tank Destroyer Battalion. It left New York for France in June of 1943, one year before D-Day, not to return until November of 1945.

As WW II dragged on, there was a Lewis County resident in every famous battle representing all the branches of the armed forces. Communities in the area were typical of those across America during the war years.

Also typical was life on the home front. During the war, the women of Napavine sewed pajamas, hospital shirts, and knit sweaters. Every drive to sell savings bonds, also known as "defense bonds", "war bonds" and "victory bonds" went "over the top" within an hour after opening the event. A big Red Cross carnival raised $1,100 in one night. Many Centralia families were involved in Civil Defense and climbed a spotting tower by Centralia College (on the field later occupied by the college library building) to watch in shifts for enemy aircraft. Spotters were located all over the county, and school children practiced making model airplanes so they could identify enemy aircraft. Nearly every home

The Great Depression, World War II, and Post-War Times

had blackout curtains and a victory garden. Rationing put limits on gas, tires, and certain foods. Scrap drives were conducted for metal, glass, and rubber. One Grand Mound resident sold a big pile of old tires to dealers from Seattle and with the cash bought a milk cow — a valuable commodity since milk, dairy products, and beef were all rationed.

In 1943 the Boeing Aircraft Company came to Chehalis, and the local versions of "Rosie the Riveter" went to work. Setting up shop on the corner of Pacific Avenue and Prindle street, Boeing employed some 600 people during its operation, many of them women. A mechanics class was offered at the Southwest Washington Fairgrounds to prepare "the girls" for their new vocation. Working up to three shifts seven days a week, they produced wing ribs and leading wing edges for the Boeing B-17, the "Flying Fortress," and later for the B-29. A detailed and personalized account of these years in Lewis County is Julie McDonald Zander's 2005 book *Life on the Home Front — Stories of Those who Worked, Waited and Worried during WW II.*

Boeing set up various operations across the state to tap into local labor pools and enhance security by spreading out production sites. Other factories were in Aberdeen, Hoquiam, Bellingham, and Tacoma. The Chehalis plant was honored with an Army-Navy Award for high production after its first year of operation. Chehalis and other regional plants contributed to Boeing's world record for production of four-engine bombers in 1944.

While the Boeing plant boosted the local economy, it also impacted the lives of those who worked there. For the first time, women were hired in large numbers as

1943 Boeing plant in Chehalis, later the Lewis County PUD offices. Photo courtesy of Boeing Company.

production workers because so many men were serving in the armed forces. Paid nearly a dollar an hour by Boeing, they sometimes earned far more than their spouses in the service, a situation that often created friction. Other couples actually met while working at the plant and later were married. Most of the employees enjoyed being with others they knew, and there was a high spirit of patriotism in their contribution to the war effort. The company formed its own baseball team and played against several former professional baseball players who were stationed at Fort Lewis during the war. One of the local workers recalled staring in astonishment as a batter hit a ball so hard that it sailed far off into a crossarm plant nearby.

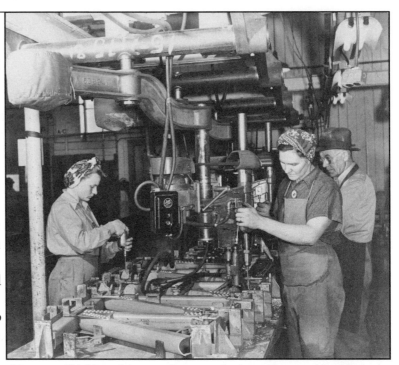

Margaret Shields and Autumn Beam work alongside an unidentified man in the Chehalis Boeing facility, circa 1943.

Margaret Shields and Margaret Langus, known for their work with the Lewis County Historical Museum, were both employed at the Boeing plant. Margaret Langus, the company nurse, remembered the day WW II ended and the jubilation at the announcement.

"We all got in our cars and headed for the streets in a victory parade," she recalled. The joy was marred only by the reminder of the 236 young Lewis County men who wouldn't be coming home. The War Memorial in Centralia's Washington Park dedicated in 1993 pays tribute to these and other fallen soldiers who died for their country.

The end of the war signaled another growth spurt in the local economy as the demand for housing soared nationwide. Because the war depleted timber on private land, the national forests, including the Gifford Pinchot, opened up large tracts to timber sales in the 1950s.

Margaret Langus by a parade float, circa 1950.

Significantly, Eastern Lewis County opened up in another way, for in 1951 the White Pass Highway to Yakima was completed. L.E. "Bud" Panco said that the road had ended about two miles above Packwood in the 1930s, and although Chinook Pass and Cayuse Pass through the Cascades were completed around 1940, the area still languished in isolation. With the White Pass Highway came the first ski lift and a rush of skiers in the early '50s. The highway allowed easy access to the sage brush deserts and orchards of Yakima and increased the population of Packwood and Randle. As an alternate route across the Cascades, the White Pass Highway continues to make Eastern Lewis County more accessible for residents and outdoor enthusiasts.

Sign in Kosmos (the town later covered by Riffe Lake) showing the White Pass Highway closed. Located next to Bristol's Grocery, circa 1951.

Chapter 19

War Memorial

The setting is purely small town America: a green, tree-lined town square with a red brick Carnegie library, and a World War I doughboy sentinel standing guard.

On a rainy Memorial Day in 1993, as American flags unfurled and patriotic music hummed in the background, Lewis County residents dedicated a war memorial to their fallen sons at Washington Park in Centralia. On the dark granite memorial are the engraved names of those men and women who sacrificed their lives for their country in a war or conflict. The roll call speaks for itself: World War I, 73 men; World War II, 236; the Korean War, 16; and Vietnam, 28. Names continue to be added including the first woman, Regina R. Clark, who died in 2005 in the Iraq War.

A parade during Operation Desert Storm gave Onalaska resident Bob Cook an idea. Lewis County had lost many of its young in wars, but nothing remained as a tribute to their bravery. A Vietnam veteran himself, Cook envisioned a memorial to the Lewis County veterans similar to the Vietnam memorial in Washington, D.C.

Soon Cook's idea spread, and numerous other volunteers from the community joined him to work on the Lewis County Freedom Walk, the name of the war memorial in Washington Park in Centralia. The idea was expanded to include those from all the wars, not just Vietnam.

After nearly two years of community planning, the memorial was dedicated on May 31, 1993, by Gov. Mike Lowry, U.S. Senator Slade Gorton, and other dignitaries. All the funds were raised locally for the memorial, which is made of some of the darkest granite available and imported from Pennsylvania. The labor and supplies were donated by local labor unions and construction companies. The location of the memorial is significant as well, for the park was given to Centralia by its founder, George Washington, and the statue of the World War I sentinel is a tribute to those veterans killed in the Armistice Day Tragedy of 1919.

The Freedom Walk entrance is marked with this memorial, 1993.

One of the biggest challenges was to make sure that the list of those killed in the line of duty was accurate. While some lists existed for World Wars I and II, the roster was by no means complete. As a collector of World War II memorabilia, Peter Lahmann became the unofficial historian whose task was to confirm all the names of Lewis County veterans killed in battle since Washington became a state in 1889. Using official War Department casualty lists, *The Chronicle* archives, and recollections of family and friends, Lahmann tabulated a total of 356 names. He was unable to substantiate the loss of any local veterans in the Spanish American War of 1898.

From there, the list grows, as each name on the memorial revealed a key player in a personal tragedy. The stories unfolded with a touching poignancy. The first known Lewis County casualty of war turned out to be Arthur Eastman, a logger from Adna, who joined the British Army in 1914. Whether he joined through commitment to the cause or a yen for adventure is not known, but he did write a letter to his mother about how bad the war was and how he longed to be home. He died in France in 1915.

Four names carry the date "Dec. 7, 1941." The four were killed when the Japanese bombed Pearl Harbor and World War II began. Also on the list was Jerry E. Stott of Pe Ell whose bad leg kept him from enlisting in the Army during World War II. He joined the Merchant Marine instead and became the only casualty when his ship was hit by an enemy torpedo. William E. Harbert of Centralia dropped out of the University of Washington engineering school during his third year to join the Army Air Force as a P-38 pilot. His plane was shot down on his next-to-the-last mission. Some 45 years after his death, Harbert's mother, Olga, was deeply touched that anyone would ask about him.

The average age of the veterans was a mere 21, and in some cases they were the last males in the family and thus carried the family name to their graves.

The Freedom Walk memorial, lying so peacefully in the park, holds many stories but most notably it is a reminder that Lewis County gives its fair share to ensure the freedom of all United States citizens.

The Freedom Walk listing of war dead, with the reflection of "The Sentinel" statue and the American flag, Centralia, 2003.

Chapter 20

Living in the Land Called Lewis

Days flow into years, years into decades, decades into centuries. Many years have passed since the boundaries of Lewis County were set to include most of Western Washington and British Columbia. Simon Plamondon, John R. and Matilda Jackson, the families of Sidney S. Ford, Joseph and Mary Borst, the Randle family, and all the other intrepid souls who so courageously settled the new land would surely be in awe if they could see it now.

But perhaps not. For if they had been around through time, they would have been contributors, if not the founders, of the institutions and organizations that make up the fiber of Lewis County communities and enrich the lives of those who live in them.

Schools form the character of any community—and who cannot relate to the nostalgia of the bygone school years? The schools of Lewis County—from roughly hewn, one-room schools in the woods to contemporary facilities comparable to any in America—have shaped the lives of thousands. Most of the little rural schoolhouses attended by pioneer children were absorbed by as many as 14 school districts.

The largest two are the Centralia and Chehalis

Schoolhouse at Forest, circa 1890.

School Districts with a combined enrollment of over 6,000 students, bigger than the population of most Lewis County towns. The smallest district is Evaline, a district that has maintained its personal, country style with only 40 students. Several private schools and the rise of home schooling have added another dimension to education.

The first schoolhouse in Centralia, on Rock, south of Cherry, circa 1885.

Green Hill School, the first of its type in the state, was founded because of a juvenile horse thief in the 1880s and because of frustrated state officials who had no recourse for incarcerating him. A grand jury found the boy a case of "almost total depravity" and recommended that the state establish a house of corrections for such cases. As a result the legislature in 1890 appropriated $65,000 and acquired 50 acres in Chehalis for a school. First called the Washington State Reform School, it opened June 10, 1891, for both boys and girls. Most were sent there for incorrigibility, but some came because they had no family and no other place to go. They received vocational and academic training; they made their own shoes and clothing, raised crops and milked cows.

In 1911 an investigation revealed deplorable conditions at the school, particularly for girls who were confined by day to a large room without exercise or fresh air. Milk was scarce; eggs, poultry and even apples were a luxury. Severe overcrowding was a common condition, and discipline was harsh. These nightmarish conditions led to the creation of a separate school for girls at Grand Mound, which opened in 1914 as Maple Lane School. Girls were the sole residents there until 1977 when it was converted to coed. It became an all-male facility in 1981.

As the years passed, Green Hill School added a barn, milk house and, in 1924, a granary which operated for many years, along with a greenhouse, carpentry shop, and auto and paint shops in 1932. In the 1950s an administration building, recreational building and cottages were added. The facility was upgraded with new cottages in the late 1990s. The name was changed to Washington State Training School, then Green Hill Academy, and finally Green Hill School.

Local legend claims that the familiar song, "I'll Take You Home Again, Kathleen," came from Green Hill School in Chehalis, not from Ireland as many believe. The first superintendent of the school was T.P. Westendorf who brought his wife Jennie Kathleen to Chehalis. She was so homesick the first winter, she nearly died. To cheer her, so the lore goes, he wrote the memorable song, and every time he caught her crying, he sang it to her. (An article by Pat Jones of *The Chronicle* in March, 2006, indicates the song was actually written in 1875 and copyrighted in 1876; the Westendorfs moved to Chehalis in 1891. Wherever the song was written, it still remains deeply tied to local history.)

The 1907 "Training School" which later became Green Hill School. Mt. St. Helens is faintly visible on the right.

The Land Called Lewis

The old Centralia High School building when Centralia College was using the third floor, August 10, 1928. The college campus now includes the land on which the high school building once stood.

Another institution, Centralia College, has contributed to advancement of thousands of Lewis County residents. It also is the oldest continuously existing institution of its type in the state. When Centralia Junior College, as it was called then, opened its doors in 1925 to 15 students on the third floor of the old Centralia High School building, there were no other community colleges in the state. Within two years its enrollment had jumped to 85 students. During the Depression, when local banks took a "holiday," community business people banded together to guarantee the financing of the fledgling institution.

Minnie Lingreen, who signed her first contract at the college in 1939, taught for 32 years at both Centralia High School and the college.

"As young men went off to war (World War II), classes became smaller," said Lingreen in an interview in 1989. "As the war ended and the veterans returned (to take advantage of the G.I. Bill) and enrolled at the college, the faculty also grew."

In 1945 the state established junior colleges as part of the state educational system and paid a total of $75 per student. The college expanded in 1950 and moved into its own building, Kemp Hall, named for Katharine Kemp, a foreign language instructor for 36 years. In 1958 Ehret Hall, named for Art Ehret, chemistry instructor and registrar, was added. A student union building came in 1963. In 1990 a classroom building was named in recognition of Minnie Lingreen. The Kirk Library Building, named for former college president Dr. Henry Kirk; the technical arts building and a new version of Corbet Theater (named for Margaret Corbet, the first college dean who served from 1925 to 1947) were built in the 1990s and early 2000s.

Centralia College has enabled hometown youth to obtain college degrees and advance to substantial careers that reach far beyond the boundaries of Lewis County. The college has responded to layoffs and economic changes by offering programs to retrain workers. It has brought performing arts and culture to a rural setting. Its campus and classes have come to symbolize hope and a doorway to the world for Lewis County residents.

The face of health care has changed a great deal from the time when the Sisters of Providence helped to create the first hospital, and a handful of country doctors made house calls. Two modern hospitals, Providence Centralia Hospital and Morton General Hospital, serve residents, while at least 50 medical doctors and about 18 offices list their services either as clinics for general patient visits or for specialties such as urology, radiology, and MRIs. Police, firefighters, and aid units are quick to respond, even in the most remote parts of the county.

Sisters of Providence financed their charitable works through "begging tours" by boat, stagecoach or horseback. Photo courtesy of Sisters of Providence archives.

When the Northwest's first licensed aviator, Clyde Berlin, flew over brand new buildings in Centralia in 1912 to christen them from his amazing "flying machine," he signaled the new era of air travel. Within a decade a turf airstrip, known as Donahoe Field, was built between the towns of Centralia and Chehalis, and in 1928 Centralia had its own airport dedication, too—on a 48-acre field near Borst Park. In 1941 Chehalis was joined by Lewis County in forming the County-City Airport. World War II brought increased air traffic, and in 1943 the federal government completed construction of the airport runway. Ten thousand spectators came to see a Boeing B-17 bomber at the expanded airport in 1944. The U.S. Navy operated the airport as a training facility and an emergency landing area during the war but returned it to local jurisdiction in 1945.

Land acquisition expanded the airport to 325 acres, some of which has been leased to Wal-Mart Stores, Inc., and other retail stores and developers.

The hangar at Donahoe Field, Chehalis was on land originally owned by Francis Donahoe, pioneer businessman.

Fords Prairie Grange exhibit at the Southwest Washington Fair, circa 1928. Granges have long been a unifying force for rural communities.

Life in any culture is reflected through its celebrations. One of the oldest festivities in the state is the Southwest Washington Fair, dating back to 1877 when a group met to advance the agricultural needs of the county. The Lewis County Agricultural Board was formed in 1882 and included the familiar names of H. Davis, (Claquato), L.A. Davis (Eastern Lewis County), William Urquhart, and John Dobson (both from Chehalis) as signers. The first recorded fair was known to have been in 1891, but when a group of citizens met in 1908, the fair became official. Land was purchased midway between Centralia and Chehalis, and with state funding, the first official Southwest Washington Fair was held in 1909. There were lapses in the fair's history, though; it was discontinued during the Depression and opened again after the Works Progress Administration (WPA) reconstructed some buildings. It closed at the outbreak of World War II, and started again after the war was over. Since then, the tradition of the fair has been ingrained into generations of families in Southwest Washington.

The rich timber history of Lewis County comes to the forefront each year in Morton with the Loggers Jubilee. It all began with climbing competition on a limbed tree on the outskirts of town in the late 1930s. In following years other events were added, such as bucking logs with a "misery whip" (cross-cut saw). One event was based on the railroad tie industry when men transferred a load of ties from one flatbed truck to another. Ax throwing, choker setting,

Competitors at the Morton Loggers Jubilee, circa 1968.

log rolling, and power sawing are just a sampling of the events that have drawn competitors and crowds of spectators to the scenic Lewis County town and the Loggers Jubilee.

Life is punctuated by memorable events, especially those involving natural disasters. The land of Lewis was shaken considerably by the earthquake of 1949 which caused one death and considerable damage. Although the impact of the Nisqually earthquake of 2001 was minimal, it alerted many residents to potential hazards. Floods have been an ongoing issue throughout the years, but perhaps the most damaging one occurred in 1996 when hundreds of homes were flooded and Interstate 5 closed for three days. And no one who lived in the Northwest in 1980 will forget the blast of Mt. St. Helens which took the lives of 58 people near the mountain on May 18, 1980. Local residents were blanketed by a blizzard of falling gray ash in a subsequent eruption on May 25, 1980.

Throughout its history the development of Lewis County has been linked to transportation. From the days of Indian trails to nearly impassable muddy roads to the steamboat era, the movement of people and goods has been a major issue. The trials and tribulations the settlers endured in their efforts to get roads were culminated when I-5 was completed through Lewis County in 1958. Those who witnessed the impact of the railroads opening up the land for development would view with bittersweet nostalgia the expansion in transportation from trains to thousands of huge trucks roaring along I-5.

Ash from the eruption of Mt. St. Helens disrupted life of Washington residents for weeks.

Interstate 5 from the 13th Street overpass, 1958. Green Hill School is in the upper right.

May Randle of Randle and Katherine Mauermann of Pe Ell, spent years of relative isolation in the wilderness. In the era of updated highways, they could have zipped into Chehalis, Olympia, or even Portland or Seattle, for a day's shopping to return to their comfortable, modern homes by evening.

Centralia's founding father George Washington named his little town Centerville knowing that it would be "the hub," when the railroad came through in the 1870s. Little did he know that major retailers would grasp that very concept when they chose Lewis County as their distribution centers between Portland and Seattle.

The cultural and geographical isolation of Eastern Lewis County ended when Highway 12 across White Pass opened in 1951. Moreover, the new highway was an avenue for delivering millions of board feet of finished wood products to markets in Eastern Washington. It opened up ski areas at White Pass and infinite recreational possibilities for tourism during the summer months. Local people were delighted to get Yakima's fresh produce nearly the same day it was picked. In later years the highway has provided accessibility for those who choose to live a rural life style and commute to jobs elsewhere. And throughout Lewis County, those who live in unincorporated areas now have the luxury of 1,000 miles of well-maintained, paved roads.

Anticipating the need to keep their young people in the community and sustain the economy, a group of far-sighted individuals have worked doggedly to create industrial parks and port districts since the 1950s. Based on a community development study by the University of

Randle's main street, 1915, was the future path of Highway 12.

Washington in 1954, the Chehalis Industrial Commission rallied the community to create a railroad spur to the new Chehalis Industrial Park near Bishop Road south of the city. The volunteer labor of the amateur "gandy-dancers" (railroad laborers) in the 1950s has enticed dozens of industries to locate in the park. The Lewis County Economic Development Council, formed in

Volunteer "gandy-dancers" building the rail line to the new industrial park south of Chehalis, 1958.

1983, continues its search to draw in new industry throughout the county.

The Industrial Port Commissions of both Centralia and Chehalis are attune to the theme of diversification as they work hand-in-hand with other entities to bring new industries to the area. Their goal: family wage jobs.

Exhibiting a trend toward services and retail trade, in 1988 Centralia experienced a historic event with the establishment of the first factory outlet store. Some fifty factory outlet stores draw in a steady stream of shoppers and freeway travelers from Canada, Oregon, and other areas. Centralia's downtown businesses have captured a market from the past with dozens of attractive antique stores and the preserved Olympic Club and Hotel, alive again from the colorful days of railroading and lumber mills when it was a "gentleman's club."

Meanwhile Chehalis has maintained its small-town charm. It has become the town of museums with the Veterans Memorial Museum, the Lewis County Historical Museum, the Frank Mason Motorcycle Museum and the home of the steam train rides each summer.

While new businesses revitalize the economy, the stability of several established firms continue their ethic of service to the community. Security State Bank, dating back to 1903 with a long connection to the Alexander family, is the only community-owned bank in the area. John W. Alexander, Sr. became its president in 1910 after working at

Interior of Security State Bank, 1913.

Coffman-Dobson Bank, the first financial institution in the area. John W. Alexander Jr. became president in 1972 and Chairman of the Board in 2001.

In the business of information, *The Chronicle* continues to be a major source of news for some 15,000 subscribers since its predecessor, the county's first newspaper, the *Centralia News,* appeared in 1885. The

The (then) Daily Chronicle press room, in 1941. Predecessors of the newspaper date back to 1885.

The Land Called Lewis

Washington Governor Mon C. Wallgren and Vice-President Harry Truman at KELA, Centralia, 1944.

and society's use, and forests that enhance our quality of life by offering recreation to an urban society. While timber is no longer king, it maintains a steady influence with some mills and harvest from private and public timberlands.

As Lewis County moves through its second century, its leaders and citizens define—and defend—their historical values. Traditionally a conservative area, Lewis County is in the grip of urban growth which brings about changes in the uses of the land and concerns about environmental impact.

The original land claims offered settlers independence from their neighbors and the freedom to develop their land.

radio station KELA AM 1470 first hit the air waves in 1937, and a second radio station, KITI AM 1420, came on board in 1950.

The wood products industry, which dominated the economy for a century, has faced peaks and valleys impacted by both economic and environmental factors. The issue of timber resources continues to be a sensitive one. Forest land is viewed in three ways: old-growth forests which must be preserved as a link to our natural heritage, forests that are strictly for harvest

Jim McCash, Tony Duckwitz and Billy Duckwitz felling a tree for the Mutual Lumber Company, Bucoda, 1907.

The individualistic spirit of the past is threatened by population growth and regulation.

Farms and timberlands were once the focus of the local economy and workforce. Now the economy is more focused on businesses near the I-5 corridor. Residential developments replace family farms and crop up in previously unpopulated areas.

Resources such as timber, coal, and salmon, were once in such awe-inspiring abundance that they could be harvested without end. Those very resources that drew people at first now face depletion.

In the face of urbanization, maintaining the character and personality of local communities is critical. Understanding and even capitalizing on the past is the key to planning for the future.

Through the challenges of change, the legacy of The Land Called Lewis is solid. It should be viewed with pride, for it is so recent, so tangible that we can still touch it.

The vision of the pioneers will remain. We owe our heritage to those who have gone before.

Pioneer Picnic, Borst Park, Centralia, 1935.

Chapter 21

Rotogravure

The photographs in this book have been lovingly restored with computer technology and hundreds of hours of detailed work to repair damage and eliminate defects in the originals. This chapter contains photographs that didn't fit the text, but couldn't be left out…

Original and restored image of the Farmer's Exchange on Main Street in Centralia, 1889.

Rotogravure

Napavine School May Day celebration, 1918.

Napavine School girl's baseball team, 1918. Back row: Pauline Morton, center field; Cecil Meyers, third base; Ellen Johnson, manager & pitcher; Vivian Breloer, left field; Doris Kohl, second base & captain. Front row: Paula Olsen, catcher; Erma Moore, right field, Dorothy Dickinson, shortstop; Evelyn Balestra, first base.

The Dryad High School basketball team, 1923.

The Land Called Lewis

The Pe Ell town band and others on the way to the Polish Cemetery. The priest's house is visible at right, 1906.

Chehalis Fire Department horses, Deg and Prince, held by Clyde Truett in front of the Chehalis Fire Department. The doorway of the Brunswig Opera House is in the background, 1910.

McKinley "Red Crown" Service at N.E. corner of Tower and Main, 1925, later a home appliance business.

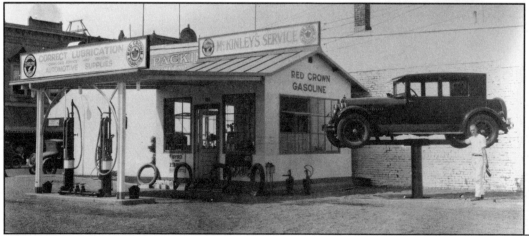

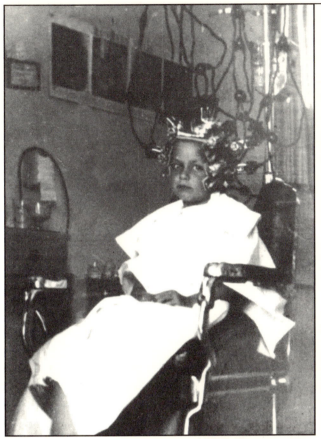
Receiving a permanent wave, circa 1940.

"Miss Ella Field, 107 N. Tower, HATS to $5.00"

Motorcyclists, near Centralia, Dec 25, 1914.

Clara and Oren Armstrong on the right, with friends in 1905.

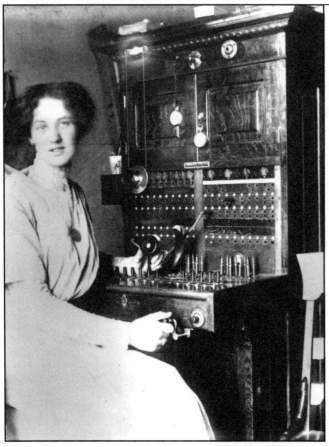

The first local telephone exchange in operation, circa 1905.

Indian Saunders and wife, residents of the land that was once the Smith Donation Land Claim.

The dance hall at Claquato, circa 1970.

Rotogravure

Workers begin tearing down the left part of the St. Helen Hotel to make way for the new brick structure, circa 1912.

The first stage of the brick St. Helens Hotel, 1916. Later the building was extended to replace the original hotel on the right and two additional stories were added.

The completed new hotel served as a resting place for tens of thousands of travelers between Seattle and Portland on "old" Highway 99.

Levi Adrian Davis farm, Claquato, 1894.

Paving St. Helens Avenue with concrete, Chehalis, 1911.

4th grade, Lincoln School, Centralia, 1942.

Rotogravure

The Ellsbury survey crew moving their camp west from Centralia towards Grays Harbor, 1887. See page 51.

The Pe Ell School wagon in Walville.

Grace Seminary, later Centralia General Hospital, lives on in the name of Seminary Hill and Seminary Hill Road.

Toledo High School graduating class, 1900.

China Creek flooding Main Street, Centralia, 1933.

"Grace Bechly, wife of Ernst Bechly."

An evening of reading. The Armstrong family, 1905.

Local taxi operated by George Kepper and Joe Aust, Chehalis, 1940s.

Loading logs on the North Fork of the Newaukum for Robert M. Shaver's Shingle & Sawmill, 1920.

A student pilot at Donahoe Field stands by his 1926 coupe, 1928.

Southwest Washington Fairgrounds carnival, 1936.

Rotogravure

John Rice, owner of The Dream Theater, Chehalis, later The Ben Franklin Store, later an indoor mall. The theater is showing "House of 1,000 Candles," released in 1915.

Night lights in Centralia, 1940.

Time Line — The Land Called Lewis

Pre-recorded history: Native Americans live on the land for perhaps 10,000 years

1700s
1700s Britain, United States, Spain, and Russia vie for rights to the Northwest
1792 Robert Gray discovers the Columbia River and establishes U.S. claim

1800s
1803 Louisiana Purchase
1804-06 Lewis and Clark Expedition notes the Cowlitz River
1811 American John Jacob Astor establishes Astoria as a fur-trading post
1818-20 Simon Plamondon, French Canadian trapper, explores region, marries daughter of Chief Scanewa of Cowlitz Tribe
1818 U.S.-Great Britain agree on joint occupation of Oregon region (includes present state of Washington)

**1818-1846
British era**
1820-40s British-owned Hudson's Bay Company develops fur trade north of the Columbia River
- Fort Vancouver established 1825, Fort Nisqually 1833
- Fur Brigades travel into present Lewis County
- Trade established with Chehalis, Cowlitz, and Nisqually tribes
- Indian trails and rivers are major routes
- French Canadians settle on prairies
- British discourage American settlement north of Columbia River

1820s Simon Plamondon becomes first permanent white settler north of the Columbia River in the land called Lewis

1829-30 Influenza strikes Native American population
1829-30 "Intermittent flu" kills nearly 90% of the Native Americans in the Northwest and leaves many villages empty
1838 Hudson's Bay Company establishes Puget Sound Agricultural Company, demonstrating that the region contains productive farmland
1838 Black Robes (Catholic priests) arrive to establish first church north of the Columbia River at Cowlitz Landing
1841 Exploration of Northwest by American Lt. Charles Wilkes includes the Cowlitz settlement

1845 Lewis County formed; extends to Sitka, Alaska, and includes most of British Columbia
1845 John R. Jackson becomes the first American land owner north of the Columbia River
1846 Lewis County for six months is not a part of the U.S.; Britain and the U.S. still dispute ownership of the Northwest
1846 Sidney Ford party and Joseph Borst establish claims

**1846-53
Government established**
1846 Britain and U.S. sign Oregon Treaty establishing international boundary at 49 degrees north latitude; Lewis County is officially in the U.S. but in Oregon Country
1848 Oregon Country becomes the Oregon Territory; settlers from Lewis County serve in the legislature in Salem, Oregon
1850 Over 1,000 white setters live north of the Columbia River
1850 Donation Land Claim Act allows claims of 320 acres per single man, 640 per married couple in Oregon Territory
1851 Cowlitz Convention at Cowlitz Landing, Lewis County, argues for separation from Oregon Territory; ignored by U.S. Congress

**1830s-1860s
Oregon Trail era**
1852 Monticello Convention at Longview petitions Congress for separation from Oregon Territory as "Columbia Territory"; Congress approves "Washington Territory" to avoid confusion
1853 Washington Territory established; Gov. Isaac Stevens negotiates Medicine Creek Treaty with western Washington Indian tribes
1855-56 Indian War in time of unrest; settlers live in forts and blockhouses during perceived threat; most fighting occurs east of Cascade Mts.

Time Line — The Land Called Lewis

	1857 Skookumchuck post office established at future site of Centralia
	1858 Post office established in Saundersville (later Chehalis)
	1862 Claquato becomes Lewis County seat; parts of Military Road completed
	1861-65 Civil War; few settlers arrive.
	1864-1917 Steamboat era on the Cowlitz River for 50 years until World War I when motor vehicles are preferred for transport
1871 Railroad era begins	1871-73 Northern Pacific Railroad constructs first stretch of northern route of transcontinental railroad from Kalama to Tacoma. Through Lewis County, towns grow along the railroad tracks
	1873 Napavine establishes its post office
	1874 County seat moved to Saundersville
	1875 Centerville platted by George Washington, African-American settler
	1879 Saundersville name officially changed to Chehalis
	1880-91 Settlement of Eastern Lewis County; numerous post offices established from Mossyrock east to Packwood
	1883 Centerville name changed to Centralia
	1883 Winlock becomes the first incorporated city in Lewis County.
	1889 Washington becomes a state
1880-1929 Lumber mill era coincides with railroad boom years	1892 Fires in Chehalis destroy buildings belonging to Eliza Barrett, "founding mother" and business woman; businesses relocated to Market Street
	1893 Severe depression grips U.S.; many people leave Lewis County
	1893 Floyd Riffe brings 18 families by train from West Virginia and Kentucky to settle in Eastern Lewis County
	1890-1920s Roads improved in towns from wood plank streets to brick to paved streets; increasing use of motor vehicles
	1891 Washington State Reform School, the first in the state, opens on a "Green Hill" in Chehalis
	1903 President Theodore Roosevelt gives a stump speech in Chehalis
	1907-14 Coal mines lead to the creation of towns of Kopiah, Mendota, and Tono, north of Centralia
	1917-18 World War I; Lewis County citizens, "doughboys," serve in the European war theater
	1919 Centralia Tragedy results from confrontation between Industrial Workers of the World and WW I veterans; five die
1920-60s Small farm agriculture era	1919-33 Prohibition of alcohol leads to era of moonshiners and bootleggers as stills flourish in the backwoods of Lewis County
	1925 Centralia Junior College is established
	1927 Dedication of Paul Donahoe Aviation Field between Centralia and Chehalis; Centralia Airport dedicated a year later
	1929-40 The Great Depression era leads to failures of major lumber mills and banks; agriculture sustains local residents
	1941-45 World War II era; Boeing establishes a plant in Chehalis for production of airplane parts
	1954-60s Interstate 5 opens through Lewis County as part of nation-wide freeway construction during the Eisenhower administration
	1967 Opening of steam plant and coal mine in Hanaford Valley, Centralia
	1969 Dedication of Mossyrock Dam
1990s Retail and manufacturing era	1980 Mt. St. Helens volcano erupts
	1990s Shift in economy from agriculture and timber industries to retail, product distribution and manufacturing
	2006 TransAlta closes the Centralia coal mine

- compiled by George "Finn" Nikula

Sandra A. Crowell, author.

About the Author:

Writing has been a major part of Sandra Crowell's life. Wherever she has lived—from her growing-up years on a ranch high in the Colorado Rocky Mountains, to an island in Alaska, or the bottom of a canyon in North Idaho—she has combined writing with an acute sense of place. She is the author of newspaper articles, newsletters, brochures, and grants. In 1980 she and co-author David Asleson produced a pictorial history of the St. Joe River in North Idaho, *Up the Swiftwater*, which has become a classic in that area and remains in print. While she was living and working in Lewis County, Washington, she had an opportunity to write this history. Although the project was shelved for a decade, the essence of the book remains true to her original vision. During her career, Crowell has been an adult educator and manager. She lives with her husband in the country near Olympia, Washington.

John Panesko, publisher.
As a lifetime resident, attorney, politician and later radio talk show host, John recruited the group to produce a book of the history of Lewis County. He selected and restored the photographs, inserted them in the text, assembled the book and financed the publication. "My grandfather was one of those hearty pioneers who homesteaded here in the 1800s. It is a privilege to finally tell their story in such a wonderful book."

Edna Fund, historian.
Active in the community on many projects, Edna was the lead researcher for the book. She found dozens of stories, information and photos hidden in local archives. Additionally she tracked down rare photographs to supplement those of the museum. Her constant optimism and encouragement helped the group get through long hours of editorial meetings. "I was so glad to be part of the recognition of the pioneers whose story has yet to be told. Now, here it is!"

John Martin, editor.
As former managing editor of *The Chronicle* John brought his extensive knowledge of local history to this project, helping sort the truth from the rumors. John's professional eye for the language usage and punctuation is evident on every page, helping to make the text a pleasure to read. "I've always wanted a comprehensive book of Lewis County history, so I jumped at the chance to help make it happen. "

The Lewis County Historical Museum, resources.

Over the decades, dedicated members of the Lewis County Historical Society and volunteers at the museum have archived the valuable history included in this book. This and other history books are available at the museum in Chehalis or online at: LewisCountyMuseum.org.

Acknowledgments by the author, Sandra A. Crowell

The manuscript for this book was an unfinished dream lying in a box of outdated computer disks, and then one day it came back to life. Its final publication would not have been possible without the tireless dedication of John Panesko, publisher and producer, who spent thousands of hours reconstructing a work written a decade before and bringing it to life with carefully chosen photographs. Nor would it have been accomplished without John Martin whose editing made it a polished product and Edna Fund, enthusiastic researcher who verified hundreds of facts. Many others have shared their knowledge and support: Rose Bowman, Craig Nelson, Cheryl Murray, and Lee Coumbs who initiated the original project; Judith Irving and Dr. James Vosper who wrote specific sections of the original text; and LaVonne Sparkman who gave permission to quote her works from East Lewis County. Dozens of people were interviewed for the book, many of whom may not be mentioned here but who were greatly appreciated nonetheless. The partial list includes Harold Borovec, Marjorie Aldrich, Margaret McIntire, Jeannette Ward, "Bud" Panco, Bert Woodland, descendants of Simon Plamondon, Peter Lahmann, Vic Kucera, Bob O'Neill, Bob Thompson, Finley Hays, Roy Wilson, and the DeGoede family. Thanks to Karen Johnson for editing, Brett Shackleford and Centralia College for technical assistance, and to my husband, George "Finn" Nikula for his continual patience and support. For the rich historical information and photographs, the Lewis County Historical Museum opened its files to a wealth of information, thanks to the support of Debbie Knapp, director, and enhanced by the extensive knowledge of "the Margarets," Margaret Shields and Margaret Langus. Most of all, thank you to all the people whose wonderful stories make this history come alive.

Selected Bibliography

Books

Adams, Kramer A. *Logging Railroads of the West.* Seattle: Superior Publishing Company, 1961.

Asay, Jeff. *Union Pacific Northwest.* Edmonds, WA: Pacific Fast Mail, 1998.

Barkan, Frances. *The Wilkes Expedition: Puget Sound and the Oregon Country.* Olympia, WA: Washington State Capital Museum, 1987.

Chaplin, Ralph. *The Centralia Case: Three Views of the Armistice Day Tragedy at Centralia, November 11, 1919.* New York: Da Capo Press, 1971.

Crowell, Sandra A. and David O. Asleson. *Up the Swiftwater.* Coeur d'Alene, ID: Museum of North Idaho, 1995.

Galvin, Wayne. *The Timber Baron of Winlock.* Chehalis, WA: Lewis County Historical Society, 2002.

Graves, Ray. *A History of Pe Ell, Washington and the Upper Chehalis Valley.* Rochester, WA: Gorham Printing, 2006.

Gullick, Bill. *Traveler's History of Washington.* Caldwell, ID: The Caxton Printers, 1996.

Hannon, Trudy R. *John R. Jackson: Washington's First American Pioneer*, Chehalis, WA: Advocate Printing, 1998.

Hays, Finley. *Finley's Rigging Shack.* Chehalis, WA: Rigging Shack, 1996.

Hendrickson, Peter; Jane Long, Veronica Livingston, ed. *Centralia, City at the Center: a Textbook of Local History for Centralia Third Grades.* Centralia, WA: Centralia School District, 1986.

Kirk, Ruth and Carmela Alexander. *Exploring Washington's Past: A Road Guide to History.* Seattle and London: University of Washington Press, 1995.

Lampman, Ben Hur. *Centralia: Tragedy and Trial.* Seattle: Shorey Book Store, 1985.

Lavender, David. *Land of Giants: The Drive to the Pacific Northwest 1750-1950.* Lincoln and London: University of Nebraska Press, 1958.

Lingreen, Minnie & Tiller, Priscilla. *Hop Cultivation in Lewis County, Washington, 1888 to 1940.* Centralia, WA: Washington State Commission for the Humanities, 1981.

Mackie, Robert Somerset. *Trading Beyond the Mountains: the British Fur Trade on the Pacific, 1793-1843.* Vancouver, B.C.: UBC Press, 1997.

Markam, John. *Seventy-five Years in Northwest Forests.* Chehalis, WA: Loggers World Publications, 1977.

McCelland, John, Jr. *Wobbly War.* Tacoma: Washington State Historical Society, 1987.

Mumford, Ester Hall. *The Man Who Founded a Town.* Seattle: Ananse Press, 1990.

Nix, Alma and John, ed. *The History of Lewis County, Washington.* Chehalis, WA: Lewis County Historical Society, 1985.

Nix, Alma and John, ed. *The History of Lewis County, Washington, Volume II.* Chehalis, WA: Lewis County Historical Society, 1987.

Our Hometowns: A Historical Photo Album of Greater Lewis County. Centralia, WA: *The Chronicle*: Vol. 1, 2003.

Our Hometowns: A Historical Photo Album of Greater Lewis County. Centralia, WA: *The Chronicle*: Vol. 2, 2005.

Phillips, James W. *Washington State Place Names.* Seattle and London: University of Washington Press, 1980.

Riegel, Robert Edgar. *The Story of the Western Railroads from 1852 through the Reign of the Giants.* Lincoln and London: University of Nebraska Press, 1970.

Ramsey, Guy Reed. *Postmarked Washington: Lewis and Cowlitz Counties.* Chehalis, WA: Lewis County Historical Society, 1978.

Schwantes, Carlos Arnaldo. *Long Day's Journey: The Steamboat & Stagecoach Era in the Northern West.* Seattle and London: University of Washington Press, 1999.

Smith, Herndon, compiled by. *Centralia: The First Fifty Years, 1845-1900.* Centralia, WA: Centralia American Revolution Bicentennial Committee, 1995.

Smith, Walker C., *Was It Murder?* Seattle, Shorey Book Store, 1966.

Speidel, Bill. *The Wet Side of the Mountains (or Prowling Western Washington).* Seattle: Nettle Creek Publishing Co., 1981.

Sparkman, Lavonne M. *Before It's Gone—Old Timer's Tales.* Rochester, WA: Sparkman Publications, 1998.

Sparkman, Lavonne M. *From Homestead to Lakebed, Kosmos: The Town That Drowned.* Bend, OR: Maverick Publications, 1994.

Sparkman, Lavonne M. *The Trees were so Thick There was Nowhere to Look But Up!* Bend, OR: Maverick Publications, 1989.

Sparkman, Lavonne M. *Where the Big Bottom Begins: A Randle History.* Rochester, WA: Sparkman Publishing Company, 1995.

Telewki, Frank W., Scott D. Barrett. *Logging Railroads of Weyerhaeuser's Vail-McDonald Operation.* Hamilton, MT: Oso Publishing Co, 1955.

Toledo History Committee. *The Toledo Community Story 1776-1976.* Toledo, WA: The Toledo Parent-Teacher Organization, 1976.

Wilson, Roy I. *Cheholtz and Mary Kiona of the Cowlitz.* Lima, OH; Express Press, 2001.

Wilson, Roy I. *The History of the Cowlitz Tribe.* Published by the author, 2006.

Wilson, Roy I. *Legends of the Cowlitz Indian Tribe.* Bremerton, WA: Cowlitz Indian Tribe, 1998.

Wood, Charles. *Lines West.* Seattle: Superior Publishing Company: 1967.

Wood, Charles. *Northern Pacific.* Seattle: Superior Publishing Company, 1968.

Zander, Julie McDonald. *Life on the Homefront: Stories of Those who Worked, Waited, and Worried during WWII.* Toledo, WA: Chapters of Life Memory Books, 2005.

Zander, Julie McDonald. *Legacy of Two Lumbermen: The Hemphill-O'Neill Company History.* Toledo, WA: Chapters of Life Memory Books, 2006.

Files, Collections, Letters

For topical information, see collected files at the Lewis County Historical Museum, Washington State Archives, Southwest Region and Timberland Regional Library system, including branch local history collections.

Files from private industry: C.A. Callison Company; Tacoma City Light; National Frozen Foods; Weyerhaeuser Company; WIDCO and TransAlta.

Kletsch, Albert G. "Steamboat on the Cowlitz." Series of articles *The Daily Chronicle*, 1968.

Plamondon family collection.

Newspapers

For specific topical information, see collected files at the Lewis County Historical Museum and the Centralia Timberland Library.

Pamphlets, Brochures

Hanson, Linda, comp. *History and Favorite Recipes of Onalaskans.* Second Printing, 1997.

Kangas, Jill. *Railroad Depot to Museum: A Community Project Through Time.* Chehalis: Lewis County Historical Society, 1981.

Marr, Carolyn, Donna Hicks, and Kay Francis. *The Chehalis People.* Oakville, WA: Confederated Tribes of the Chehalis Reservation, 1989.

McClelland, John M., Jr. *Cowlitz Corridor: Historical River Highway of the Pacific Northwest.* Longview, Washington: Longview Publishing Co., 1953 and 1984.

Miles, Charles. *Letters and History of Lewis County. History of Claquato Landmarks.* Circa 1960s.

Washington Centennial Association, *1845-1945: A Commemorative Booklet.* Olympia, WA: State Department of Conservation and Development, 1945.

Unpublished documents

Aldrich, Marjorie. "Mossyrock Memories," 1976.

Bemisdarfer, Kathy. "History of Riffe and Riffe Family," undated.

Browne, Betsy. "History of Winlock, Washington," 1974.

Crowell, Sandra A., ed. "Looking Back," Centralia College: 1994.

Evans, Eugene. "History of Napavine," 1933. Additional material added by Reba Milam in 1953. "Cutting Family," undated.

Hale, Janet A. "Winlock, Washington Territory," History Thesis Linfield College, McMinnville, OR: 1948.

MacDonald, J. W. "Napavine," circa 1900-1910.

Miles, Charles. "Claquato Roads in the Stage Days," (undated) circa 1938.

Randt, Tenna Smith. "Bits of Winlock History," circa 1931.

"Remembrances and Recipes: Onalaska PTO Cook Book," Compiled by the Onalaska Parent-Teacher Organization. Onalaska; Onalaska High School Graphic Arts Department, 1975.

Wall, C.C. "A History of Winlock, Washington," 1952.

Index

A

Adna, 80
African-Americans, 152
Agnew, S.A., Lumber Co., 105
Agnew, Sam, 105
Ahlstrand, August, 101
Ahlstrand, Emil, 88
Ainslie Lumber Co., 151
Ainslie, David, 107
Alder school, 30
Aldrich, Neal, 136
Alexander, John T., 57
Alexander, John W., 177
Alpha, 85, 115
Annonen, Sylvia, 138
Armistice Day Parade, 120

B

Barnett, Eugene, 122
Barrett, Eliza, 57, 72-74
Barrett, John, 73
Barszchowski, Rev. F., 155
Baw Faw Peak, 25
Bear Canyon, 86
Becker, Ray, 122, 123
Bercier, Emilie Fenlay, 13
Berlin, Clyde, 173
Berry Prairie, 134
Big Bottom Country, 59, 84, 85
Black Prince Mine, 126
Black Robes, 14
Black settlers, 152
Blanchet, Rev. Francis, 14
Bland, Bert, 122
Bland, O.C., 122
Blankenship, Thomas, 85
Blaser, 153
Boeing Aircraft Co., 165, 166
Boistfort, 25, 26
Boistfort Valley, 143
Bootleggers, 162, 163
Borden Milk Co., 118, 139, 140
Borovec, Harold, 67
Borst blockhouse, 34
Borst home, 22
Borst, Joseph, 22, 23, 34
Borst, Mary A., 22, 23
Bremer, 85, 140
Bremgartner, 153
Breuse, Peter, 81
Bristol's Grocery, 167
Brown Brothers Lumber Co., 102
Brown's Coal Creek Lumber Co., 107
Brun, M.W., 137

Bucey, Henry, 35
Burlington Northern Railroad, 69
Bush, George, 19
Busie, Henry, 27, 35

C

Callison, I.P., 139
Carlisle Lake, 116
Carlisle, William, 115
Carlisle, William A., 115
Carlisle-Pennell Lumber Co., 116-118
Carlson, Johann, 101
Carnation Milk Co., 118, 141
Carnegie Library, 76
Casagranda, Ben, 120
Cascara, 139
Centerville, 27, 28, 29, 55
Centralia, 27-29, 56, 65, 74-76, 119-122, 168, 169
Centralia Airport, 173
Centralia College, 172
Centralia High School, 172
Centralia Millwork & Supply Co., 103
Centralia Providence Hospital, 173
Centralia schoolhouse, 170
Centralia Steam-Electric Plant, 124, 131
Centralia Train Station, 56
Ceres, 144
Champion Logging Co., 113
Charles, Pierre, 25, 26
Cheese Day, 142
Chehalis, 30, 57, 62, 65, 70-72, 74, 117, 139, 165
Chehalis Airport, 161
Chehalis Coal Co., 126
Chehalis Cooperative Creamery, 141
Chehalis Furniture & Manufacturing Co., 102
Chehalis Indian Reservation, 36
Chehalis Industrial Commission, 176
Chehalis River, 2, 22, 28, 45, 100
Chehalis River, frozen, 121
Chehalis Tribe, 2-4, 7, 19, 28, 42, 92
Chehalis Western Railroad, 63
Chehalis-Centralia Railroad Assn., 67
Chickens, 137
Chief Scanewa, 6, 8, 9, 13, 24, 149
Chilcoat family, 88
China Creek, 53
Chronicle, The, 177
Cinebar, 85, 129
Cispus, 161
Citizens Unemployment League, 158
Civil Defense, 164
Civilian Conservation Corps, 161, 162
Claquato, 35, 42-45, 57, 71, 83
Claquato Church, 21
Claquato Courthouse, 21
Clark, Regina R., 168
Clark, William, 10

Clevinger, 90
Climax locomotive, 97
Coal Creek, 126, 128
Cochran, James, 27
Cochran's Landing, 28
Coffman, N.B., 157
Coffman, N.B. & Margaret, 71
Cole Sick, 13
Colored Church, 152
Columbia River, 1, 10, 11
Columbia Territory, 41
Columbia, ship, 10
Cooness, Mary Jane, 29
Cora, 85
Corbet, Margaret, 172
Cowlitz Convention, 24, 41
Cowlitz Falls Project, 149
Cowlitz Farm, 16, 17, 18
Cowlitz Landing, 16, 31, 41, 42, 46, 47, 82
Cowlitz Prairie, 12, 16, 92, 132
Cowlitz Produce, Co., 138
Cowlitz River, 2, 10-12, 15, 42, 43, 45-49, 84, 85, 89, 100, 132, 146, 149
Cowlitz River Milling Co., 81
Cowlitz Trail, 45
Cowlitz Tribe, 2-7, 9, 11, 19, 35, 36, 42, 84, 92, 133
Cowlitz Valley Cheese Assn., 142
Cowlitz, Chehalis & Cascade Railroad, 65-67, 117
Crescent Coal Company, 127
Crown, Bertha, 128
Cutting Family, 24
Cutting, John, 25
Cutting, Otis Plant, 25

D

Dairies, 140
Darigold Co., 141
Darigold Creamery, 140
Davis, Levi Adrian, 86
Davis, Lewis Hawkins, 21, 35, 45, 134
Davisson Lake, 148
Dawes, Vice-Pres. Charles, 123
Deggeller, Sheriff Edward, 163
DeGoede Bulb Farm, 136
DeGoede, Henry, 136
Demers, Rev. Medeste, 14
Depression, Great, 158-161
Dobyns, Lloyd, 142
Doernbecher, F.E., 107
Donahoe Field, 161, 173
Donation Land Claim Act, 30, 31, 38
Doss, Dode, 90
Doty, 111, 162
Doty Lumber & Shingle Co., 63
Doty, C.A., 111
Dryad, 62, 111

E

Eadonia, 81
Eastern Railway & Lumber Co., 104, 105
Eastman, Arthur, 169
Egbert, Gordon, 139
Egg Day, 138, 139
Eggs, 137-139
Ehret, Art, 172
Ellsbury survey crew, 51
Emery & Nelson Lumber Co., 67, 106, 164
England, J.H., 108
Ethel, 87
Evaline, 163, 170
Everest, Wesley, 121-123
Ewald, Mark, 135

F

Fair, Southwest Wash., 65, 174, 190
Far West Homes, 105
Farmer's & Merchant's Picnic, 134
Farmers and Merchants Picnic, 142
Faulkner, Bert, 123
Faver, 153
Fern Hill Cemetery, 20
Ferry, 85
Finnish Lutheran Church, 151
Finnish settlers, 150
Foch, Gen. Ferdinand, 123
Ford, Helen, 23
Ford, Sidney S., 23, 24, 32, 34, 40, 133
Ford, Tom, 24
Ford's Prairie, 133
Florence Mine, 124
Forest schoolhouse, 170
Foron at Fords Prairie Mine, 127
Fort Borst, 34
Fort George, 13
Fort Henness, 33, 34
Fort Nisqually, 16
Fort Steilacoom, 43
Fort Vancouver, 13, 16, 19, 43
Fort Victoria, 39
Fox Theater, 159
Frances, 153
Franchere, Gabriel, 11
Freedom Walk, 168, 169
Frost, Frank, 77
Frosty's Tavern, 68
Fulton, 85
Furrer, 153

G

Galloping Goose, 117
Ghosn Store, 136
Ghosn, G., 136
Gilchrist, Jim, 95
Gilmore, Eva, 128
Gisler, 153
Gleneden, 83
Glenoma, 88
Gorton, U.S. Senator Slade, 168
Graham Land Co., 117
Grand Mound, 33, 34
Grand Mound Fruit Growers Coop., 160
Gray, Captain Robert, 10
Great Depression, 158-161
Greek settlement, 153
Green Hill School, 171
Grimm, Warren, 120
Guerrier's Logging Co., 96

H

Hagle, Bertha, 128
Hanaford Valley, 124, 130
Hangman's Bridge, 121
Harbert, William E., 169
Harding, Pres. Warren, 123
Harmony, 85
Harms, Frank D., 102
Haywood, Big Bill, 120
Helsing Junction, 151
Hemphill-O'Neill Lumber Co., 106, 107
Highton, John, 33
Highway 12, 176
Highway 508, 116
Holman Lumber Co., 106
Hops, 143
Hospitals, 173
Hubbard, Dale, 121
Hubbard, F.B., 104
Huckleberry Mountain, 133
Hudson's Bay Co., 12, 13, 16, 18, 39, 92
Huntting family, 136

I

Imperial Powder Co., 128
Indian War, 32-36
Industrial Workers of the World, 119-123
Influenza, Indians, 13
Interstate 5, 175

J

Jackson Courthouse, 20, 21, 40
Jackson, John R., 19, 20, 40, 43, 44
Jackson, Matilda, 20
Japanese farmers, 154
Japanese mill-workers, 154
Japanese settlers, 153
Jefferson, Thomas, 10
Jewish community, 156
Joerk, William, 88
Jones, Bert E., 127

K

Kalama, 53
Kehoe, John, 133
KELA AM 1470, 178
Kelsey, N.B., 124
Kemp, Katharine, 172
Kiona, Mary, 5, 8, 9, 146
Kirk, Dr. Henry, 172
KITI AM 1420, 178
Klaber farm, 145
Klaber Valley, 143
Klaber, Herman, 143-145
Klickitat Prairie, 144
Kolenen, Nick, 150
Koontz, Matilda, 20
Kopiah, 124, 125, 128
Kosmos, 112, 113, 146, 167
Kosmos Logging Co., 112
Kraft Co., 141
Krebs, John, 133
Ku Klux Klan, 156, 157
Kwalhiokwa, 4

L

Ladd, 129
Lady Washington, ship, 10
Lake Scanewa, 149
Lamb, John, 122
Lang's gold mine, 128
Langus, Margaret, 166
Legionnaires, 121
Leudinghaus Brothers, 111
Lewis and Clark, 11
Lewis County courthouse, 74
Lewis County Historical Museum, 58, 177
Lewis County Map, 37
Lewis County PUD, 149
Lewis, Meriwether, 10, 39
Lewis-Pacific Dairymens' Assn., 141, 142
Liberty Loans, 164
Liberty Theater, 159
Liederkrantz Hall, 127
Limmer, 153
Lincoln Creek, 28
Lincoln Creek Log Co., 98
Lincoln Creek Lumber Co., 105
Lingreen, Minnie, 172
Littell, 101
Little Falls, 80, 81
Logan Hill, 134
Loggers Jubilee, 174
Longhouses, 5
Longmire, James, 84
Longview, Portland & Northern Railway Co., 68
Louisiana Purchase, 10
Lowry, Gov. Mike, 168

Loyal Legion of Loggers and Lumbermen, 118
Lynch, Thomas, 152

M

MacDonald, 24
Mack's Log & Timber Co., 93
Maple Lane School, 171
Marcotte, John, 137, 138
Martalla, Charles, 150
Martin, H.H., Lumber Co., 103
Martins' Mine at Tono, 127
Mason, Frank, Motorcycle Museum, 177
Mauermann family, 26
Mauermann, Katherine, 176
Mayfield, 128, 129, 146, 147
Mayfield Bridge, 147
Mayfield Dam, 66, 146, 147
Mayfield, Henry Clay, 147
McCaffray, William Sr., 135
McCormick, 64, 158
McCormick Lumber Co., 109
McCormick Mill, 110, 111
McCormick, Harry, 110
McElfresh, Arthur, 120
McFadden, Judge Obadiah B., 70
McInerney, James, 122, 123
McKinley Stump, 70
McLoughlin, John, 16, 19
McMahan, Jim, 91
McMahan, May Randle, 90, 91
Medicine Creek Treaty, 32
Meeker, Ezra, 72
Meir, 153
Memorial, War, 168, 169
Mendota, 124, 125, 128
Mendota Coal Mine, 125
Meskill, 61
Metsker, Charles, 77
Mexican-born residents, 157
Meyer, "Rock Creek", 109
Military Road, 42-46, 50
Miller, General Winlock W., 76
Milwaukee Railroad, 60
Mineral, 59, 85, 129
Mineral Lake, 84, 101
Minnetonka, 52, 53
Mint, 139
Mission, St. Francis Xavier, 14, 15, 17
Mission, Whitman, 20
Monarch Mine, 124, 125
Monticello, 46
Monticello Convention, 24, 41
Moonshine, 162, 163, 164
Moorhead, Joseph, 87
Morton, 59, 83-88, 113, 129, 140, 141
Morton General Hospital, 173
Morton Loggers Jubilee, 174
Mossyrock, 27, 89, 128, 135, 160
Mossyrock Dam, 89, 148

Mound Prairie, 33
Mt. St. Helens, 175
Mueller brothers, 109
Mueller, John K., 153
Mulford, Vera, 128
Museum, Lewis Co. Historical, 58
Mutual Lumber Co., 178

N

Nalewaja, Frank, 155
Napavine, 24, 25, 54, 62, 67, 68, 79, 106
National Fruit Canning Co., 135
National Guard, 122
National Polish Catholic Church, 155
Nealy, Jack, 76, 77
New Consolidated Mercury Mining Co., 129
Newaukum, 57
Newaukum Valley Railroad, 67, 68
Nikula, Martha, 150
North West Fur Co., 12, 13
Northern Pacific Railroad, 51-58, 60, 61, 79, 93
Nudd and Taylor, 102

O

O'Connell, M.T., 108
Old Colored Church, 152
Olympia Club, 57
Onalaska, 115, 117, 118, 158
Onalaska Theater, 160
O'Neill, Bob, 107
Oregon Territory, 28, 40, 41
Oregon Trail, 20, 38
Outlet stores, 177
Oxen plowing, 137

P

Pacific Highway, 44
PacifiCorp, 130
Packwood, 42, 161
Packwood, William, 84
Pagett, Dr. C.C., 76
Palmer Lumber Co., 103, 105
Paniczko, Vincent, 155
Payton, Margaret, O., 159
Pe Ell, 25, 26, 61, 62, 64, 109, 111, 155
Pearl Harbor, 164
Pearson Ranch, 144
Peterbilt, 113
Petterman, Al, 113
Pinto, Horace H., 25
Pioneer Picnic, 179
Pistnen, Henry, 150
Pitcher, Hamilton, 67, 106
Plamondon, Simon, 2, 9, 12-16, 35, 37, 39, 40, 84
Plamondon, Simon Jr., 31

Plamondon, Veronica, 13
Plums, 137
Polish Catholic Church, 155
Polish immigrants, 155
Pope and Talbot, 93
Port of Centralia, 177
Port of Chehalis, 177
Poultry, 139
Powell, Dick, 151
Prohibition, 162
Providence, Sisters of, 173
Prunes, 137
Puget Sound Agricultural Co., 14, 16-18, 40, 132

R

Rainier National Forest Reserve, 162
Randle, 42, 45, 88, 133
Randle Bridge, 91
Randle family, 90
Randle, May, 176
Rankin, 115
Riffe, 85, 88, 89, 146
Riffe Baptist Church, 89
Riffe Lake, 112, 148, 149
Riffe, Floyd, 89, 148
Roberts, George, 16-18, 24
Roberts, Loren, 122
Robinson, David and Isaac, 156
Rocky Point tunnel, 68
Roosevelt, Teddy, 70
Rosbach, Tilly, 128
Rosie the Riveter, 165
Roundtree, Mary Adeline, 23
Roundtree, Turner R., 26
Russian/Ukrainian refugees, 157
Ryderwood, 158

S

S.W. Washington Fair, 65, 174, 190
Saari, Gertrude, 150
Scanewa, Chief, 6, 8, 9, 13, 24, 149
Salzer Valley, 62, 94
Salzer Valley Lumber Co., 95, 96
Samson tractor, 137
Satsop, 2
Saunders' Bottom, 57
Saunders Prairie, 70
Saunders, Schuyler, 73
Saunders, Shuyler and Elizabeth, 70
Saundersville, 30
Scanewa, Chief, 6, 9, 13, 24
Schools, 170
Security State Bank, 177
See-See-Nah, 7
Sentinel, The, 123, 168, 169
Shaffer Brothers, 111
Shaner, Daniel, 128
Shanty town, 158

Shay locomotive, 97
Sheehan, Mike, 122
Shelton, John S., 24
Shields, Margaret, 166
Shingle bolt drivers, 98, 99
Silver Shirts, 157
Simmons, Michael T., 19, 93
Simpson Co., 95
Sisters of Providence, 173
Skookumchuck River, 28
Smith, Britt, 122
Smith, Elmer, 120, 122
Smith, Levi, 95
Snow Log and Shingle Co., 102
Snow Mill, 101
Sommerville Mill, 79, 106
Sopenah, 80, 81
South Bend, 60, 61
Southwest Wash. Fair, 65, 174, 190
Southerland, Jack, 112
Sprague, General J.W., 57
St. Francis Xavier Mission, 14, 15, 17
St. Helens eruption, 175
St. Helens Hotel, 72
St. Mary's Center, 15
St. Urban, 153
St. Urban Church, 30
Steamboats, 46-50
Stearns, Henry S., 80
Steele, Orland, 121
Stevens, Gov. Isaac, 23, 24, 32, 33, 35, 41, 51
Stillman, Henry, 26
Stiltner, 90
Stockum, Mary, 7
Stoker Coal Co., 126
Stott, Jerry E., 169
Studhalter family, 140
Sulphur Springs, 85
Superior Coal Co., 126, 127
Swiss families, 153
Swofford, 85

T

Tacoma, 54
Tacoma City Light, 146, 148
Tacoma, Olympia & Chehalis Valley Railroad, 124
Tansunshun, 23
Temple family, 87
Temple, Henry Clay, 86
Tenino, 53
Tharp, Ethel, 128
The Sentinel, 123, 168, 169
Theaters, 159
Thompson, William and Byrd, 105
Thrash Creek, 128
Thrash Opera House, 62
Tililikish, Kitty, 7
Tilton River, 84

Titanic, 145
Tobacco, 137
Toledo, 17, 47, 48, 81, 82, 132, 142, 143, 149
Toledo Bridge, 82
Tono, 124, 126, 128
Tono Mine, 126
Tower Lumber and Manufacturing Co., 104
Tower, Charlemagne, 104
Training School, 171
TransAlta, 131
Treat, Vernon, Lloyd and Glenn, 121
Trolley, Centralia-Chehalis, 65
Truman, Harry, 164
Twin City Railroad Co., 65

U

Union Pacific Railroad, 126
University of Washington, 26
Urban, St., 153
Urquhart store, 68
Urquhart, James, 25

V

Vader, 80, 81
Vader Parade, 156
Vader, Martin, 80
Vance, 133
Vancouver County, 39
Vancouver District, 39
Veness, J.A. "Jack", 107
Veness, J.A., Lumber Co., 108
Verndale, 85, 89
Veterans Memorial Museum, 177
Villard, Henry, 55
Volcano, 175

W

Waller, 153
Walville, 110, 111, 158
Walville Lumber Co., 64
Walworth & Neville, 110
War Memorial, 168, 169
Warbass, Edward D., 31, 46
Warbassport, 42
Ward, Garland, 91
Washington Co-op Poultry and Egg Assn., 138
Washington Fruit Growers Assn., 134
Washington Iron Works, 96
Washington map, 1
Washington Packers, Inc., 134
Washington Park, 123, 168, 169
Washington Territory, 37, 41
Washington, George, 27-29, 34, 75, 76, 168, 176
Washington, Mary Jane, 29

Webster, 115
West Coast Mills, 105
West, Johnnie, 134
West, W.F., 71
West, William F., 57, 71, 72
Westendorf, T. P., 171
Western Crossarm and Manufacturing Co., 105
Westfall, Sadie, 128
Weyerhaeuser Co., 94, 114
Weyerhaeuser, Fredrick, 93
White Pass Highway, 167, 176
White, Charles F., 25
White, Dave, 100
Whiteside, Andy, 152
Whitman massacre, 32
Whitman Mission, 20
WIDCO, 130
Wilkes, Lt. Charles, 12
Willamette Meridian, 38, 39
Willapa Valley Cheese Assn., 141
Williams, Sam and Harriet, 24
Wilson, 85
Wilson Coal Co., 125
Wilson, Judge John M., 122
Wilson, L.C., 125
Winlock, 76-78, 106, 137-139, 150-152
Winlock Cooperative Creamery, 141
Winlock School, 77
Wobblies, 120-123
Works Progress Administration, 161
World's Largest Omelet, 142
World's Largest Strawberry Shortcake, 134
WW I, 119, 135, 141, 168
WW II, 146, 154, 158, 164-169, 173, 174

Y

Yakima, 167
Yeoman Lumber Co., 92

Z

Zeek, Joe, 101

The information in this book came from hundreds of sources, some of which contradicted each other. If you have documentation which may clarify information in this book for future editions, please write to Panesko Publishing, 222 S.E. Spring Street, Chehalis, WA 98532. Thank you.

You can buy additional copies of this book at local retail outlets or at the Lewis County Museum in Chehalis or online at LewisCountyMuseum.org.

For orders of ten or more books write to Panesko Publishing at the address above.